Project Whirlwind

The History of a Pioneer Computer

Digital Press History of Computing Series

PROJECT WHIRLWIND

The History of a Pioneer Computer

KENT C. REDMOND & THOMAS M. SMITH

Digital Press

Design by David Ford
Printed in U.S.A.
1st printing, June 1980
Documentation number AX009-DP-001
ISBN 0-932376-09-6

Library of Congress Cataloging in Publication Data

Redmond, Kent C.   1914-
   Project Whirlwind.

   Includes index.
   1. Whirlwind computer. 2. Electronic digital
computers–History. I. Smith, Thomas Malcolm,
1921-   joint author. II. Title.
TK7889.W47R43   621.3819'58   80-14852

The text was created on a DEC Word Processing System and, via a translation program, was
automatically typeset on Digital's DECset-8000 Typesetting System.

TO

Historian Harry C. Jordan
who first saw the virtue of such a history

Historian Howard Murphy
who picked up the phone and made it possible

Administrator Clare Farr
who answered the phone and made it practical

to undertake the history of Project Whirlwind

Preface

Because the future is unpredictable and because research and development projects must attempt to craft their portions of that future by converting options and uncertainties to accomplished facts, we present the story of Project Whirlwind, as it developed, from the end of World War II.

This is not a technical engineering history. Rather, it is the story of how technical, financial, and administrative problems vied for solution in an enterprise conducted in war and peace, the outcome of which was by no means foreordained or routine.

Before readers, however, become caught up in the historical details that explain the course of Project Whirlwind, they are advised to bear in mind that the emergence of the new and the unexpected follows a logic all its own. One has to be willing to change the subject, so to speak, and go where the past went as it moved toward the present, if one is to understand how the research and development process can force the state of the art and produce, as it did in this case, so significant an item of novelty as the first high-speed electronic digital computer able to operate in "real time." Possessing this ability, the Whirlwind computer could not only carry out mathematical and logical operations of value to scientific research but also accomplish these with such speed and reliability that it could keep up with physical events and physical and mechanical motions and processes as rapidly as they occurred, monitoring or directing or changing their course of action at the will of the human operator. Whirlwind was the first digital computer that could be put to use as a practical device for, say, controlling manufacturing processes or directing airplane traffic.

As the story of the making of Whirlwind unfolds, it will become clear that events proceeded simultaneously on two levels. There was the essential, dynamic level of informal communication and decision-making among the participants. And because institutions—military, governmental, and higher education—were involved, there was the level of formal communication and commitment without which the innovative events on the informal level could not continue or produce the action required. The informal events are never so well documented as the institutional, but anyone familiar with research and development, American style, can infer the operation and sometimes the character of these. We have sought to incorporate both levels whenever possible, since to describe only the documented institutional events is to portray a sanitized past that never really existed and that offers no lessons.

Project Whirlwind contributed more than a machine that advanced the state of the art in computer technology, it also contributed a number of trained, experienced, and enthusiastic engineers who were to carry over into their post-Whirlwind careers that élan and dedication which was so obvious in the Whirlwind technical staff of carefully selected engineers and bright young graduate students looking for subjects for master's theses in electrical engineering. Whether in Project Whirlwind they had always used their time and energies wisely is difficult to determine. Certainly they had worked hard, and time was to demonstrate they had learned a great deal.

We have reprinted at the end of the book articles written by the two principals in the story of Project Whirlwind. The papers reflect the computer state of the art and Whirlwind's place in it as regarded by Jay W. Forrester in 1948 and Robert R. Everett in 1951, after Whirlwind was in operation. We are grateful to both men for permission to publish their work.

We have illustrated our study with photographs and diagrams made by the project staff as Whirlwind was being developed and built. These interesting contemporary materials were generously supplied by the MITRE Corporation of Bedford, Massachusetts. Edward L. Galvin gathered photographs from the MITRE Archives and Stuart A. Bemis processed them. J.A. O'Brien, formerly of Project Whirlwind and now of the MITRE Corporation, gave invaluable advice on the selection of illustrations.

We convey our thanks to all those who contributed to this history and deserve a share in whatever merit it may possess. Howard Murphy, chief historian for the Air Force Cambridge Research Center when the study was commenced, was a major force in getting the study underway and continued a source of advice and encouragement after his return to the university campus. He and Harry Jordan, also of the Air Force historical program, critically reviewed the first draft of the manuscript and offered beneficial suggestions for subsequent revisions. Clare Farr, Ellie Fitts, Louise

Sullivan, and J. P. Hastings of the MITRE Corporation provided materials, services, and facilities while we were pursuing the study in the Cambridge-Bedford area of Massachusetts.

Both the MITRE Corporation and Digital Press of Bedford, Massachusetts, deserve a special note of appreciation: the former for services, assistance, and encouragement vital to the completion of the history; the latter for intelligent editorial supervision and the study's inclusion as the first of a series of publications on the history of computer development.

To those whom we interviewed and who gave so generously of time and knowledge and thus permitted insights otherwise unobtainable, we are particularly grateful. Regardless of position or opinion, all were sympathetic to our efforts. Many in subsequent discussion gave wise counsel which assisted greatly in later revisions of the draft. The contending views were sharply articulated by four participants in particular and to them go special thanks for their candor: Mina Rees of the Office of Naval Research, Perry Crawford, Jr., of the Special Devices Division, and Robert R. Everett and Jay W. Forrester of Project Whirlwind.

Last here, but always first, we appreciatively note the sympathetic encouragement of our respective families who shared not only the pleasures but also the frustrations of re-creating Project Whirlwind.

Kent C. Redmond
Thomas M. Smith

Contents

Illustrations

Project Whirlwind

The History of a Pioneer Computer

1

The Beginning

The project that came to be called "Whirlwind" got its start during World War II, when a brilliant, flamboyant engineer named Luis de Florez asked his alma mater, the Massachusetts Institute of Technology, to build a new kind of machine to help train naval bomber flight crews. The enterprise got under way routinely enough, but those were extraordinary times, and they permitted the investigation to become an extraordinary research and development project pursued with extraordinary vigor, ingenuity, and flair at apparently extraordinary cost and with extraordinary returns.

The times were extraordinary because the world powers in Europe, Asia, and North America were embroiled in a war so ferocious and bitter that it swept up the total resources of the nations involved and changed the daily living patterns of millions of men and women, civilians and combatants alike, as long as it lasted. It was in these extraordinary circumstances that MIT responded to de Florez's request.

The machine that de Florez asked for was not the machine that the MIT engineers in Cambridge, Massachusetts, ultimately built. He was interested in a dual-purpose flight simulator, not in a digital computer. In 1943 it was taking far too much time and money to train flight crews to man the more complex, newer warcraft in production, and it was taking far too much time and money to design high-performance airplanes. A possible solution to both problems had been suggested by the recent successful development of ground-anchored flight trainers.

The massive trained-manpower need of World War II confirmed the inadequacies of contemporary methods and equipment for the training of crews of military aircraft. Both British and Americans had sought to eliminate this major weakness by the initiation of research and development programs designed to create superior equipment and methods. The programs led to the operational flight trainer which, without ever leaving the ground, simulated the flight characteristics of a particular existing warplane. Such trainers had proved useful in training flight crews at inestimable savings in time, money, and lives. An early British trainer, the "Silloth," was pneumatically operated. The Americans subsequently applied the same technique, but when further investigation disclosed that variations in temperature and humidity affected pneumatic operation too drastically to permit realistic operation of the trainer's complicated systems, they turned to electrical networks and motor circuits and obtained the greater reliability and versatility they desired.[1]

If, in the manner of the flight trainers, a mock airplane cabin or cockpit could be put through the motions that wind-tunnel tests and calculations indicated a new and untried design might exhibit, the responses of a pilot at the mockup controls would provide valuable data regarding the promise of the untried design. These data, when integrated with further wind-tunnel tests and calculations, could effectively accelerate the development and production of wholly new and superior airplanes. At least, such was the reasoning of MIT engineers when they joined in active discussions with United States Navy personnel in 1943 and 1944.

The Navy planners approached the problem from a more practical military view. They saw it as an opportunity to reduce the increasing cost in dollars and man-hours of providing a new and different flight trainer for each warplane model in combat use. They wanted instead to develop a protean, versatile, master ground trainer that could be adjusted to simulate the flying behavior of any one of a number of warplanes. Such a prototype trainer would provide the configurations and specifications to which cheaper individual-model trainers might be built in desired numbers for their flying schools.[2]

So Navy and MIT engineers, for their separate but mutually reinforcing reasons, made common cause and in 1944 embarked on a common project utilizing Navy funds and MIT technical competence: the development of the Airplane Stability and Control Analyzer (ASCA).

As we have indicated, ASCA was never built. A series of consequences that no one foresaw intervened, Whirlwind I appeared instead, and it was put to a wholly different use involving the aerial defense of the continental United States.

The key figure to set these events in motion was the naval officer who, more than any other man, brought the ASCA project into being, Captain Luis de Florez, director of the Special Devices Division of the Bureau of Aeronautics. Captain de Florez was one of those who in the very early days of World War II had decided to forsake a lucrative civilian career in order to serve the national cause. An engineer with an international reputation for his work in aviation and oil refining, he joined the Navy in 1939. There, until his return to civilian life in 1946, he pioneered in the development of "synthetic" training devices, some of which one congressional sub-committee report called "little short of miraculous."[3] In 1944 he received the Robert J. Collier Trophy of the National Aeronautics Association for his contributions to the preparation of combat crews during World War II.

In 1940, after flight training at Pensacola, Captain—then Com-mander—de Florez was brought to Washington as special assistant to the head of the Bureau of Aeronautics, Vice Admiral John Towers, a friend of long standing. By April 1941 de Florez had won recognition for his ad-vanced training concepts. Later in the same year he went to London to study British developments in synthetic training devices, and it was presumably upon that occasion that he had the opportunity to study the Silloth trainer.

Returning to the United States just before Pearl Harbor, he was placed in charge of a section in the training division of the Navy. Subsequently, he was promoted and granted authority to establish the Special Devices Divi-sion within the Bureau of Aeronautics with an initial appropriation of $50,000. Before the year's end the figure had been increased to $1 million; by the end of the following year, 1942, it had reached $10 million. As of No-vember 1944 the division was well established with a staff of some 250 tech-nical officers and 150 enlisted men and civilians.[4]

For Captain de Florez the trainer-analyzer was a logical and proper ex-tension of existing operational flight trainers that the Bell Telephone Labor-atories in Murray Hill, New Jersey, had developed for the Navy, notably trainers for the PBM, PB4Y2, and F6F aircraft. These simulators permitted the reproduction of typical operational flight conditions by means of in-strument readings. The instruments within the cockpit of the trainer were fed data by an "electromechanical computing system" that responded to both simulated aircraft performance and crew reaction. Sufficient realism was attained to familiarize the flight crew with the operational character-istics of the type of aircraft for which they were preparing.

Operational flight trainers were expensive, but they had proved a techni-cal and practical training success. It seemed only natural to Navy and MIT planners, prodded by Captain de Florez, to extend the concept "into the generalized field of aircraft simulation" by investigating a "universal trainer into which constants for various types of aircraft could be set."[5]

During the fall and winter of 1943 de Florez discussed the dual-purpose simulator with members of his technical staff and also with representatives of the Bell Telephone Laboratories and the Massachusetts Institute of Tech-nology. Bell's involvement was the obvious consequence of its contempo-rary work in operational flight trainers. MIT's involvement stemmed from its own personnel's interest in the problem and from the reputation of its impressive technical resources. The latter made the institute a source of ad-vice and guidance that Captain de Florez as a graduate found natural and easy to tap. Initially, he had anticipated using MIT personnel in a consulting capacity only; the actual engineering development would be performed by the Bell Telephone Laboratories.[6]

While engaged in discussion with Captain de Florez and his staff, the administrators and professors at MIT proceeded to expand their own investigations into the matter. On December 8, N. McL. ("Nat") Sage, director of the institute's Division of Industrial Cooperation, sent an official letter to Captain de Florez, notifying him that MIT had appointed Professor John R. Markham as project engineer for research on an "Airplane Stability and Control Analyzer."[7] While the Navy's Special Devices Division investigated the dimensions of the enterprise that was taking shape, examining projected costs and identifying industrial laboratories that might be willing to develop such a trainer-analyzer, Markham, together with Joseph Bicknell and Otto C. Koppen, made a study of more detailed technical aspects of the problem. They drew up a report the following April on what they called "a proposed method of ensuring satisfactory handling characteristics of new airplanes," and circulated it to interested parties. Of particular significance for the dawning Whirlwind story is their assertion that "a specialized calculating machine could be built that could be set up for a particular airplane according to data obtained by experimental means, and the pilot's control motions could be fed into the system by actually having the pilot fly the resulting airplane."[8]

The MIT study was incorporated into the Navy program as the result of a conference called in January 1944 to discuss the feasibility of using the PBM-3 trainer, then under development at the Bell Telephone Laboratories, as the basis for the proposed dual-purpose simulator. The conferees agreed to defer further discussion until specifications had been prepared by the MIT group. Once this had been done, discussions would be resumed, after which the recommended specifications would be forwarded to the Western Electric Company for a proposal to be drawn up on the required engineering work.[9]

By mid-April the MIT report was completed and sent to the Special Devices Division. It contained the reasoned conclusion of aeronautical engineering specialists Markham, Bicknell, and Koppen that it was practicable to design and construct an aircraft control and stability analyzer. The success of existing flight trainers, they noted, permitted the assumption that "a similar mock-up and calculating machine could be used to develop the flying characteristics of a projected airplane." Save for the construction of a flying prototype, the proposed simulator, they concluded, "should provide the best means of determining flying characteristics of large airplanes whether the design be conventional or unconventional." They warned, however, that adoption of the proposed simulator would require the expansion and improvement of existing wind-tunnel techniques and equipment in order to secure more and superior data.[10]

A copy of the report was sent directly to Captain de Florez with an accompanying letter from Professor Jerome C. Hunsaker, head of MIT's Department of Mechanical Engineering. Professor Hunsaker stated that the proposed simulator offered "a new tool of very great research significance," and would permit for the first time, if the details could be worked out, "the controlled motion (handling characteristics) of an airplane" to be estimated prior to construction. The heart of the simulator, the analyzer, would be difficult to design and build, he acknowledged, but the Bell laboratories possessed the ability if they would make the effort. If the Navy undertook the proposal, MIT would for its part enthusiastically continue to cooperate and would make available, at its own expense, the Wright Brothers Wind Tunnel for development of the equipment required to determine "the unusual aerodynamic coefficients needed to feed into the analyzer."[11]

Once the concept had been endorsed by the findings of the MIT study group, the Special Devices Division proceeded during the following month to establish a formal program for its implementation, identifying the proposed simulator as "Device 2-K, Aircraft Stability and Control Analyzer."[12] On August 11 specifications for both the computer and the cockpit were published, and the procedures for the selection of a qualified contractor were instituted. Curiously, the specifications contained no reference to the use of the simulator as a master operational flight trainer, but described it as a means "to obtain quantitative measurements of the stability, control, and handling characteristics of large multi-engined aircraft" prior to construction, thus permitting the distinct inference that if the MIT engineers had not prepared the specifications, their recommendations had been influential.[13] The omission, however, was in no way a reflection of any change in purpose on the part of Captain de Florez, for during the years that followed he continued to regard the proposed device as the prototype of both a master operational flight trainer and an experimental-aircraft simulator.

De Florez initially had anticipated that the project would be undertaken jointly by the Bell Telephone Laboratories and its manufacturing associate, the Western Electric Company, but ultimately the task was given to the Massachusetts Institute of Technology. All in all, some twenty-five commercial and industrial organizations were considered in the original canvass, but these either were eliminated or withdrew for various reasons.[14] Apparently, both Bell and Western Electric were reluctant to undertake the program lest it interfere with Navy contracts of greater immediacy.[15] Furthermore, by the fall of 1944 victory was visible over the horizon, and the two companies may have preferred not to commit their facilities to a long-term military responsibility rather remote from their primary peacetime mission of servicing the needs of their parent organization, the American Telephone and Telegraph Company.

Intended or not, the selection of MIT was logical and natural. As part of its contribution to the war against fascism, before America became formally involved, MIT had enlarged its areas of scientific research and engineering development by the addition of programs and facilities designed to seek solutions to technical problems arising from the need for new and improved weapons. One of these facilities was the Servomechanisms Laboratory of the Department of Electrical Engineering. The special competence developed by the laboratory and its personnel, coupled with MIT's immense technical resources, had formed by 1944 a combination of talent uniquely qualified to undertake for the United States Navy a project that ultimately was to make a major contribution to computer technology.

MIT also had participated in the ASCA project from the very beginning. In addition, Navy negotiators anticipated a substantial reduction in cost, since as a nonprofit corporation MIT had lower direct costs and overhead than did private industrial organizations.[16] Whatever the reasons, the Special Devices Division was authorized in November 1944 to undertake with MIT a preliminary investigation into the trainer-analyzer.[17]

Captain de Florez's course of action did not go unchallenged. From the very beginning of his Navy career his advocacy of technical innovation had met criticism, opposition, and even outright hostility, but it is to be remembered that the history of innovation is also the history of resistance to change, especially where institutional officers and custodians are involved.[18] Since institutions exist to preserve what men value, they draw some of their strength and substance and vitality from tradition as well as from innovation. Opposition to innovation has generally been sincere, finding its roots, as Elting Morison has noted, in adherence to the traditional, to the familiar, to the fear of change and of the impact of change upon one's career if not one's entire way of life. When exercised in a military institution and carried to an extreme, it can, as history shows, confound statecraft and endanger the very security of a modern nation.[19]

Luis de Florez was neither the first nor the most conspicuous to encounter such resistance while encouraging technical progress. The First Sea Lord of the British Admiralty, Sir John Fisher, had encountered opposition and hostility in the decade preceding World War I, when he pushed through the dreadnought construction program and spent millions on the submarine.[20] Proponents of the German U-boat as an offensive weapon were unable to win the support of the guiding genius of German sea power, Admiral von Tirpitz, and thus Germany neglected to realize the potential of the weapon that might have brought her victory in World War I.[21] Opprobrium was heaped upon the Board of Ordnance and Fortification of the United States

War Department for wasting its limited funds on Samuel Langley's unsuccessful experiments in heavier-than-air flight.[22] Admiral William S. Sims, one of the creators of the modern American Navy, was in constant difficulty because of his support of innovation.[23] De Florez was in good company.

The opposition to de Florez's proposed trainer-analyzer was sharp and articulate. It was given voice by Captain W. S. Diehl, chief of the Aerodynamics and Hydrodynamics Branch of the Bureau of Aeronautics, who, acting under oral instructions, had investigated the feasibility and value of the proposed trainer-analyzer. Captain Diehl's report to his superiors was bitterly negative, describing the projected device as "essentially a physicist's dream and an engineer's nightmare." The claims made for it, Diehl argued, were technically unsupportable. Furthermore, the proposal was both inappropriate and redundant, since it encroached upon work already in process under the aegis of the National Advisory Committee for Aeronautics. These views, Diehl asserted, were shared by other engineers within both the Navy and the National Advisory Committee for Aeronautics.[24]

To counter Diehl's criticism de Florez marshaled his forces within both the Massachusetts Institute of Technology and his own organization, the Special Devices Division of the Bureau of Aeronautics. The counter-arguments from the MIT study group reiterated the initial conclusions that the trainer-analyzer was technically feasible, valid, and of great promise. Professor Jerome Hunsaker, then on leave to serve the National Advisory Committee for Aeronautics as its chairman, responded in that capacity, rejecting the charge that the proposed program would encroach upon the committee's work. Instead, Hunsaker encouraged the Navy to proceed with the project, not only because of its great practical promise but because the research was important for itself.[25]

For his own part, de Florez replied that the proposed generalized trainer was a natural outgrowth of the operational flight trainer. It would eliminate about 80 percent of the work required for the design and construction of a specific flight trainer. A substantial reduction in cost would result at the same time that a means would be provided to accelerate the successful design and development of new airplanes. The criticism voiced by Captain Diehl, he implied, was just as invalid and unsubstantial as had been earlier criticism of the projected development of the now successful operational flight trainer. He recommended, therefore, that his division be authorized to continue with the project in cooperation with the Massachusetts Institute of Technology.[26]

Captain de Florez was persuasive. His arguments were undergirded by a record of demonstrated accomplishment. On November 28, Rear Admiral D. C. Ramsey, chief of the Bureau of Aeronautics, granted the requested permission.[27]

Anticipating that approval to continue with the project and to enter into contractual negotiations with MIT would be forthcoming, representatives of the Special Devices Division had met in mid-October with technical and administrative representatives of the institute for preliminary discussions. Present at this conference was another who would play a key role in the developing Whirlwind story, Nathaniel Sage. As director of the Division of Industrial Cooperation at MIT, Sage was responsible for the negotiation and administration of externally sponsored research and development projects conducted by the institute.[28] He was to serve as a sympathetic and protective liaison agent between the project and its Navy sponsors, as well as between Project Whirlwind and the MIT administration. Considered an excellent judge of men, Sage was more apt to support the man than the project, in the belief fortified by his experience that a good man meant a good project. His support of Whirlwind and its leadership was a reflection of his willingness to aid younger men who had gained his confidence and respect.[29] It is extremely doubtful whether Whirlwind could have survived the stormy years of 1947–1949 had not Nat Sage given it unswerving and resourceful support in his dealings both within the MIT community and with the Navy.

Sage's influence extended beyond MIT. His was a strong, dynamic personality. His policy views helped mold the pattern of the relationships that evolved during the war years between the federal government and MIT. These relationships were not peculiar to MIT but were representative of those which evolved between American educational institutions and the government in the wartime research and development effort. Sage was a penetrating observer who understood well the attitudes, the institutional commitments, the frailties and foibles, as well as the strengths and insights, of both career military minds and civilian-in-for-the-duration administrators and contract officers with whom he had to deal. Since this wartime cooperation was unprecedented, Sage had a relatively free hand as he charted unfamiliar seas in establishing the procedures and forms that were to guide the contractual relationships between MIT and the government. The novelty of these relationships, the exigencies of the war, and Sage's experience and resourcefulness cumulatively gave him the power to induce the government to accept many of his suggestions concerning contractual arrangements.[30] One consequence of this state of affairs was the broad latitude of options subsequently made available to the new ASCA project in the early conduct of its operations. Indeed, by conservative institutional and corporate standards the project enjoyed unusual freedom of choice.

Another influential MIT representative present at the discussions in October 1944 was Professor Gordon S. Brown, director of the Servomechanisms Laboratory.[31] Brown's presence indicated that if MIT chose to proceed with the next phase of the ASCA project, the Servomechanisms Laboratory might well be involved. This was understandable, for the nature of the work

Left to right, Captain Luis de Florez (courtesy National Archives), Gordon S. Brown and Nathaniel McL. Sage (both courtesy MIT Historical Collections).

lay within the laboratory's competence and experience. The laboratory had been established in December 1940 under the direction of Gordon S. Brown, assisted by Albert C. Hall, John O. Silvey, and Jay W. Forrester. It grew out of a training program for United States Naval Fire Control Officers begun in 1939 in MIT's Department of Electrical Engineering and arrangements made with MIT by the Sperry Gyroscope Company for a research and development program to produce a remote control system for antiaircraft guns on merchant ships.

In the fall and winter of 1940–1941 Nazi dive bombers had become a primary menace to the supply ships approaching the United Kingdom from the United States and elsewhere. The Sperry Gyroscope Company was developing a defense system that required a servomechanism to link a computing sight to the 37mm guns with which merchant vessels were to be armed. Rather than retool to manufacture an already existing British remote-control system, the company had chosen to develop a system that would utilize components already in domestic production and had arranged with MIT to conduct the necessary research.[32] Responsibility for the research program was given to the Department of Electrical Engineering because of its experience in servomechanisms; in turn the department organized the Servomechanisms Laboratory.[33]

From the beginning the new laboratory was a loosely controlled organization, for it played a very special role in Professor Brown's thinking. Believing that research and development flourished most creatively when free from tight and arbitrary lines of administrative control, he refused to employ the procedures and controls that many would have considered mandatory features of good management practice. From a conservative critic's point of view, Brown provided a dangerously decentralized "every man for himself" environment that was neither practical nor safely businesslike. Within the laboratory each project director could organize the work according to his individual peculiarities and capabilities. Carried to the next logical step, this practice left to each investigator all the latitude he could wish for in the conduct of his work. If the man's talents were not up to the task to be performed, deficiencies became quickly apparent.

From Brown's point of view it was a matter of finding a good man and backing him by turning him loose to make his own mistakes. In the case of the Servomechanisms Laboratory on the MIT campus, the good man preferably took the form of a brilliant and promising graduate student in electrical engineering who seemed able to avoid the gross mistakes and to profit rapidly from the small ones. Brown's surveillance was perhaps deceptively loose. The more astute students soon realized that this procedure gave them all the rope they needed to hang themselves spectacularly. One effect of this realization was the exercise of caution and careful planning without sacrificing the paramount aim to be innovative.

The unconventional management techniques and procedures Brown applied were so inconspicuous as to seem almost absent. Some of his own subordinates in the laboratory became convinced that he really did not know what was going on, so often did his back seem to be turned. This apparently casual supervision was deliberate, however, reflecting Brown's philosophy of education and his ideas on the proper conduct of advanced research and development. Brown was convinced that the loosely structured but, for his purposes, highly communicative interchange of ideas and experience not only contributed to the growing maturity of the student but also enabled older faculty members to remain more innovative and more critical of their own technical views. A net result would be the enhancement of engineering knowledge, for professors and students alike were stimulated by their mutual contacts and exchanges of views.

Brown felt then and in after years that it was not enough to provide the intellectual milieu, the intellectual challenges, the new horizons that a first-rate educational and training program could offer. Necessary preliminaries as these were, they were too protectively academic. The harsher, more realistic practical experience of the bona fide research and development laboratory committed to solving nonacademic problems was also necessary, nor should such experiences be postponed until after graduate degrees had been obtained. Brown saw no reason why carefully selected predoctoral and premaster's degree students of the caliber that MIT attracted should not be exposed to the novel blend of the sheltered, academic instructional program and the playing-for-keeps, practical, research and development program that they would later encounter as professional engineers. In his direction of the Servomechanisms Laboratory, Brown sought to implement these con-

Machine shop, Servomechanisms Laboratory, MIT.

victions.[34] The measure of his success was demonstrated not only by the considerable performance of the laboratory itself but also by the performances of former students and assistants in later years.

The spirit of the laboratory was high, in part because it was the product of Professor Brown's inconspicuous leadership, but also in part because of such factors as the élan of the graduate student and research assistant determined to demonstrate his creative abilities and to find new worlds to conquer. This élan Brown sought to further and exploit. Another factor, equally strong, was the personal dedication the war evoked. Whether this sense of personal commitment stemmed from pure patriotism or the desire to get a "dirty" job done, it was as much a stimulant to the young neophyte in the laboratory as it was to his mentors and senior colleagues of the scientific and engineering community. After the Japanese attacked Pearl Harbor on December 7, 1941, the American people committed themselves wholly to the war effort, in a national mood of determination and self-sacrifice difficult to imagine by those who have not experienced it. The response to the nation's call when it mobilized its scientific and engineering manpower to aid the prosecution of the war attests to the power of this mood. It was a mood that left no room for a "business as usual" philosophy.

The operational latitude within the Servomechanisms Laboratory encouraged the exercise of both wartime and professional motivations and enthusiasms. Much of the same psychological atmosphere, the same spirit, the same personal response were to be carried over into Project Whirlwind—and years later were recalled with nostalgia by those who had been participants.

In the years following its establishment in 1940 the Servomechanisms Laboratory had expanded both in programs and in personnel. By the time MIT was discussing the ASCA project with the Special Devices Division in 1944, the laboratory had a staff of approximately 100, including 35 engineers. It had since its creation "developed remote control systems for 40mm gun drives; for radar ship antenna drives; for airborne radar and turret equipment; and for stabilized antennas, directors, and gun mounts; as well as having cooperated in a number of other instrument problems."[35] As a consequence, the laboratory had in its four years acquired extensive experience in the research, design, development, and practical testing of that general class of machines, an example of which it was anticipated would form the heart and brain of the projected trainer-analyzer.

During the month that followed the October 1944 conference between MIT and Navy personnel, both the Special Devices Division and the Servomechanisms Laboratory sought to arrive at an unofficial understanding that could serve as the basis for official contractual negotiations. The laboratory prepared a tentative proposal in early November, providing for a research and development program to be carried to the "breadboard model" stage over a one-year period at an estimated cost of $200,000. The construction of the final simulator would be undertaken only after the program had then been reevaluated and the decision to continue had been made.[36] A conference held on November 15 disclosed, however, that both parties had come to the opinion that the initial proposal was both too extensive and too expensive. Consequently, they jointly worked out a new proposal, for a more modest preliminary study at a cost of about $75,000. This study would provide, they felt, a sufficiently accurate appraisal of the feasibility and ultimate cost of the trainer-analyzer.

The terms of this agreement were incorporated in the Special Devices Division's application to the Bureau of Aeronautics for approval of the project. On December 14, 1944, the Navy issued a formal Letter of Intent for Contract NOa(s)-5216. Four days later MIT officially accepted the letter of intent, and the program for the development of the airplane stability and control analyzer was launched.[37]

None of the participants anticipated a major change in course in the ASCA project. They were quite reasonable and quite wrong, for no one could anticipate, before the research was undertaken, that the difficulties inherent in realizing the initial purpose would be so profound or that the efforts of both MIT and Navy experts to reach a solution would generate a different enterprise superseding the first. Even the prophetic Captain Diehl, who had called the project "a physicist's dream and an engineer's nightmare," did not allow for a change in course; after all, his solution had been to refrain from embarking on it at all.

2

Computing Problems

The letter of intent of December 1944 marked the end of feasibility studies and the formulation of a program of design and implementation. It was a shift from the field of aerodynamics and aeronautical engineering to the field of electrical engineering and electromechanical control systems, and it placed final and full responsibility for the project in the Servomechanisms Laboratory. While the project's feasibility was still under study during the fall of 1944, Brown had brought it to the attention of one of his assistant directors, Jay W. Forrester, who had managed earlier projects in the laboratory.[1] Forrester became interested in this provocative engineering challenge, as Brown had hoped he would, and agreed to direct the project if it became a reality. He began work on it immediately and assumed a responsibility he was not to relinquish until 1956.

Forrester soon brought Robert R. Everett into the project. In a very special way, reflecting the complementary temperaments of the two young men, Everett came to share the responsibility and the technical direction of the project with Forrester. These were the two engineers whose leadership gave the project its basic character during the following decade. There was never any question that Forrester was in charge, exercising administrative authority and technical leadership, and there was never any question that Everett was second in command, exercising continuing technical leadership and administrative authority when Forrester was preoccupied with external affairs. Linked by a deep mutual respect and understanding, they worked together in unusual harmony, without always employing the same means to reach their common goal.

A native of Anselmo, Nebraska, Forrester had obtained a Bachelor of Science degree in engineering at the University of Nebraska in 1939. In the fall of that eventful year, about the time that Hitler's troops invaded Poland

and set off World War II, Forrester came to MIT as a graduate student and research assistant in electrical engineering. He was already on hand when Brown set up the Servomechanisms Laboratory in response to the looming technical demands of the war. The progress of the war expanded opportunities for original engineering research at MIT by providing the incentive, the needs, and the funds. One of the research and development fields so expanded and accelerated involved the design and development of feedback circuits, mechanical and electrical analog devices, and powerful servomechanisms responsive to remote control. Since the "Servomech Lab" had a major role in the dramatic technical progress made in this area during the war, Forrester was one of those who acquired extensive familiarity with the potentialities and limitations of servomechanisms and with associated problems of integrated system design and development. Fighter-director radar controls later placed on the USS *Lexington* were one of the systems that had given him important practical experience. Consequently, when de Florez's trainer-analyzer appeared above Forrester's horizon, he possessed both the technical experience and the administrative organizational experience to set up the project. Indeed, his experience profoundly affected his assessment of the problems and opportunities the project faced and equally profoundly influenced the design philosophy the project would follow. Yet, because of the unpredictable character of the research and development process, neither he nor anyone else at the time realized what transformations would ensue and what the project would become during the following eighteen months, not to mention ten years.

Everett, born in Yonkers, New York, had received a Bachelor of Science degree in electrical engineering at Duke University in June 1942, six months after the United States became a combatant in the war. That summer, about a month after entering MIT to seek a master's degree, Everett joined the war effort by going to work for Forrester in the Servomechanisms Laboratory.

Both young men thus were exposed to Brown's way of doing things and to the level of intellectual enterprise maintained by him and his colleagues. Under his eye they developed their respective organizational and administrative talents as well as their electrical engineering expertise. Although they did not try to duplicate Brown's personal style, it is not surprising that features of the philosophy of management followed by Brown within the Servomechanisms Laboratory influenced significantly the organization and administration of the Airplane Stability and Control Analyzer program after it became Forrester's primary responsibility. He and Everett proceeded, of course, to conduct the program in their own style.[2]

At first, however, Forrester worked on the ASCA project virtually alone and by early November had laid out his plan of attack. Basic units of the complete analyzer would include a simulator "cockpit with controls and instruments, the flight engineer-observer station, and the calculating equipment." While the specifications seemed to have purely electrical analog computing in mind, Forrester surmised that many of the integrator functions "might well be met through use of a variable-stroke hydraulic transmission." Perhaps a mixed mechanical and synchro data system, although more expensive, might avoid certain design difficulties of the all-electric system. "A combination system of synchro data, voltage data, mechanical integrators for multiplication by constants, and hydraulic transmission integrators for integrating and for multiplication by two variables" might be a suitable compromise.[3]

Obviously, he should study existing trainers, familiarize himself further with the equations embodying the aerodynamic requirements, "discuss the objective of the apparatus with the Navy sponsors . . . with commercial test pilots, designers, and wind tunnel men for detailed information on behavior and accuracy," examine "mechanical and electrical methods of continuous mathematical calculating," obtain engine-performance equations, study the physical details involving "types of signalling [and] types of amplifiers and other components," consider the types of schematic approaches available, and lay out a schematic solution that would "reduce the number and types of equipment as far as possible."[4]

On November 4 and 5 he laid out preliminary schematics "to show the solution of the equations" contained in the specifications. Familiarizing himself further in this way with the abstract statements, conditions, and quantities that the airplane analyzer would translate into suitable motions of the simulator cockpit, he considered ways and means of interpreting and restating for engineering purposes the requirements set forth the previous April at MIT by Markham, Koppen, and Bicknell and in August by the Bureau of Aeronautics.[5] His preliminary survey indicated that 92 quantities and 33 simultaneous equations were involved, just to describe the aircraft response. Further study indicated that, strictly speaking, 30 of the equations described the aircraft response, 3 related to acceleration and velocity, 8 dealt with instrument responses, and 6 applied to the control forces. So the analyzer would have to handle at least 47 equations involving 53 variables with respect to time, and none of these took into account the engines and engine controls. Since a multiengine simulator was what de Florez had in mind, the device would be complex indeed.

As Forrester familiarized himself in greater detail with the overall problem, the project became more and more elaborate. From his preliminary schematics Forrester further concluded that "the extensive use of synchro position for quantities or of mechanical multiplication seems entirely out of the question." On the other hand, "a-c voltage signals should cause much less difficulty because of the ease of isolating various circuits." By careful engineering, he noted, one ought to be able to avoid phase difficulties such as Bell Telephone Laboratories engineers had encountered when designing trainers.[6] There were pros and cons, pluses and minuses, options and trade-offs to be sorted and evaluated; these considerations kept him fully occupied as they entered into and modified his appraisal of the project.

In this manner he proceeded to shape his preliminary assessment of the ASCA problem. It was partly on the basis of this assessment that the meeting of November 15, 1944, between Navy Bureau of Aeronautics personnel and Sage, Brown, and ASCA engineers Forrester, Everett, and Hugh Boyd of MIT found both the Navy and MIT representatives ready to back away from the $200,000 breadboard-model contract that had been proposed earlier. As Forrester noted at the time, "BuAer felt from previous projects that the project would not be of such magnitude and also, after the intervening two weeks of study, MIT had a clearer picture of the requirements." It appeared more practical to think in terms of "a 4 to 6 months preliminary study to be covered by an appropriation of $75,000 . . ."[7]

What had happened was this: MIT, through the informal actions of Sage, Brown, and Forrester, had initiated the limited feasibility and cost study stipulated in Contract NOa(s)-5216 even before the letter of intent was issued by the Navy and accepted by MIT. This was neither the first nor the last time that professional involvement with the engineering problems by the engineers preceded official endorsement by the appropriate administrative and legal officers. Indeed, it was the practical thing to do: assess the problem in a preliminary way before making a commitment to undertake it in greater detail. In a very real sense Forrester's work before December was a feasibility study of the prospect of taking on the ASCA feasibility study.

This arrangement—a not infrequent characteristic of the research and development process—allowed formal fiscal and administrative agreements to rest upon the latest technical thinking and placed the entire procedure on an empirically sound basis. In consequence, the legal and monetary relationships became subsidiary means to the end of securing the engineering knowledge and the technical hardware sought. As will be seen, this subordination of fiscal and administrative factors to the engineering factors did not persist throughout the history of the project. But it was a customary way to start a project, and a wholly acceptable one in wartime. While prudent control of expenditures was always to be desired, the imperative consideration was to get on with the job, at whatever the cost in dollars.

Forrester's investigative techniques were, of course, the product of his experience since at least 1940. They were not intuitive, unexamined procedures that he was unaware of and could not explain. On the contrary, he took it for granted that he should analyze and make as explicit as possible the useful techniques that "came naturally" from his experiences. He preferred to know where he stood and why, at all times and was committed in a very self-aware way to understanding and rationalizing and systematizing the procedures of his own mind, especially where innovative intellectual ac-

tivity, such as engineering research, was involved. This trait was part of the young graduate student's immense self-possession (which some found presumptuous, if not patronizing, in one so youthful). It helped him to organize his plans of attack, it helped him to carry them out, and although it did not prevent errors in judgment, it provided continuing reexamination of that judgment and helped to minimize errors before they got out of hand. It could not forestall basic policy-level errors nor remedy the fact that the fullness of his expert knowledge in the area of mechanized analog computation and the principles of servomechanisms was also the measure of the depth of his contemporary ignorance of mechanized digital computation. There resulted a postponement in the selection of a suitable computer while Forrester underwent progressive disenchantment with the ideal device as he saw it in his mind's eye.

An example of his self-aware, analytical mode of procedure is to be seen in a report on hydraulic servomechanism developments, his master's thesis, which he began in 1941 and finished in November 1944, as he was taking up the ASCA project. The views he had expressed in 1941 he considered still appropriate in 1944. He made no apology for the fact that in the thesis "considerable emphasis is given to the mathematical analysis of the control systems which have been developed." "This has not been done because the analysis is academically fascinating," he wrote, "but because, from an engineering viewpoint, it has proven the surest and quickest way to obtain the desired results and to avoid the pitfalls so often appearing in the trial and error attempt to solve a complex problem." Forrester felt that the analysis of the device discussed in his thesis provided "an excellent example of the philosophy of the laboratory toward remote control theory."[8]

"It may seem," he continued, "that an undue amount of attention is devoted to the development and design of the early experimental and pilot models. However, it is there that the analytical approach may most effectively be shown, and the brief dismissal of many of the design and engineering problems of later work results not because these problems were easily solved, but because one with the necessary understanding and respect for the complexity of the operating principles may expect to reach the proper answer."[9]

Project engineers: Jay Forrester sits at the table to the right with a booklet before him. Robert Everett is at the upper right corner of the same table.

Forrester noted the importance of devoting a "great deal of time and attention . . . to careful measurements of the characteristics of individual pieces of equipment which are to be placed in a remote control system. These measurements and study yield information on the reliability of the components and make available numerical values of the constants appearing in the equations representing the response of a system. Such an investment of time and effort has returned substantial and satisfying dividends in the reduction of time consumed by 'cut-and-try' experimenting."[10]

Such were the technical background and perspectives that Forrester brought to bear when he opened his investigation of the ASCA problem in November 1944. By mid-December he had become sufficiently acquainted with both operational flight trainers in general and the proposed trainer-analyzer in particular to articulate the technical requirements for the analyzer, prepare a tentative time schedule, and assemble a list of personnel competent to carry out the work needed to fulfill the contract.

He sought, in addition to Everett, three other engineers: Hugh Boyd, Stephen Dodd, and George Schwartz, all of whom had been working on projects in the Servomechanisms Laboratory. As was to be expected, however, some time elapsed before Forrester was able to assemble the engineering staff he wanted. By the following February only Forrester himself and Boyd had been able to devote full time to the project; the others divided their time between the trainer-analyzer and other projects.[11]

Work on the project did get under way, nevertheless, and at the start it was paperwork analysis intermixed with examination of the state of the art. An early January examination of flight trainers for the Navy's PBM and PB4Y patrol bombers led Forrester to conclude that, impressive though they were, most of the circuits did not appear suitable for "the high precision requirements and flexibility of the proposed aircraft trainer."[12] The cockpit problem appeared to admit more straightforward solutions than did the prospect of designing the extremely complicated analog computer that the simulator would require. As the six-month preliminary study period progressed, Forrester found that the problems were proving more formidable than he and his associates had earlier thought they would be. Overall, however, the situation was under control, for the point of such research was to delineate the scope of the problems involved, and the emerging picture continued to indicate that the stumbling blocks were not insurmountable. Forrester, Brown, and Sage remained confident they could achieve a solution, although by May 1945 they were willing to admit that they had, in their earlier, relative ignorance, underestimated the development cost.[13]

In a memorandum of May 8 that never went beyond the draft stage, Forrester noted that the problem of developing certain components for the analyzer was requiring more extensive research than they had expected.[14] Many of the customary electrical and mechanical procedures of solving the appropriate differential equations could not be applied in their usual form but would have to be improved and tailored to the job at hand. Particularly was this true, Forrester felt, where speed of response was critical and where the ratio of maximum to minimum signal was extremely broad. In the former instance, the reactions of the pilot in the simulator cockpit would enter into the statement and the solution of the hypothetical aircraft's stability. His responses to simulated aerodynamic forces acting upon the pilot's controls ought to accomplish corrective actions, and these would have to take

The storage tube laboratory for Project Whirlwind.

effect as promptly in the simulator as they would in a flying airplane. Thus, the equipment had to operate within these real response times. "This is especially true," wrote Forrester, "of the integrators which convert accelerations to velocities and of the control-column loading equipment."

Again, both the normal maneuverability of an airplane and its range from smooth, level flight to sharp maneuvers imposed a corresponding range between minimum and maximum signals that no known mechanical equipment having a single scale of operation could embrace unless, by suitable mechanical and electrical means, "an automatically self-adjusting scale factor" could be incorporated. Forrester reported that "details of variable scale-factor devices have been worked out but have not yet been experimentally proven."[15]

Consequently, when Forrester contemplated the end of Phase I (the preliminary study period called for in the contract) and the beginning of Phase II (actual design and construction of ASCA itself), he recognized that he and his staff could not know where they stood in Phase I until the studies and demonstrations then in progress were completed, nor could they provide a realistic answer regarding the practicality of Phase II until they knew that suitable components existed. He felt that the components could be developed "in the next few weeks," but saw the necessity of obtaining additional laboratory and engineering time. Perhaps an extension of time on Phase I and scrutiny of the transition period between Phase I and Phase II might constitute the best course of action. However, such a course of action would require more money. For example, if $50,000 were added to the original $75,000 allotted for Phase I, a sufficient extension of time might be achieved. An additional interval of two or three months, at $25,000 per month, might take care of the transition period.[16]

This precise course of action was not taken. The Navy remained satisfied with the rate of progress made during the first five months. It was confident that the "general outlook was promising." When Sage's office—MIT's Division of Industrial Cooperation—submitted on May 22, 1945, its proposal for extension and modification of the contract, the upward revision of estimated cost that Forrester, Brown, and Sage felt was necessary omitted the complicated phasing that Forrester had toyed with and stated instead that the project could be carried through to completion within eighteen months at a cost of approximately $875,000.[17]

MIT's proposal was the expression of its determination to continue; the Navy's affirmative response, contained in Letter of Intent for Contract NOa(s)-7082, June 30, 1945, was the expression of its determination to continue. The renewal firmly committed the Navy, for the new contract not only continued but expanded the project at a cost that was too large to permit easy withdrawal. Excellent contractual and working relationships on the technical level had been established, and there was every reason to go ahead. Of course, there were unsolved problems.[18] Had there been no problems, the Navy would not have had to turn to MIT instead of a private manufacturer less interested in advanced research. As to the immediate future, no one could say how long it would take to finish the war against Japan; the empire the Japanese had begun to build in 1931 might be crumbling rapidly, but no one could be sure how long the successful invasion of Japan itself would take. And if ASCA were developed too late to help in the war, its long-run achievement would still be useful. Eighteen months and $875,000 would represent a sound prospective investment of Navy research and development funds for 1945 and 1946.

The onset of summer saw increasingly severe technical analysis by Forrester and his associates of the progress they were making and the problems they were encountering. Forrester in particular began to probe insistently the problems of the form the computer equipment should take and the appropriate representation that should be given the test data. To represent nonlinear data by mechanical linkage, for example, appeared to be neither a flexible nor a general enough method. Although such a method could be incorporated in an analog system, it posed the possibility that wasteful trial-and-error routines would have to be undertaken each time new data required adjustment of the linkage system.[19]

Forrester discussed his problems with others. Samuel Caldwell of MIT's Electrical Engineering Department had suggested in May that the work of George Stibitz and his associates at Bell Telephone Laboratories might offer suitable alternatives.[20] Stibitz, a mathematician who had obtained his Ph.D. in physics, was then involved in the design of a digital computer using telephone relays for storage of numerical data and for arithmetical operations, and the following year the Bell Relay Computer, Model 5, was put into operation.[21] But Forrester did not pursue Caldwell's lead.

By the last week of June 1945 Forrester was notifying Brown that a rough survey of staffing requirements made in anticipation of the Navy's continued support indicated that his group needed eight more electrical and electronic engineers and three mechanical engineers (they had none at the time). In addition, a building would have to be designed and built; consequently, an architect should be obtained to supervise construction through the following spring. Forrester went on to outline a schedule of the progress required to carry out Phase II: research from August 1945 until the first of the following year, mechanical development and design from August 1945 to March 1946, electrical development and design from January to March 1946, procurement and construction from January to July 1946, assembly and installation from July to December 1946, testing and trouble-shooting from January to March 1947, and delivery of the equipment to the Navy on March 31, 1947.[22]

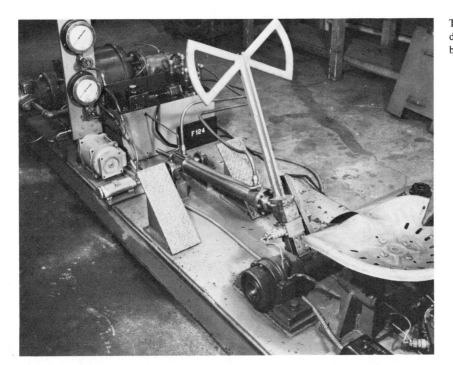

The control force demonstrator developed by the ASCA project.

Robert Everett and the control force demonstrator.

As June passed into July and July into August during that summer of 1945, Forrester became increasingly disenchanted with the lack of flexibility and versatility of the elaborate servomechanism system that was taking tentative shape. The real-time response problem still defied forthright solution, and unless certain design features were changed, the units of the ASCA would remain permanently interconnected in the pattern imposed by the equations of motion of the aircraft. In consequence, the analog computer portion of the analyzer would be unavailable for use on other problems between simulation tests. The result would be a grossly uneconomical waste of potentially one of the most powerful such computers to come into existence. Perhaps prewired, removable plugboards could be employed, with the result that operating characteristics of the computer circuits might be explored between tests and provide important information on the potentialities of the computer for simulator work.[23]

In August the apparent need to make several changes in the integrator circuits of the analyzer represented additional problems, while success with experimental tests on a variable-oscillator design suggested a feasible three-phase motor could be developed for a variable-frequency servo application that the analyzer required. The project was making reasonable progress on some details—Stephen Dodd was studying the properties of the aerodynamic equations, George Schwartz was investigating ways and means of representing aircraft piston-engine performances, and others were examining aspects of radio noise level, cathode follower characteristics, and analyzer component interconnections—but progress with many of the detailed design chores did not keep Forrester from pondering upon the overall characteristics and limitations of the simulator.

In retrospect it should be noted that the wartime design experiences of the graduate students in the Servomechanisms Laboratory, unusually rich and varied though they had been, had not placed them at the forefront of innovative, analog computer design activity in the manner that their postwar experience in Project Whirlwind was to give them pioneering competence and preeminence in digital design work. Their relatively heavy-handed, brute-force engineering approach to the design of analog computation machinery contrasted with the light touch manifested at the end of 1945 in the analog computer approach taken, for example, by Arthur Vance and his associates at RCA. Expert in designing low-drift amplifiers, the latter group developed driftless, direct-current amplifiers that proved essential to later analog computer development. Here they possessed a degree of experience and competence that the Servomechanisms Laboratory engineers lacked, and de Florez's engineers in the Special Devices Division of the Navy were aware of these differences.[24]

The SDD program managers were also increasingly preoccupied with the dawning missile and rocket technology that German engineers had launched spectacularly with the V-2 rockets used to bombard London, and they were sensitive to the greater challenges lying ahead for simulator engineers in both the aircraft and missile design.[25] It would be easy to suggest, in consequence, that the Navy programmers began to encourage Forrester and his colleagues to explore other design avenues that would avoid the analog computer design problems they were encountering, but the evidence of such long-range master planning is not only lacking but also contradicted by the complex sequence and fortuitousness of related events during the remainder of 1945. Apparently aware that the course of engineering research is not explicitly predictable, the Navy engineers rested their confidence upon the already demonstrated innovative abilities of the MIT engineers and encouraged them to go whither their investigations led them, within the overall confines of the ASCA problem that had been laid down.

Meanwhile, in August 1945, as Forrester and his associates were seeking solutions to the analog engineering problems besetting them, Japan surrendered. The war was at last over, and many could move once more to pick up the threads of their peacetime lives and occupations. Forrester had to give some of his attention to the necessary goings and comings and reorganization of activities that ensued, but the dislocations of the war's end proved to be transitory in their effect upon the ASCA project.

At the same time, in the wider technical community and unknown to Forrester, a mathematician at Brown University was making arrangements to call an international conference on computers in October. R. C. Archibald, chairman of a National Research Council committee on mathematics, was readying notices that would bring together at MIT experts from England and the United States for a two-day meeting to take stock of wartime developments. Archibald and his committee were particularly interested in new "electronic devices . . . which promise astronomical speeds for numerical computing processes."

During the summer of 1945 Forrester had found time in the midst of the routine of his laboratory affairs to discuss computational techniques other than those associated with the analog computer and had found that the engineering development of none was so far advanced as to be of immediate use to him. From Perry O. Crawford, Jr., a fellow graduate student in electrical engineering, Forrester learned of the intriguing future prospects that some already saw for employing digital numerical techniques in machine calculation. At MIT during the middle thirties Professor Caldwell had introduced a course in mathematical analysis by mechanical methods, and Crawford, as a graduate student and research associate under Caldwell and Vannevar Bush, was exposed to both analog and digital machine-computation concepts when they were for the most part still in the theoretical stage, especially where digital techniques were concerned.[26]

In 1942 Crawford had submitted his master's thesis, "Automatic Control by Arithmetical Operations," discussing the application of digital techniques of computation to the automatic control and direction of antiaircraft gunfire. After indicating how recently physicists and electronic engineers had become seriously interested in methods of performing arithmetic operations using such electronic devices as the Eccles-Jordan flip-flop circuit, he restricted his discussion to the problem of predicting the future position of the target and described the sort of electronic equipment that might be useful for the automatic calculating required. The equipment would consist of electronic switching elements and circuits "for multiplying two numbers, finding a function of a variable, recording numbers, translating mechanical displacement into numerical data, and for translating numerical data into mechanical displacements."[27]

Forrester recognized that all of these operations were required of the aircraft stability and control analyzer. There was no question that Crawford understood the nature of his problem, although it was not encouraging to hear Crawford express the opinion that the successful application of these new digital techniques to the sort of problem that Forrester's group was attacking lay still too far in the future to be of any help.

These ideas, presented to Forrester in stimulating detail in mid-September, did not slip from his mind in the months that followed.[28] When Crawford left MIT in October to go to work for de Florez in the Special Devices Division of the Navy, he spent part of his last day on the campus talking with Forrester about digital calculators and the new breed of controlled-sequence devices then coming over the horizon. At the University of Pennsylvania in Philadelphia an elaborate vacuum-tube calculator, the Electronic Numerical Integrator and Computer, called ENIAC for short, was being constructed; and another, the Electronic Digital Variable Automatic Computer, or EDVAC, was under development.[29] ENIAC was nearing completion at the Moore School of Electrical Engineering under the direction of John W. Mauchly, a physicist, and J. Presper Eckert, Jr., an electrical engineer. The two men were well aware that theirs was the first enterprise committed to using vacuum-tube circuits to carry out highly complex calculations, in their case dealing with ballistics data for their sponsor, the United States Army.

Forrester was on the track of something new. He liked what he saw, and the more he saw, the more he wanted to see. He could not put it aside. In after years both he and Everett were to attribute to Perry Crawford the crucial suggestion which they came to take seriously, that digital numerical techniques merited serious study.[30]

Although Forrester had worked more extensively with analog devices, his mathematical and electrical engineering backgound permitted him to perceive and explore rapidly the prospects of digital calculation. There was nothing novel about the equivalence of the two modes of calculating, analog and digital; he was aware that these were alternative procedures, each possessing its particular virtues and defects. And if the *arrangement* of some of the electrical components that Crawford called to his attention was novel, the tubes, capacitors, resistors, and elemental circuits were familiar features that offered no trouble. The novelty thus lay less in the elements than in the *system* implications, and with these Forrester promptly began to familiarize himself. So intent were he and Crawford, and then Everett, in their contemplation of the prospects, that they paid little heed to the historical background of the state of the art as they found it, and indeed such awareness was not necessary to qualify them to carry out the technical pursuit in which they were then engaged.

3

The Shift to Digital

In the summer and fall of 1945 electronic digital computation was beginning to awaken serious technical interest at various locations in the United States and Europe. That no electronic digital *computers* were yet in operation was of little consequence. What mattered was that Western mathematicians and engineers were being caught up in a classic example of the historical phenomenon of "convergence," in which the embryonic computer technology was assuming shape and character from the merging of several diverse machine-design traditions and several abstract intellectual traditions. Personal curiosity had combined with historical circumstance to place various individuals at peculiar, strategic positions from which they could take advantage of the opportunities provided by this convergence of traditions. Among these individuals happened to be the young engineers engaged in the ASCA project at the Massachusetts Institute of Technology. Their individual exertions had helped to bring them to such positions, and the converging traditions set the boundaries within which their ingenuity would go to work.

The first of these traditions was itself a composite of several machine and device developments, each of which had a long history. They included the odometer and the abacus in diverse forms from ancient times, the slide-rule and the mechanical adder from recent times, and the electromechanical calculator traditions of the last hundred years, culminating in the relay machines of George R. Stibitz and his colleagues at the Bell Telephone Laboratories and the electromechanical Harvard Mark I built by Howard Aiken with assistance from the International Business Machines Corporation.

Among the converging intellectual traditions, as distinct from machine traditions, were those of counting and "reckoning," or calculating; other mathematical traditions that had produced the logarithm, Napier's "bones," the slide-rule, and Charles Babbage's unfinished and forgotten computer (to name only a few); and the scientific and technical traditions that produced, in one direction, theories about electrons and electromagnetic phenomena, and in the other direction, applications of electronic science in such forms as the vacuum tube, electronic circuits, and radar.

The technical machine tradition that first exploited computer techniques in the late 1930s and early 1940s was the electromechanical tradition brought into being by prior advances in the technologies of electricity, of controlled-motion machinery, of the desk calculator, and of the telephone system. At the hands of Aiken, Stibitz, and others, it provided the first machine generation of computers, but although it spawned refined and improved members of one class of relay, switch, and gear machines, it shortly proved to be a subclass of provocative but sterile computers without lasting issue. The cause lay not in any essential "hybrid sterility," but in the independent development of a more promising machine form that happened to come hard on the heels of the first. This second form permitted vastly greater calculating speeds, and it provided a second generation of computers mechanically unrelated to the first: the electronic digital computers.

The first true electronic computer was the Electronic Numerical Integrator and Computer, or ENIAC, designed and built at the University of Pennsylvania under the direction of John Mauchly and Presper Eckert. Mauchly as a physicist had found himself (without realizing it) in the same predicament in the late thirties that Aiken and then Stibitz independently suffered: he was sharply aware that great quantities of data needed mathematical processing and that existing techniques were slow, cumbersome, unreliable, and hopelessly unable to meet the challenge. He concluded that vacuum tube circuits ought to be exploited.

Mauchly knew how instantaneously electric signals could travel along a wire. He knew how incredibly rapidly a vacuum tube could block or pass or modulate an electronic signal. The next step was to determine how these properties could be exploited by suitable electronic hardware systematically arrayed. This engineering problem did not diminish his confidence in the possibility that combinations of electronic signals could be made to stand for numbers and submitted to manipulations that would produce the same numerical results that the human mind can produce when it "calculates." So in the fall of 1941 he joined the Moore School of Electrical Engineering at the University of Pennyslvania, determined to obtain the electronics design assistance he sought.

By 1943 he, Eckert, and others at the Moore School, as well as Army Ordinance representatives, were convinced that a system of vacuum tubes and radio circuits, of standard form and established characteristics, should be able to perform lengthy digital computations in the laboratory. Further, they should do so with the required speed and accuracy to provide values extremely useful for further perfecting greatly needed ballistics trajectory data. The ensuing work on the ENIAC during 1944 and 1945 was carried on under wartime secrecy, but this did not keep it from coming to the attention of the Princeton mathematician, John von Neumann, or of some of the electrical engineers at MIT. The machine went into operation in 1946 and was put to work on ballistics calculations as planned. It would multiply two ten-decimal numbers in less than three-*thousandths* of a second, compared to the three-second interval required by that earlier-generation calculator, the Harvard Mark I.

The ENIAC machine was from the start designed for a particular use rather than as a general-purpose machine of wide application, for there were many engineering problems that its designers had to solve without ambitiously extending the capacities of their projected machine. In this respect they resisted the temptations to enlarge and improve which had caused Babbage to fail a century earlier. Aiken's nonelectronic Mark I filled a wall, so to speak, no deeper than a man could reach but fifty-one feet long and eight feet high, and the Bell Aberdeen relay computer was housed in a room approximately forty by thirty feet in area. The ENIAC also was large, occupying the sides of a room approximately forty by twenty feet and including racks of assemblies on wheels in the center of the room. Some 18,000 radio tubes and 1,500 electrical relays went into its construction, together with plugboards, wiring, power units, and related equipment. Its internal storage was kept small, consonant with the mathematical chores it was expected to perform. The large size of this and other early computers was deliberately stipulated by the designers. Access to the components was what they were interested in, so that unanticipated repairs and improvements might be made easily in these pioneer machines.[1]

The ENIAC, being electronic, was not an engineering descendant of the Mark I mechanical machine. Instead, the tradition upon which its physical equipment was based traced back into the complex history of electronics in radio and telephony. The electronic computer tradition after the ENIAC rested not only on the ENIAC itself but on wartime developments in the pulsed circuitry of radar, on the well-developed state of the art in radio tubes and circuitry, which was subsequently modified by transistors and solid-state circuitry, and on the logical abstractions of a mathematical tradition that included Babbage, Edward Boole, John von Neumann, and Alan Turing.

When the lessons of the tradition of the automatic sequence-controlled calculator machines—the tradition of Stibitz and Aiken—were joined to the hitherto distinctive electronic traditions of radio and radar circuitry, their coming together seemed wholly natural. The modes of application of circuits to computation and of computational and logical concepts to electronics were so provocative that the specialists involved—Eckert, Mauchly, von Neumann, and the Britons, Wilkes, F. C. Williams, and Turing—did not even wait for the first electronic computer, the ENIAC, to be completed and in operation before they rushed on to more ambitious conceptions.

It was at this juncture of events that the MIT engineers working on the aircraft stability and control analyzer fell in with those who were engaging in the activities bringing together the calculator and the electronic traditions. It was Forrester's good fortune, as the leader of the group, to find himself standing at the intersection of the two traditions; his was also an instance of the innovative situation that Pasteur once characterized with the remark, "Chance favors the prepared mind." Forrester's mind was indeed prepared by the computer problems the aircraft analyzer was posing at the time, and he grasped at this attractive prospect of a general solution.

Everett's and Forrester's combined insight and vision enabled them to perceive, seize, and exploit the opportunities of joining the abstract, elaborate, *logical-formal tradition* of manipulating discrete numerical quantities (upon which the mechanical-calculator tradition had been resting) to the particular *engineering tradition* of producing radio and radar equipment. They were able to expand and develop further both of these traditions, especially the latter. Their intuitive and analytical assessments of the rate at which such reduction to practice (for some reason it is never called "elevation to practice") could be accomplished was one key factor that was to make their particular computer unique in its time. A second key factor was the type of task they designed their computer to perform. In this respect their computer was so unlike all the others that for a while it appeared it would find no use to justify either its cost or its existence. Then once again an independent and separate tradition over which Forrester and his group had had neither control nor influence—this time taking the form of certain highly specialized preparations for waging war—joined with and made use of the brand-new electronic-computer tradition to further advance the state of the art.

But that is getting ahead of the story. At the end of summer in 1945 the prospect confronting the MIT engineers was still that of a cockpit or control cabin connected, somehow, to an analog computer related to the design tradition of the electromechanical differential analyzer developed at MIT by Vannevar Bush and Samuel Caldwell between 1935 and 1942.[2]

News of the successful operation of the MIT differential analyzer had been withheld during the war, lest the enemy learn how useful and practical it was. Instead, intimations were deliberately "leaked" that it had failed to live up to expectations. The end of hostilities permitted MIT to celebrate the true achievements of the analyzer at the meeting of computer experts that has already been mentioned—that which R. C. Archibald of Brown University had called as chairman of the National Research Council's Committee on Mathematical Tables and Other Aids to Computation.

This historic first conference on digital computer techniques took place at MIT October 30–31, 1945, under the auspices of Subcommittee Z on Calculating Machines and Mechanical Computation. Its purpose was expressed in its formal title: "Conference on Advanced Computation Techniques."[3] Among those who attended were Perry Crawford and Jay Forrester. The latter was particularly interested in reports of the design activity occurring at the University of Pennsylvania. Prepared by his conversations with Crawford and anyone else he had encountered who was knowledgeable, he was keenly receptive to the stated object of the conference: "To familiarize each member of the Group with present potentialities in the field, and to make known future developments." The program of papers to be delivered and especially the roster of expected conferees redoubled both his curiosity and his growing commitment to the emerging digital tradition.

Before two weeks had passed, he had visited the University of Pennsylvania to obtain more information and was inquiring into the design details of the ENIAC and its projected successor, the EDVAC.

It is difficult, if not impossible, to say confidently just when the realization struck Forrester that a novel solution—the electronic digital instead of the analog mode—had presented itself. Caldwell's suggestion in May that Forrester might find Stibitz's work significant did not precipitate the vital moment. Did the conversation with Perry Crawford in September, then? Or was it their discussion on the day Crawford left in October? In after years Forrester recalled standing on the steps in front of one of the MIT buildings talking with Crawford, when the latter's remarks turned on a light in his mind.[4] His recollection is that from that time on he began to consider the digital mode seriously.

The turn of events that strategically affected Forrester's prosecution of the ASCA project is visible in internal developments within the project, in the hiring practices and the efforts to secure the assistance of certain MIT departments, in the renegotiation of the Navy contract, and in Forrester's and Crawford's separate and joint efforts to explore the prospective application to other uses of a digital computer sophisticated enough to meet the requirements of the airplane analyzer.

The months of November and December following Archibald's computer conference were put to use by Forrester in testing the immediate import and implications of the digital concept. It was a period during which he tested, revised, examined, and reexamined the value of the ideas he had held regarding a solution to his problem. If those ideas were glitter without substance or too wild a dream, then they must be dismissed. If the digital prospects continued to show promise, the grounds for this promise must be laid out and at least prospected in a preliminary way.

Accordingly, on November 9, 1945, Forrester, as part of his effort to shift the attention of his staff, held a conference of his project engineers on the general subject of techniques in computation. The opening paragraph of the report of this conference, written by one of the project engineers, reveals how fundamental was the reexamination and the reorientation that Forrester was initiating:

Analogy type of computation has been under consideration, but there are other approaches which are highly thought of in mathematical circles throughout the country at present. It is the purpose of the present discussion to consider certain features of some of these.[5]

After indicating the basic modes of calculation of the Harvard Mark I and noting that its mechanical calculating speeds were quite slow, the report turned to the "Pennsylvania technique" of calculating electronically with vacuum tubes. Even though the machine being built along these lines is not yet working, the report stated, "there is already a proposal to make another one which contains other features of importance to the aircraft analyzer problem." The latter machine was the EDVAC, which was intended to employ pulses in temporal, linear sequence and store its information "by the use of a thin column of mercury, referred to as a 'tank'"—a mercury delay line.[6]

The report discussed a possible method of adding, using vacuum tube circuits, then turned to the subject of using the tubes to multiply by a procedure that would take only two or three times as long as a single addition. "These digital techniques are fundamentally processes of doing one thing at a time," the report noted. "Techniques for high speed electronic computation have not been worked out, and several months' work will be necessary to properly evaluate the process."

Actually, the evaluation was already under way in the Servomechanisms Laboratory, as the engineers set about familiarizing themselves with the principles of this novel type of machine that would consist of five major components systematically linked to work together: an input unit that would receive the numbers to be processed, an arithmetic unit that would perform the necessary calculations, an internal storage unit in which data, operating instructions, and results could be stored, an output unit that would produce the information the machine had processed, and a control unit that would regulate and integrate all the operations of the other four units of the machine.

These were the major subdivisions of the computer. Babbage had first conceived them in the nineteenth century and then they had been all but lost to sight. Aiken had reinvented them and embodied them in his electro-mechanical Harvard Mark I that used no vacuum tubes. Eckert and Mau-

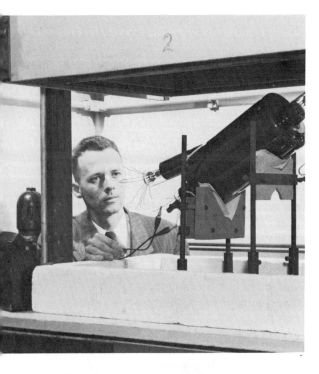

Above left, Forrester with a storage tube of the type eventually used in Whirlwind. Above right, technicians insert a high-voltage electron gun. Opposite, Forrester, Stephen Dodd, and Pat Youtz compare storage tubes.

chly were embodying them in their electronic ENIAC. And now Forrester and his engineers were examining their principles of operation, their merits and deficiencies, and turning their thoughts toward the technical details of how each unit should be built.

Especially attractive was the fundamental simplicity of the ultimate working parts of the machine. If one imagined, say, four vacuum tubes in a row and switched on the fourth tube on the right, that signal could stand for the number "1." If the third tube was on and the other three were off, that would signify "2." If tubes three and four were both on, that would signify "3." If only the second tube was on, that would signify "4." If the second and fourth tubes were on, the number would be "5." If tubes two and three were on, that would stand for "6." If tubes two, three, and four were all on, that would signify "7," and if only tube one were on, that would be "8." And so on. There was no necessary end to this logical pattern; one could encode as large a number as he wished by this binary digital system of notation.

Two features that strongly attracted Forrester and his group were the fact that *patterned* arrangements of energized tubes symbolized numbers and the fact that these patterns were built up from modular units of two tubes, a design that could be repeated over and over again. Just as bricks could be used to build a wall, so could elementary circuit designs be repeated to build a computer. As the conference report remarked, "These digital techniques are fundamentally processes of doing one thing at a time." The engineers were exhilarated at the possibilities opening up before them. With bricks, so to speak, they could build not just a wall but a house, a city.

Forrester, on November 13, sent an airmail, special delivery letter requesting from the Pentagon access to published technical reports on the EDVAC. He pointed out that his Navy aircraft research contract involved "the simultaneous solution of many differential equations, and the techniques visualized by the University of Pennsylvania on their EDVAC computer show considerable promise."[7]

In November he also was looking for new people to add to the project staff. He sought talented graduate students or well-qualified radar experts who could move with the present staff members in the new direction they were heading. He would consider only candidates of exceptional promise; they ought to be between 25 and 40 years old, he specified, "and of doctor's degree caliber, although selection will be based on the man's experience, cleverness, ingenuity, and references rather than on his academic degrees." Thus, in a letter of November 16 to the MIT Radiation Laboratory he asked for men with a radar design background, "experienced in the generation and handling of low-power level signal pulses, in applications which will require pulses a part of a microsecond long and spaced a microsecond apart."[8] He

J. A. O'Brien at work on the test control element for Whirlwind.

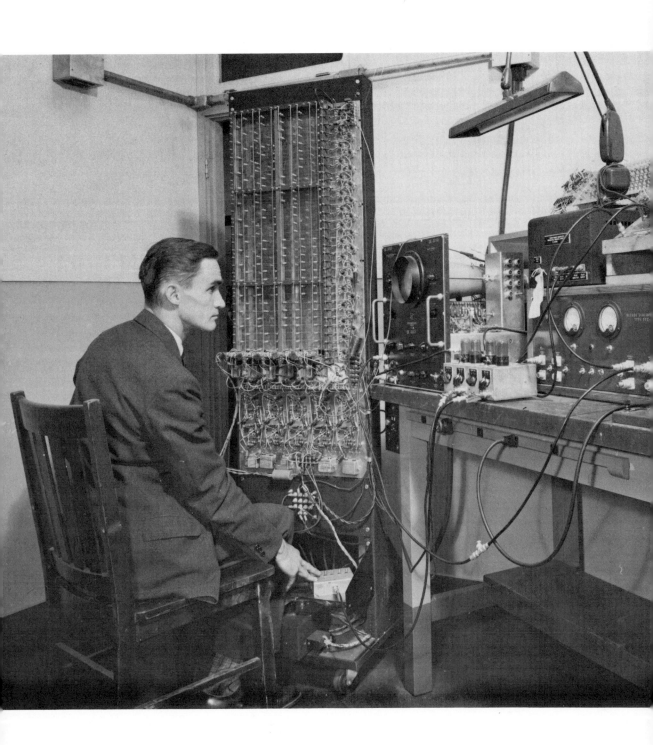

closed the letter on a characteristic note: "I wish to stress the need for cleverness and ingenuity in the field of coded pulses."

Forrester was convinced, from his wartime experience, that it was more efficient to pay a higher price for one really good man and then give him his head, than it was to pay less for three average men and have to lead them by the hand. He felt he possessed the experience and the judgment to enable him to recognize the difference, and although he did not expect his every selection of a new man to be error free, he was adamant about maintaining exceptional standards in choosing design and test engineers and mathematicians. Over the years ahead this policy brought in many promising men, some of whom went on to important industrial, engineering, and consultative achievements in their subsequent careers.

The high standards that Forrester and his associates came to insist upon, with the endorsement of Brown and Sage in the background, inevitably attracted unfavorable comment from some outsiders as time passed, eliciting off-the-records remarks that the project personnel, who worked in a building closed by security regulations to outsiders, were arrogantly high-hat and snobbish; that they were as unrealistic about what they were doing as they were young and immature; and that theirs was a "gold-plated boondoggle," extravagant in its demands, in its personal rewards, and in its raids upon the taxpayer's purse.

Unquestionably, the project members evolved a deliberate policy of saving development time and money in the long run by figuratively insisting on going "first class." Drawing together as it did young men of ambition, ability, and spirit, and reinforced by a habit of daily operations that stressed, and for the most part obtained, intelligently planned and coordinated operations, this policy produced an unusually high esprit de corps. As one project member, Kenneth Olsen, recalled years later, viewing the operation from the perspective of a personally successful administrative and engineering career as founder of a computer manufacturing company, "We were cocky. Oh, we were cocky! We were going to show everybody! And we did. But we had to lose some of the cockiness in the sweat it took to pull it off."[9]

Forrester's philosophy of acquiring high-caliber staff members became the project's continuing policy, and representative events that helped bring this about are to be seen in measures he took late in 1945 to enlist the aid of certain departments at MIT as he began to explore in earnest the possibility of using the new-fangled digital computer, a successful electronic model of which had not yet been put into operation. A week before Christmas he was suggesting active consultative arrangements. "I feel," he wrote to Professor Henry B. Phillips, "that the Mathematics Department can make an outstanding contribution to our work in studying proper set-up procedures and techniques to be used in digital computation," and he suggested that exploratory conferences with specified individuals be arranged to generate momentum. Already, since early December, lecture notes on mathematical analysis by mechanical methods were being provided to ASCA personnel from a course given by Professor Samuel Caldwell of the Electrical Engineering Department.[10]

Forrester's letter requesting cooperation from the Physics Department revealed his awareness of the prowess a digital computer would possess if it could meet the requirements of the airplane stability and control analyzer: "It is our hope that the solution of the equations involved can be accomplished by electronic techniques. If so, the computer also will be capable of solving many other problems in the fields of mathematics and physics." Such a computer, he recognized, would be "of much greater scope than any other now in existence or being considered for the immediate future."[11] He hoped that the ASCA project could obtain the "active participation of certain men whose primary interest is in physics, but with a secondary interest in our work." He named a couple of graduate students then matriculating for the doctorate as the kind of talent he was seeking and indicated that appointments could be made either through the Electrical Engineering Department (with which the Servomechanisms Laboratory was affiliated) or through the Physics Department.

At that time Forrester thought of the program in prospect as comprising two major parts: a six-month "preliminary survey of electronic computation possibilities," and a three-year design and construction phase.[12] This view, which had come out of discussions and personal reflections before the end of November, rested ultimately upon the classic distinction in mathematics between continuous and discontinuous quantities. Traditionally, geometry dealt with continuous magnitudes (lines, surfaces, and volumes), and arithmetic dealt with discontinuous magnitudes (numbers). By convention, a clock with its hands and circular face is an *analog* device that reports time in terms of continuous quantities, regardless of the fact that numbers may appear on its face. A digital clock is (obviously) a *digital* device that reports time in terms of discontinuous quantities, i.e., numbers instead of segments of a circle. Similarly, an analog device, whether it be as simple as an old-fashioned clock or as complex as Caldwell and Bush's differential analyzer, calculates with continuous quantities, while a hand-held calculator calculates with discontinuous quantities, employing not the decimal digital mode taught to schoolchildren but the binary digital mode.

Forrester, at ease with both the continuous and the discontinuous modes of calculation, proceeded to sift out the following considerations: If the analog method of calculation were pursued, entailing the use of a differential analyzer type of machine, it might—contrary to his original expectations—be unsuitable for the ASCA purpose. To represent the quantities by electrically interconnected mechanical shaft rotations, for example, would require an analog device of extreme complexity. Further, the period of time to accomplish a solution would be too long "because equipment will not respond fast enough to give the pilot proper 'feel' of the cockpit controls."[13]

On the other hand, if ASCA computations were performed by electrical voltage analogy instead of mechanical shaft-rotation analogy, then one encountered the technical difficulties of insufficient signal range. These along with the factors of the physical tolerances that could be achieved and of the friction that would be encountered might severely limit sensitivity and accuracy of solution. A change in equations or problems would require an elaborate new physical hookup of the operating components. However, analog solutions ought to be exact, in theory, and the analogy technique was well known and well established for relatively simple problems. Such were the pros and cons on the analog side of the question.

On the digital side, numerical analysis by arithmetical processes would replace continuous with discontinuous quantities and could solve the entire set of ASCA equations, given time enough. If there were not time enough, then there would have to be speed enough, of the sort that electronic circuits might well provide. There would be no physical tolerances or friction to contend with, and although digital techniques were not so well established as analog, experience was being acquired with the Harvard Mark I, the Bell Telephone Relay Computer, and the University of Pennsylvania ENIAC then approaching completion. "Most new plans," Forrester observed, "lean toward the binary system," and the vacuum tube, he knew, was a more reliable—and incredibly faster—binary (on-off) device than a relay.[14] A hypothetical electronic machine, then, might indeed be fast enough, and one might proceed to anticipate two types of storage, either mercury delay lines or electrostatic tubes, along with suitable computation and control circuitry, as constituting suitable designs.

He saw various mathematical and engineering advantages in digital computation, not the least of which were the prospects that construction costs might be less and trouble location easier. Problems could be set up more rapidly, and since their solution must progress one step at a time in the digital mode, then "the problems of a large, interconnected, simultaneously operating analog computer network are avoided." Finally, the computer could be "used for many problems other than aircraft analysis."[15]

Nevertheless, the digital disadvantages were formidable. Although construction costs might be lower, development costs would be higher, for digital techniques and corresponding electronic devices were not well known or their design well established. Development would take more time, but construction should take less. Further, he reflected realistically, the ASCA problem "requires pushing the digital technique well beyond anything even contemplated up to the present time."[16]

Although many circuits appeared to be ready for development and use, it would take five or six months of intensive study to discover whether the first promise was as substantial as it appeared. Forrester concluded that such a study must be made. The prospects were sufficiently attractive and enough people were optimistic about the future of electronic digital computation to warrant proceeding a step further. Was this a prudent decision? It certainly was not without risk. "This group at the present time," he wrote, "has no concrete information on which to predict the outcome of an investigation."[17] Upon such considerations Forrester contemplated a six-month "preliminary survey of electronic computation possibilities" and a three-year design and construction phase.

By mid-January 1946 the investigations which Forrester and his associates had been carrying on since October gave them sufficient confidence to recommend to the Navy that "numerical electronic methods as applied to the aircraft analyzer be carefully investigated." If the digital computer could be successfully developed, their proposal noted, the rewards would include "more reliable performance, higher accuracy, lower cost, smaller size, and more flexible operation." In addition, the digital computer would permit the "solution of many scientific and engineering problems other than those associated with aircraft flight."[18] This last comment contained the embryo of the general multipurpose computer that was increasingly to become the primary goal of the project.

Digital computation techniques and methods, however, were not accepted immediately as a panacea. Extensive research was necessary to explore the ramifications. To this end MIT proposed a contract that sought the accomplishment of two tasks: (1) the design of a digital type computer adequate to the requirements of the aircraft analyzer; (2) the adaptation of the computer to the analyzer, and the design of required associate equipment. The two tasks would overlap chronologically. The first would commence immediately and pursue intermediate objectives until December 1949, when the whole project was to be completed. The second would phase in toward the end of 1946, but only after a "final decision on the practicability of electronic computation as related to the aircraft analyzer" had been made. Task one, it was estimated, would cost $1,910,000; task two $477,600—a total of $2,388,000 for the completed project.[19] Such was Forrester's and Sage's thinking at the beginning of 1946. If the projected rate of progress was overly optimistic, it nevertheless provided timed goals at which to aim.

Simultaneously with the submission of the proposal to the Navy's Office of Research and Inventions (ORI), Forrester replied to a request made earlier by Lieutenant Commander H. C. Knutson of ORI's Special Devices Division for "comments on the applications of high-speed electronic computation."[20] Forrester's reply contained much of the substance of ideas that had emerged from previous discussions he had held with Perry Crawford on the subject. The digital computer, Forrester predicted, would possess a flexibility not possible with the analog computer, permitting therefore the construction of a "Universal Computer" with definite possibilities for military application in both tactics and research. In tactical use it would replace the analog computer then used in "offensive and defensive fire control" systems, and furthermore, it would make possible a "coordinated CIC (Combat Information Center)," possessing "automatic defensive" capabilities, an essential factor in "rocket and guided missile warfare." In military research, electronic computation held promise of possible wide and diversified research programs in "dynamic-systems": (1) aircraft stability and control; (2) automatic radar tracking and fire control; (3) stability and trajectories of guided missiles; (4) study of aerial and submarine torpedoes, including launching characteristics; (5) servomechanisms systems; and (6) stability and control characteristics of surface ships. Digital computation, furthermore, would allow the "study of both interior and exterior ballistics" and "stress and deflection studies in ship and aircraft structures."

Leaving the areas of possible military application, Forrester turned to the implications of high-speed electronic computation for scientific and technical research in general. Here he predicted widespread opportunities in the fields of (1) nuclear physics, (2) thermodynamics, (3) compressible fluid mechanics, (4) electrodynamics, (5) mechanical engineering, and (6) civil engineering. He further considered its application to statistical studies in both the physical and social sciences. In the social sciences alone, he observed, it would be of value to government agencies and departments. He concluded with the following comment:

The development of electronic digital computation is only beginning, and considerable effort and money will be expended in achieving the equipment to meet the above objectives. Once sufficient development is completed, however, the cost of duplicating electronic computing equipment will be less than for other forms of computers. Beginning with a suitable basic design, new computers could be built with facilities for a specific magnitude of problem by adding or omitting standardized memory or storage units without requiring significant redesign.[21]

The proposal that had been made in January 1946 to the chief of the Office of Research and Inventions was revised and resubmitted the following March. Substantively, the revision differed little from the original: it requested that the date of completion be extended to June 1950 and that the total allowable expenditures be increased from $2,388,000 to $2,434,000. It also included a summary of Forrester's letter to Knutson and presented the research-and-development challenge in terms of an overlapping sequence of four activities or phases:

1. "Research, development and construction necessary to demonstrate digital techniques of the type required for the final computer."
2. "Design of a computer which is adequate for the aircraft analyzer problem."
3. "Construct and assemble the computer and associated equipment for control and stability studies on aircraft."
4. "Operation of the complete equipment for the solution of aircraft stability problems and application of the computer to other types of scientific computation."[22]

Although the revised proposal submitted to the Office of Research and Inventions was an MIT document, it also reflected the influence and ideas of those at the Navy's Special Devices Division who were immediately responsible for federal administration of the trainer-analyzer project. The rapport between the two groups was sufficient to produce fruitful joint discussions in which a proposal acceptable to the Navy could be worked out. Actually, the Special Devices Division in February 1946 had recommended to its parent organization, the Office of Research and Inventions, that the MIT proposal be accepted and implemented. Hence it is probable that the March revision reflected the Office of Research and Inventions's reactions to the original proposal. The revision was then transmitted to the institute by the Special Devices Division. As a consequence of whatever internal adjustments were made, the Office of Research and Inventions incorporated the first two phases of the March proposal into Contract N5ori-60. This contract superseded the earlier Letter of Intent for former Contract NOa(s)-7082 and became retroactively effective to June 30, 1945.

Under Task Order No. 1 of the new contract, MIT was to undertake first the construction of "a small digital computer involving investigation of electric circuits, video amplifiers, electrostatic storage tubes, electronic switching and mathematical studies of digital computation and the adaptation of problems to this method of solution." Second, it was "to design an electronic computer and aircraft analyzer based on Phase I of this Task Order."

Phase I was to commence as of the date of the contract and was to terminate June 30, 1947. Phase II, commencing July 1, 1947, was to terminate June 30, 1948. The first phase would cost $666,000, the second $528,360. The total cost of the contract was set slightly larger than the sum of the two phases: $1,194,420.[23] These costs were in agreement with the amounts set by MIT in its revised proposal of March 1946. In that month, also, the Navy revised its initial specifications to conform to the changed conditions and goals. Finally, in the revised specifications, the project was given the name by which it was to be known thenceforth: "Whirlwind."[24] It was one of a group of new computer projects that the Special Devices Division funded and designated by such names as Whirlwind, Tornado, and Hurricane.

Preliminary Design Efforts

Two and a half years had passed since MIT had responded in December 1943 to Captain de Florez's original request and set John Markham and his associates to work on the aerodynamics problems of the airplane stability and control analyzer. Forrester had taken up the challenge in the fall of 1944, with the result that MIT and the Navy were formally committed by the end of the first year to the development of an ASCA prototype.

During the second year Forrester became totally immersed in the project, in the detailed difficulties involved in fashioning the analog computer that his experience told him he would need, and then in the theoretical alternative of a digital computer before there were any such computers in operation. By the end of the second year Forrester was switching to digital, the young engineers and funding supervisors in the Navy's Special Devices Division were enthusiastically encouraging the change, and the stage was being set for Project Whirlwind.

During those two and a half years larger winds of change were also blowing. The titanic struggle of World War II came to an end, and there followed the profound transformation of returning to peacetime routines and the prudent conduct of business as usual. These efforts occupied the attention of most Americans and their institutions. But ASCA-Whirlwind was an exception. Forrester, with Nat Sage's and Gordon Brown's support, continued to pursue his goal with unabated drive and singleness of purpose. The research and development project that had begun routinely by the wartime standards of 1943 became extraordinary in the conduct of its affairs by the peacetime standards of 1946 and 1947. Major elements of these peacetime standards were a drastic shrinkage in military funds and extensive reorganization of military planning for research and development in order to accommodate the more leisurely peacetime tempo. These shifts imposed constraints that Project Whirlwind tried to ignore.

The novel and extensive collaboration that had sprung up during the war between the national military establishment and civilian engineers and scientists appeared to some to be no longer needed, since there were no more battles to be fought; it evaporated at a rate that pleased military and civilian traditionalists and disturbed those who saw some lessons to be learned from the experience. The latter sought to continue the collaboration.

Project Whirlwind was not to thrive unscathed through this "sea change" that set in when peace returned, but its engineers were too busy with immediate technical challenges to pay much attention to larger affairs. By the end of 1945 the computer was still the tail of the dog, so to speak, and the aircraft stability and control analyzer was the dog. A year later, judging by events within the Servomechanisms Laboratory, the tail had passed through and beyond the point of wagging the dog and had become the dog. The analyzer became the tail, and even that was cropped in 1948 when the cockpit was junked.

It could be argued in after years that abandonment of work on the rest of the analyzer was a serious tactical mistake, for as the airplane analyzer faded further into the background, so did the once-obvious immediate practical relevance of the untried computer become more remote and more nebulous. The overriding pragmatic question in the spending of military funds was, classically, "What's it good for?" Although the answer became dazzlingly clear to Forrester and his project associates and was perhaps earlier as clear to Perry Crawford in the Special Devices Division, as the months and years passed it seemed to become less clear to others, almost in proportion to the rising costs. Early in 1946 Forrester and Crawford separately saw five years of research and development work ahead before success would be demonstrated and appreciated. To Forrester it became a goal that required the sort of pace a $100,000-a-month budget would provide.

At the end of the first week in January 1946 he was still pressing his search for the men he needed. "The general type of man whom we need," he wrote in a letter asking Nat Sage for assistance, "should have originality and what is often referred to as 'genius.' He should not be bound by the traditional approach . . . I do not know of suitable prospects."[1]

While he was beating the bushes for personnel, he set up ten divisions in the laboratory—seven to carry on the technical work and three to support these—ordered a weekly meeting of each division at a time when he could be present, created a coordinating committee of his divisional leaders, and called for a stepped-up delivery of reports on technical progress and problems. "The Navy expects, and rightly so, to be informed of research and development progress through suitable reports," he pointed out to his staff in an early Conference Note.[2]

By the end of February he had a firm enough schedule, based on discussions with the Navy, to call several tasks and their time schedules to the attention of the engineers on the project. These tasks were allocated to cover a period from the preceding July to June 1950.[3] According to the new schedules, the last six months of 1945 had been devoted to completion of studies in analog computation, to preliminary investigation of digital electronic methods, and to plans for carrying on the latter. Characterized in this manner, the project gave the impression of being routinely in command of its situation at all times, and this was an impression that Forrester sought naturally and by design to convey to his staff.

But *had* they been in command of the situation at all times? This was a question that Navy programmers and administrators were later to raise more than once, not only regarding this particular period in the affairs of the project but subsequent periods as well. There were some critics who came to feel that Forrester was attempting to gloss over the brute fact that the project had had to abandon its first intention to build an analog computer, just as, later, it abandoned the aircraft analyzer. Forrester and his associates had made a false start, ran this argument. What was to be gained, then, beyond self-deception and false impressions conveyed, by describing the situation otherwise? And why try to deceive his own engineers, many of whom had been intimately involved, by such statements in his published schedule?

The answer is to be found in part in Forrester's style of conducting his affairs and in part in the character of the research and development process. He saw himself as best carrying out his directorial function by shielding his men from potential outside interference that would interrupt their progress and, at worst, demoralize their enterprise. It was his responsibility to see that the project had what it needed to proceed with its investigations and to avoid making the personnel of the project privy to external administrative, policy, and fiscal problems that they were not prepared to handle, that they were not hired to handle, and that they could do nothing about in any event. Forrester saw no reason to allocate time for his engineers to stand wringing their hands.

Since both he and his staff understood the difference between the known and the unknown and between the predictable and the unpredictable in engineering research, no false illusions were being generated within the organization by putting the best face on the fact that preliminary views and preliminary investigation had yielded unforeseen negative information that stimulated the discovery of an affirmative alternative. As Forrester well knew, an engineering problem was also an engineering opportunity, the validity of which could be affirmed only by finding a solution. The digital computer offered a challenging and exciting solution indeed. So he chose to regard the last six months of 1945 as a period devoted to analog and digital computation studies rather than as a period of crisis, and although it had been a time when far-reaching decisions were made, these did not constitute a serious crisis in his view.[4]

He gave his team a year to lay its plans for building a digital computer, another half year on simulator cockpit studies and equipment and on logical designs and bench-test models, a third year to work up final equipment and circuit designs and to begin work on final components, a fourth year to build the prototype computer and receive the cockpit from the Navy as an item of "Government-Furnished Equipment," and a fifth year to finish, test, and deliver to the Navy the completed analyzer. In the middle of 1950 the machine would go into full operation.

Forrester visualized four tasks that included but expanded upon the phases delineated in the March 1946 proposal. The first would accomplish basic theoretical work by the middle of 1947 and would produce a small digital computer that could perform essential basic functions. The second task would begin before the first ended, would last for a year, and would lay out the basic designs for the cockpit and prototype computer. The third task would overlap the second and in a year produce these components of the prototype airplane analyzer, and the fourth task would produce the working, tested analyzer a year later.

To control the schedule but permit technical and administrative adjustments, Forrester stipulated a policy of periodic review "because of the indefinite nature of the problem and dependence upon ideas which have not yet been formulated." He also made it clear to project personnel that the schedules and tasks described were not fixed for all time, that indeed the arrangement simply reflected present thinking.

By the middle of March 1946 Forrester had set up a flow of internal information among the project engineers that he intended would indicate every two weeks what each investigator was doing along various of the following lines of investigation:

Block Diagrams
Computing Circuits
Mathematics
Mechanical, including Cockpit
Mercury Delay Lines
Storage Tube Research
Other Electronic Problems

He took for granted that this beginning arrangement would be improved upon, and it was altered as necessary in the following years.[5]

Of the lines of investigation indicated, only the "Mechanical, including Cockpit" represented a continuation of an earlier line of inquiry, and even that was affected by the knowledge that devices must be developed to convert the digital, electronic-pulse data into mechanical forces and motions affecting the pilot and the cockpit. Further, the responsive forces generated by the pilot's movements of the mock controls must be converted back into corresponding digital pulse data. These problems were not impossible, but neither did established solutions exist. The digital computer was too new.

Forrester's appraisal of the overall situation with respect to computer design caused him to consider more than one aspect of the storage problem; while mercury delay lines as proposed for the EDVAC appeared very promising, so did the use of special electrostatic storage tubes. Forrester and his associates began to survey the state of the art in this specialized area. The mercury, or acoustical, delay line employed the stratagem of providing a looped electrical circuit in which was inserted a "tank" of mercury. An electric pulse introduced into this circuit could be preserved by circulating it around and around such a loop until needed. The electric pulse would generate a sound wave at one end of the mercury tank, and the sound wave would regenerate the electric pulse at the other end of the tank. Because sound travels more slowly than an electric pulse, a delay would result in the continuing propagation of the signal, hence the name. The Project Whirlwind engineers learned that this device was being considered for both the Moore School EDVAC and the British EDSAC, which were lineal design descendants of the Moore School ENIAC. It might provide alterable high-speed, internal storage of the sort the ASCA digital computer would need.

Another storage device that appeared equally promising was the electrostatic storage tube. In principle, the face of a cathode ray tube (TV picture tube) could be divided into a grid of squares over which a controlled electron beam could sweep, charging, recharging, or discharging each square upon command. It would thus provide an alterable, electromagnetized memory surface for internal storage purposes. While both the mercury delay line and the electrostatic tube appeared theoretically adequate at first glance, each needed to be studied, and neither yet existed as a practical physical device. Forrester and his engineers realized they faced intensive research and development activity before they could say they had an acceptable internal storage unit.

Computing circuits composed a category worthy of several engineers' attention, for these circuits would carry out the electronic operations that would perform the appropriate arithmetic and calculating operations in the digital mode.

It was visualized at first that the Block Diagrams Group, the Mathematics Group, and the Electronics Group, especially, would construct a symbiotic relationship in which each would create necessary information for the other. But in the state of engineering art as it then existed, so unformed with respect, on the one hand, to an aircraft analyzer, and on the other hand, to a digital computer, their relatively vast mutual ignorance imposed contingent

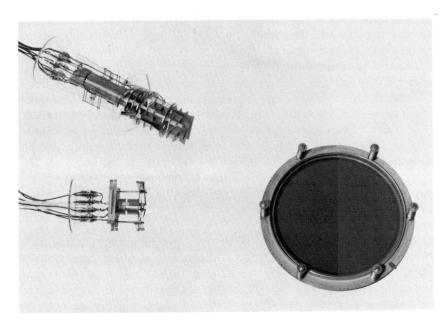

The main parts of an electrostatic storage tube are (left) the two electron guns and (right) the collector screen and the surface on which the binary digits are stored.

restraints that hobbled them together. The Mathematics Group sought to work its way out of their mutual predicament of ignorance by considering ways and means of attacking the aircraft equations that Markham, Koppen, and Bicknell had provided, as modified and extended by L. Bernbaum and Bicknell.[6] "We have decided," reported the head of the group, Hugh R. Boyd, "to work on rather short specific problems and gradually build up sufficient data and experience in numerical methods to enable us to attack the aircraft problem effectively. This preliminary work would also serve to build up our knowledge of other types of problems which our computer would solve effectively."[7]

The Electronics Group became several groups, oriented to particular problems and components, such as circuits, pulse transformers, mercury delay lines, and electrostatic tubes. They realized that decisions from the Block Diagrams Group would give them information about more elaborate components and their systemic relationships. A demonstration adder, clock pulse generator, switching arrangements, and electrostatic tubes were among the devices under study and construction during the spring.[8]

The task of the Block Diagrams Group, as described by its head, Robert Everett, was "in general, to devise a complete computer system, including definitions of all components, interconnections of these components, [and the] sequence of operations."[9] At the same time that the Mathematics Group would be a source of information about computer requirements, the Block Diagrams Group would be ascertaining machine computing tech-

The MIT 400-series electrostatic storage tube.

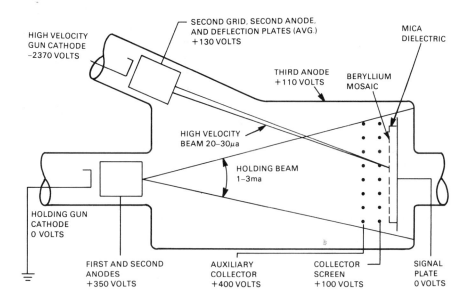

HIGH VELOCITY GUN CATHODE
−2370 VOLTS

SECOND GRID, SECOND ANODE, AND DEFLECTION PLATES (AVG.)
+130 VOLTS

MICA DIELECTRIC

THIRD ANODE
+110 VOLTS

BERYLLIUM MOSAIC

HIGH VELOCITY BEAM 20–30μa

HOLDING BEAM
1–3ma

HOLDING GUN CATHODE
0 VOLTS

FIRST AND SECOND ANODES
+350 VOLTS

AUXILIARY COLLECTOR
+400 VOLTS

COLLECTOR SCREEN
+100 VOLTS

SIGNAL PLATE
0 VOLTS

niques, programming techniques, and component designs for accomplishing computing, storing, switching, and programming.

Hindsight shows the attempted correlations of the responsibilities of these groups to have been at once reasonable and naive. Had they been mathematicians instead of engineers, the young men involved might have placed the power and responsibility to lead the way in the hands of the Mathematics Group. Here, too, they would have been reasonable and naive. But they did not, and as time passed the Block Diagrams Group became the leader.

The Block Diagrams Group meanwhile began to analyze possible ways to proceed. In early April, with Everett assigned to the job full time, Steve Dodd assigned one-fifth time, Pat Youtz three-eighths time, and P. Tilton one-half time, the group found open to it "a great number of system possibilities ranging all the way from the completely serial or sequential method described by von Neumann, where no two operations are performed at once, to a completely parallel method where all operations are carried out at once, including digit transmission."[10] The latter method would be equivalent in complexity to an analogy type solution, Everett felt. He saw that the range of possibilities represented "a complete range of solution time and a complete range of complexity and duplication of equipment. Some intermediate complexity must eventually be chosen, the criterion being that the total equipment must be as simple as possible but still provide the required solutions."[11]

Everett went on to point out that three considerations dictated the course of action of the Block Diagrams Group. (1) The Mathematics Group had to determine the mathematical phrasing and solution procedures of the aircraft analyzer equations, in order to know the "maximum expected total of operations required in a fixed time period." (2) The Electronics Group had to ascertain "the time required for a single operation." (3) The Block Diagrams Group had to acquire a knowledge of components that would "allow the most efficient paralleling of equipment, to satisfy" the requirements with which the other two groups were working. These strictures made it apparent to Everett that "no final system block diagrams can be developed for a long time," although final designs of components could probably be estimated closely enough to provide these elements of the system when they were needed.

Since explicit system parameters were as yet unavailable, Everett proceeded to consider the order of magnitude of data, orders, and solution procedures a computer might be expected to handle when coping with operations of the aircraft analyzer. With these considerations in mind and proceeding in the direction indicated by the ENIAC and EDVAC enterprises of Eckert and Mauchly, Everett envisioned a machine that would have a total storage of about 8,200 words or less. It would accommodate a word length of about 30 binary digits. It would round off numbers as a fixed policy to begin with (the problem of errors resulting from rounding off would be taken up later). Its storage tubes would operate serially. It would incorporate a high-speed multiplier as its arithmetic unit. Input and output operations would be carried on simultaneously. Finally, it would operate as a sequential machine.[12] Such were the preliminary design parameters. They did not remain unchanged.

Everett suffered no illusions about what he and his group did *not* know; a first purpose of their early efforts would be "to learn as much as possible about computer techniques and problems." At the same time, they would be providing the Electronics Group with "preliminary specifications to enable them to better direct their efforts."[13]

Thus the young engineers under Forrester's direction spent the year of 1946 exploring possibilities, selecting from these the arrangements, designs, requirements, practical limits, characteristics, theoretical models, and bench-test items they found promising. Some worked on hardware designs. Some worked on mathematical procedures that would be amenable to machine handling and machine solution. Some worked on the problems peculiar to creating a machine—the analyzer and its computer—that, to work properly, must consist of an integrated system of component electronic and mechanical mechanisms and submechanisms. However efficiently and reliably a particular circuit or subassembly might perform its functions when tested by itself, how would it work when interconnected with other circuits?

Would an array of these generate sufficient "noise"—residual currents, stray impedances and interference, back emf's, and the like—to cause a theoretically simple arrangement to become inordinately complex as a consequence of making it work in practice?

Especially important were the policy-level design decisions that would give the system its basic character. Should a storage assembly acquire its unit of information (technically called a "word") bit by bit or should it acquire it all at once? If mercury delay lines were used, means of inserting information essential to the calculating processes of the computer (interpolating) must be provided, complicating the circuitry. Since pulses of electric current constituted the basic signals the computer would use, the timing and routing of these must be finely controlled at all times. Since the digital mode of operation meant that fresh signals were used either to alter the character of earlier signals or to alter the character of a patterned arrangement of earlier signals, a "domino" effect was a prevailing feature. If just one "domino" fell the wrong way, if just one signal were mistimed, misrouted, or were to cause a wrong radio tube to operate, or if one tube or circuit malfunctioned and no "back up" component were there to compensate for the failure, then *all of the rest of the calculations* to follow would be in error. In homely analogy, the computer was an intricate array of "bucket brigades," and if one bucket failed to be passed on, then the entire operation was nullified.

On the other hand, even though for want of a nail a kingdom could be lost, reliability and coherence were practical possibilities because of the "building-block," or modular, construction of circuits that was possible. A reliable gate circuit could be inserted wherever it was needed, to block or to pass a signal to a given circuit. The digital computer would be a more complex piece of machinery than, say, any automobile, yet it could employ the same submechanisms over and over, as a tree does by employing not one leaf but hundreds simultaneously. Unlike the tree, the computer must have its modular submechanisms—its multivibrator "flip-flops," its gate circuits, and so on—interconnected in such a way that the static hookup of tubes, wires, resistors, condensers, diodes, and the like could accommodate and effect a dynamic, ordered pattern of flow of radio pulses.

Long before the spring of 1946, the project engineers had passed beyond these simple considerations, which have been represented here in oversimplified language, to the more sophisticated design and construction challenges of working on the detailed technical specifications. Forrester had suspected at the start that although the mercury-delay-line storage principle possessed many attractive features, it might prove too slow for the real-time response needs of the airplane analyzer, especially when part of a serial, or sequential-pulse, machine. Theoretically, flip-flops could be used instead as storage devices, but in a simultaneous-pulse machine, so many tubes would be involved that keeping them all replaced and operating would be well-nigh impossible.

Electrostatic storage offered an attractive alternative principle. Various investigators in the field of vacuum tube research were working upon applications of this principle, by which a minute spot on a signal plate could be negatively or positively charged and hold, or store, that charge long enough to be useful. The RCA "Selectron" tube, the Williams tube (named after its British inventor, F. C. Williams), and an electrostatic tube developed by another MIT laboratory, the Radiation Laboratory, were among applications that attracted Forrester's attention as 1946 wore on, and by autumn, he, Steve Dodd, who had been carrying on preliminary tests, and their associates decided to modify the MIT tube design to fit their particular needs.[14]

In the meantime, Everett and his group had found compelling reasons to discard the sequential mode of pulse operation and adopt the higher speed, simultaneous, or parallel, transmission of digits (pulses) among the circuits of the machine.[15] A high-speed, parallel-digit multiplier appeared promising for the same reasons, the most important of which was the speed of computation required if the aircraft simulator were to work.[16]

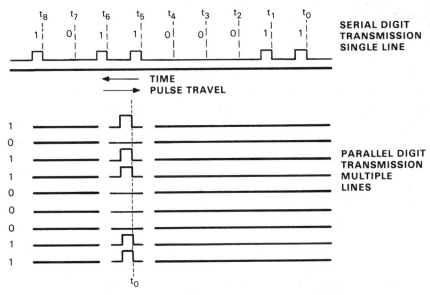

SERIAL DIGIT TRANSMISSION SINGLE LINE

PARALLEL DIGIT TRANSMISSION MULTIPLE LINES

A project diagram comparing serial and parallel digit transmission time.

Not only did the parallel-signals computer look both promising and feasible, but also the project staff knew that the time was rapidly approaching when they must "either fish or cut bait." Forrester had pointed out in early June that "we are not yet in a position to decide what must be built by next June until we know the basic principles we are to use as a foundation."[17]

Viewing the performance limits within which the first computer they proposed to build must operate, Forrester pointed out that the contract with the Navy "calls for a model computer which will, at the very minimum, demonstrate operating principles which we plan to incorporate in the aircraft analyzer. At most, it may become a computer which will be useful for solving a variety of other problems." If the latter multipurpose type of computer were decided upon, Forrester noted that the estimated terminal date for Phase I of the contract might have to be extended beyond June 1947.[18]

What technical information might conceivably guide them in establishing the basic design parameters, so that they might proceed to build their first computer? Forrester was ready with a provisional answer: it would depend "largely upon the information forthcoming from the electrostatics field."[19] This policy view of June 1946 had hardened by December into the decision to build a preprototype computer, "in view of the probable complexity of the prototype computer which might include some 3,000 tubes."[20] The preprototype, a "simpler experimental computer," would "test the components of the computer and a system made up of them, the system being capable of doing test computations." It would "provide a system in which to test new components or types of operations as they become available." It would "check reliability and evaluate mechanical design and maintenance problems." And it would be operating in six months.[21]

When electrostatic storage tubes had been perfected, these could be substituted for the more primitive storage devices, such as toggle switches, which initially would be provided for test purposes. Since mercury delay lines were too slow, they would not be used. Standard electronic and relay racks, accommodating removable assembly bases (plug-in chassis) 17 inches deep and 10 inches wide, were readily available. They would permit easy access to and testing of the hardware of which the computer would be composed.

Project supervisor of the preprototype computer would be Forrester. Harris Fahnestock (who had joined the staff earlier in 1946) would be in charge of production. Everett would head the Block Diagrams Division, Leon D. Wilson the Computer Division, and David R. Brown the Electronic Engineering Division.[22] Within the already existing organization of Project 6345, this redirection of operations was an evolutionary phasing-in of more specialized activity; it did not abruptly alter the entire conduct of affairs. It represented the sharper focusing of operations that Forrester and his associates felt was now possible after a year of engineering research.

The extent and magnitude and detail to which their studies had carried them have only been suggested in this nontechnical account. They had worked hard, and they had learned a great deal. They had added carefully selected engineers to their staff, as well as bright young graduate students looking for subjects for master's theses in electrical engineering. When Forrester encountered a "business as usual" attitude among government sup-

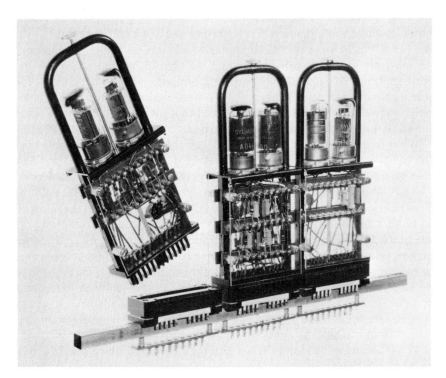

Plug-in unit prototypes: gate circuit, flip-flop, and switch tubes.

pliers of surplus equipment his project needed, he waited until he had clear evidence the responses were less than reasonably prompt and intelligent and then used it to clear up the "bottlenecks" and to ensure that, for a while, at least, they would get better service. This was a never-ending battle and a normal one with private and governmental suppliers; from the point of view of the project workers, they were never long in need of what they required, nor were they continually being held up by lack of funds and materials and technical facilities.

"We got what we needed," recalled one engineer, "and since there was such an extensive exchange of information going on, it was hard to get out of line or to order something that no one else could imagine why you'd need it. We were given our heads, but we were held accountable." "You never knew in the early days," remarked another, "when Jay [Forrester] or your supervisor would stop by to see how you were doing. There was never any question but that they were there to help, and there was never any question but that they expected you to know what you were doing. Those that didn't, somehow moved on out. Jay was pretty good at figuring out what it was that a man could do that would help the work along. Many of us were going to class and had homework, and once things really got going, we could work

An assemblage of plug-in units in a decoder panel.

morning, afternoon, or evening. You just followed the most intelligent course of action."

Whatever efficiency of the project is attested to by remembered high morale, the fact remained that as the end of 1946 approached, it began to look increasingly as though the six-months completion date of the preprototype computer could not possibly be met.[23] The details simply could not be worked out rapidly and reliably enough. In the longer run of affairs, however, the overall progress of the project hinged less upon any specific practical problem and accomplishment than upon the concurrent investigation of many paths that appeared promising. These investigations, from the spring of 1946 to June of 1948, involved the exploration of both phases of Contract N5ori-60 as outlined in Task Order No. 1. But increasingly the emphasis was placed upon Phase I, development and construction of the digital computer.

As their efforts came to be more and more completely devoted to working out the engineering intricacies of the projected computer, the airplane stability and control analyzer assumed a position of lesser importance in their minds. It was but one example of the practical applications to which Whirlwind might be turned.

In the fall of 1947, following conversations that Forrester and Everett had been carrying on with Navy Special Devices technical personnel at Sands Point, the two young engineers prepared two technical reports offering possible applications of the digital computer to naval warfare. The first of these was "a brief study of a simplified version of the anti-submarine problem." The second, issued two weeks later, was more ambitious in its scope and followed naturally from the first. It presented "in rather general terms some possibilities in the arrangement and use of high-speed digital computers for the analysis, evaluation and intercommunication of information in an anti-submarine naval group."[24] To the best of their knowledge at the time and in after years, Forrester and Everett knew of no earlier practical engineering work on how the logic of computers could be applied to interpret radar data.[25]

The two reports taken together represented an informal proposal for practical military application of a computer the like of which had not yet been built, although Forrester and Everett specifically had Whirlwind in mind. "For the simplified problem selected," they wrote in Report L-1, "the Whirlwind I computer is entirely adequate for a problem involving 10 ships, 5 submarines, interconnecting radar and sonar data, and depth charges in any number up to 20 preset units and 20 proximity-fuze units in the water at one time."[26] While the first report primarily focused on examining how a destroyer could acquire target data and translate these by means of a computer into depth-charge firing orders, the second report was concerned with communication among the ships of an antisubmarine task group in order to provide true combat information and control as a battle situation was developing. Accordingly, the second report examined the following example in detail: "Five surface ships and one aircraft are illustrated with two targets, one surface and one submerged. All units collect such information as they are able by the various methods noted. The computation and information system must make use of this total body of information to the best possible advantage."[27] The problem they then set up and explored in detail would require, they concluded, "one-half the storage capacity and one-third the operating time of WWI."[28]

There was no question in their minds that the computer they were getting ready to build would be able to handle such problems with capacity and time to spare. Both they and the Navy Special Devices engineers realized that they were contemplating a revolutionary device that would contribute immeasurably to the efficiency and accuracy of solving target problems in actual battle operation, but both groups knew also that they could as yet only talk about "paper operation." Actual testing in practice lay in the problematic future, and while the Whirlwind engineers were convinced more than ever, after these detailed studies, that they had a general-purpose computer of a practical type truly in prospect, their more immediate problems late in 1947 lay in the realm of translating their ideas further into engineering designs and these designs further into working elements of the computer.

The airplane stability and control analyzer still posed severe development problems in its own right. But the engineers' innovative predilections, the amount of funds, and the scale of enterprise carried on in Project Whirlwind produced a "first things first" attitude that reasonably centered the engineers' attention upon the computer itself. Engineering development of the cockpit and its ancillary gear for ASCA continued until June 1948. Then the decision was finally reached to discontinue that phase of the project entirely. This decision recognized the course that the program had been following and marked the total preoccupation of the project engineers with the effort to develop a general-purpose digital computer.

The formal announcement of termination of the cockpit program gave two reasons for the decision: (1) This phase of the total program had been carried forward as far as possible under the existing state of the art. Further information regarding the conversion of digital quantities to analog quantities was required, but the research to accomplish this end could not be pursued because other phases of the total program more urgently demanded the engineering and financial resources available. (2) Continuation of the cockpit phase of the total program was really unnecessary at this time, since the pace that had been followed in the design and construction of the simulation equipment would have resulted in its availability prior to completion of the computer.[29]

The decision to discontinue the cockpit phase of the project was not unanticipated. Work had slowed on the cockpit throughout the winter and early spring of 1948, and Forrester had brought the reduction in effort to the attention of both the Navy and the MIT administration.[30] The decision was also in accord with recommendations made by Perry Crawford in December of 1947 that the work on the cockpit be discontinued as "not essential to the program."[31] The cockpit was absorbing money and engineering talent that could be applied with greater benefit to development of the computer.

Official naval acceptance of the decision was acknowledged in August 1948, and its necessity was justified on the grounds that the research effort required to develop the digital computer "for comprehensive real-time simulation for synthetic evaluation was too enormous."[32] The truth of the matter was that the Navy was running low on research and development monies, and Special Devices personnel were well aware of the fact.[33]

The change in emphasis did not go completely unchallenged. During the course of a conference held September 22, 1948, with the Office of Naval Research (ONR)—which had replaced the Office of Research and Inventions as the parent organization for the Special Devices Unit—the question of the initial goal of the project was raised, and some of the Navy participants expressed the hope that the project would not "deviate too far from its original aim of producing a high-performance facility for analyzing proposed aircraft." In response to these doubts Forrester explained that the digital computer anticipated had never been intended to *be* the airplane analyzer, but rather a working model of the type of computer which could be used *in* the airplane stability and control analyzer. The working model, he cautioned, would have limited applicability to the analyzer. Throughout his remarks was the implication that he and his associates were seeking to design and construct a computer that would be in truth a general-purpose computer which could be applied to "limited, real-time aircraft simulation." In addition, it could be used for scientific calculations.[34]

In October, Navy Special Devices personnel proposed that the cockpit which the MIT group had acquired earlier from the Air Force be disposed of as surplus.[35] But in November 1948 there was still further scrutiny by the Office of Naval Research of the pros and cons of discarding the cockpit. In one sense, discarding the cockpit could be taken as discontinuing work on the airplane analyzer. To concentrate exclusively on the computer was to shift attention from the whole of ASCA to only part of it and in this way subtly change the character of the project and its goals. ONR questioned if ASCA should not remain the focus of the contract instead of yielding to Whirlwind. The Mathematics Branch of ONR, whose head, Dr. Mina Rees, had expressed some reservations concerning Forrester's comments at the September conference, investigated the possibility of realizing the original purpose of the project through the use of analog equipment being developed under another Navy program.

The investigation, conducted by Dr. C. V. L. Smith of the Mathematics Branch, reached a negative conclusion, but it was a qualified negative. Smith stated in his report that if the equations initially supplied by MIT's Department of Aeronautical Engineering were to be used, analog equipment could not perform the necessary computations in the time required. He then proceeded to question whether the "mathematical formulation of the 'Whirlwind' problem" had not been too elaborate, thereby opening the possibility that more simplified equations might not only meet the requirements of the device but might also permit the use of analog computational techniques.[36]

Ultimately the decision to discontinue work on the cockpit prevailed. In December, after the useful spare parts had been removed, the fuselage, cockpit, and turret were consigned to the scrap heap.[37] Subsequent events were to suggest that perhaps Smith's report was less the final shot in defense of the analyzer than it was the opening shot in a conflict between engineer and mathematician that was to characterize future relations between the MIT group and the Navy.

In retrospect it would appear that throughout this early formative period in Project Whirlwind's history, the Special Devices Division represented effectively both MIT's cause and its own as it sought and obtained from higher naval authority the permission and funds necessary to change and expand the program. It is arguable that the Navy's acceptance of the revised program represented a tacit, although not explicit, encouragement of concentration of effort upon the development of a "universal" computer rather than one peculiar to the aircraft analyzer. If so, it would follow that the investigators engaged in the project would feel justified in placing primary emphasis on the computer research and development phase of the program and in subordinating the aircraft analyzer to a secondary requirement that would be met later, if at all.

The policies developed and followed during this early period were acceptable to both MIT and Navy leadership, and so were the improvisations and modifications of these policies. The shift of emphasis from aircraft analyzer to universal-purpose computer was not always destined to receive Navy endorsement, for the times changed and so did the Navy personnel. Among the factors contributing to a deterioration of sympathetic support were reduction in Navy research and development budgets after the war, appearance of a new philosophy of research and development sponsorship in the Navy, the consequent emergence of the Office of Naval Research, and the inevitable personnel changes in the offices designated to oversee the Navy's role as fiscal sponsor of Project Whirlwind. These factors caused the early rapport between Servomechanisms Laboratory personnel and Navy personnel to be dimmed, if not extinguished. Unfortunately, the powerful operation of these factors could not be checked. They increasingly obscured the merit and promise of the unique Whirlwind configuration of the digital computer.

5

Pressure from ONR

The progress of technical events from 1946 to 1948 stemmed from the built-in dynamics of the research and development activities that the project engineers were carrying on, quite apart from the inevitable organizational arrangements and rearrangements and the equally inevitable legal contractual agreements drawn up and modified from time to time. An observer, depending upon his expectations, could take the view, say at the start of 1947, that Project Whirlwind was making due progress or that it was falling behind. In either case, the selection of a proper scale against which to measure the activities of the project remained a complicated, intuitive, and obscure task of judgment, further complicated by the joint practice followed by MIT and the Navy of establishing goals and schedules to be met. In this respect, Project Whirlwind was like most research and development projects. Goals and schedules were set, providing a timetable for exploring the unknown and the partly known. Since the timetable was the product of mixed ignorance and knowledge, subsequent investigation often showed the goals to be less attainable and more remote than earlier had been thought. Revised goals were necessary, and these called for further investigation, further research and development effort that yielded additional information. Inevitably, some of the new information, in its turn, further modified, transformed, or even destroyed some of the revised goals.

It was from the predicaments created by modifications in the timetable that Jay Forrester sought to extricate himself when writing a semiannual review of the status of the Whirlwind contract as of January 1947. While he and his associates were able to keep their heads above water, there was also a larger current of events that continued inexorably, slowly, steadily to carry the project toward certain shoals that were forming as a consequence of actions taken by the Navy during the transition from wartime to peacetime

operations. Pursuant to requirements imposed by the Truman administration and the Congress, the Navy reorganized its policies for supervising
and funding research and development projects. Forrester had to contend
with these changes along with his scheduling problems, and the changes
only compounded his scheduling problems.

First, the scheduling problems: Mindful of the scheduling dates for the
two phases of Task Order No. 1 that had been written into Contract N5ori-
60 a year earlier, Forrester was willing to admit to Special Devices program
managers and to their superiors in the new Office of Naval Research (ONR)
that Phase II would commence six months later than planned. The project
would need to provide sufficient development time to construct the preprototype computer called for in Phase I. Only in this way could the configurations of the Phase II prototype computer and airplane analyzer be
firmly established. The construction of the prototype computer would commence not in July 1947, as planned, but in January 1948.[1]

The computation speeds of the machine would have to be "well above
those originally anticipated," and although the general nature of the computer block diagrams had been established under Everett's leadership, much
new work involving "the advancement of electronic techniques in the fields
of video circuits, electronic switching, trigger circuits, and pulse transformers" lay ahead. Furthermore, since reliability was crucial in a computer
hooked up to an aircraft simulator, time should be allowed for the design
and incorporation of "checking and trouble-shooting circuits similar to
those required in the final electronic computer."[2] MIT believed, said Forrester, that the preprototype ought to possess the operating speeds and approximate circuits the final machine would feature.

Forrester believed that in view of existing circumstances the design of the
preprototype could be firmly established by the end of the next eight or nine
months, and construction of its many parts could be completed three or four
months later (having begun well before October). Such would be the state of
the project at the end of 1947, and it would permit the preprototype to be
assembled and put into preliminary operation "early in 1948."[3]

Forrester was careful to exclude the electrostatic storage tubes for
Whirlwind's "memory" from this schedule. They might be available in time,
but sufficient data were "not now available to make firm time estimates," so
manual-switch storage and flip-flop storage would be incorporated until
such time as the electrostatic tubes became available. The plans called for
about 25,000 binary digits of future electrostatic storage.

To accomplish the revised, stretched-out schedule would require the expenditure of $30,000 per month for the coming year; most of these expenses
would be charged to the preprototype of Phase I of the contract. As both
MIT and SDC representatives well knew, Phase I had never really been
intended to "define the nature or extent of this pre-prototype computer."

Forrester could nevertheless assure the Navy that "the project is now prepared to embark upon the specific system design of a pre-prototype electronic computer which is the end objective of Phase 1."[4]

Benefiting from the past year's researches, the preprototype would employ parallel, or simultaneous, transmission of digits. The block diagrams that Everett had developed for a serial-transmission computer—inspired

This "breadboard" multiplier was one of the first elements developed by Project Whirlwind.

A project diagram: electronic binary multiplication using a gate tube with two control grids.

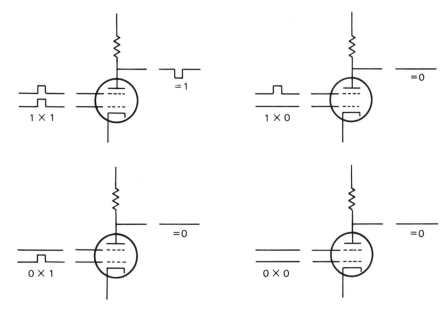

originally by the proposed EDVAC machine—had convinced the engineers that, despite relatively simple and easy-to-maintain circuits, such a device would be too slow for the airplane analyzer's real-time demands. So block diagrams had been developed for a faster, parallel-transmission computer, in which the input signals (digits) would be simultaneously transmitted from one part of the machine to another. In comparison, a serial machine was like a man with only one hand, who could handle only one item at a time. A parallel computer could have as many hands as its designer wished, and these could operate all at once.

Registers large enough to accommodate 16 binary digits would be employed. "Sixteen digits are considered sufficient for testing and demonstrating electronic operation and for a certain few investigations into the mathematical applications of digital computers," Forrester observed, but realizing how much more useful in mathematical investigation such an instrument might be if it could handle larger numbers, he added that the computer would be so designed as to carry out its operations "in multiples of 16 digits in length," specifically, 32 binary digits.[5]

Forrester's well-composed letter was packed with information; it presented the good news with the less than satisfactory and put the latter softly, so as not to disturb. Nevertheless, it was a letter that said progress was slower than had been scheduled, and when one paused and reflected upon just what sort of slow progress it was, one could see that it was progress to the tune of $305,000 already spent, progress to the further tune of another $200,000 anticipated for the next six months, and progress to still another tune of $528,000 for the year after that, with no assurance when the storage tubes would be ready. For over a million dollars it promised ultrahigh computer speeds, only 16-digit operation to begin with, and some kind of internal storage some time.

Nevertheless, this state of affairs represented not unreasonable progress to those Navy program managers who had been involved at the start of the engineering project to develop an aircraft stability and control analyzer; nor was it cause for special concern to those, like de Florez, Peter Gratiot, or Perry Crawford, who had entertained a rather visionary and aggressively dynamic engineering philosophy with regard to technical developments they considered desirable and feasible. To them, Project Whirlwind's behavior, changing schedules, and modified goals could be accounted for by the very character of the research and development process it was engaged in.

But elsewhere in the Navy there was a changing attitude. Manifested in ONR, it was caused by those fundamental organizational and policy changes which accompanied the Navy's transition to the condition and structure of peacetime operations. These changes were generated by circumstances that historically and genetically had nothing to do with aircraft analyzers and digital computers, and they were too profound to be affected by the small influence that the Navy Special Devices personnel and MIT's Project Whirlwind engineers could exert. The accumulating impact of these changes upon the Special Devices Center and Project Whirlwind, put in strongest terms, emasculated the former and drove the latter to the wall. Put in milder terms, these changes inevitably effected a major reassessment of some of the projects in which the Navy and civilian advanced research and development teams were jointly engaged, and one of these projects happened to be Project Whirlwind.

At the inception of the aircraft analyzer program at MIT in 1944, Navy supervision and funding of the program had been a primary responsibility of the Special Devices Division. This unit was initially a branch of the Bureau of Aeronautics, but it was transferred in May 1945, along with other Navy research and development facilities, to the internally established Office of Research and Inventions and again a year later to the congressionally created Office of Naval Research. Under both the Bureau of Aeronautics and the Office of Research and Inventions, the Special Devices Division had been permitted a wide latitude of authority and freedom of action. Once under the control of the Office of Naval Research, however, the division was phased out and its facility at Sands Point on Long Island was designated as the Special Devices *Center* of the Office of Naval Research. Until February of 1949, nevertheless, Navy responsibility for the supervision of Project Whirlwind was to remain with the Special Devices Center, thus ensuring a continuity of supervision up to that time.[6]

Prior to the appearance of the Office of Naval Research there had developed between the engineers of Project Whirlwind and the engineers of the Special Devices Division a reciprocal confidence and sympathy that was to decrease proportionately to the increase in ONR's exercise of authority over the Special Devices Center and its programs. The relatively harmonious relations established early in the program were given additional strength and substance when Perry Crawford left MIT in October 1945 to join the staff of the Special Devices Division. Crawford, who subsequently suggested the use of the digital computer as a solution to the real-time problem which was besetting Forrester and his colleagues, brought to SDD additional familiarity with the ASCA project, but more importantly, he brought with him an imaginative and enthusiastic confidence in the potential utility and versatility of the digital computer. As head of the Special Devices Center's computer section, Crawford was to prove an imaginative, able, and influential ally to Project Whirlwind until ONR took full command.[7]

As the Special Devices Center became more and more the instrument of ONR, however, the relations between Project Whirlwind and the center became increasingly strained and critical, to such a degree that in the winter of 1947 Forrester even questioned the center's competence "to provide the proper administrative, technical and financial assistance to the work and to properly relate the interests of all Navy groups." Undoubtedly, Forrester was becoming increasingly restive under the more critical supervision emanating from SDC in response to the increasing pressures generated by ONR. The earlier rapport was being submerged by the tensions that were created as ONR asserted its authority.[8]

The years 1947 through 1949 were difficult ones for Forrester and Project Whirlwind, for in addition to the increasing tempo and severity of Navy criticism, Project Whirlwind found itself under closer and more penetrating scrutiny by MIT's top administration. The project had become a source of contention, caught up in the struggle that accompanied ONR's efforts to implement the authority inherent within its enabling legislation. It was caught up also in the struggle between mathematician and engineer that accompanied the pioneering research and development phase of digital computation. Finally, it was caught up in the struggle over funds that accompanied postwar retrenchment.

Jay Forrester's direction of the project also became involved in the controversy. Dedicated to Project Whirlwind and determined to secure its success, Forrester aggressively and single-mindedly pursued the course he believed would most quickly reach that end. Without doubt, his aggressiveness and determination offended many, but without this sense of purpose behind it the project could very likely have failed. His superiors both within MIT and the Navy no doubt were pleased by his determination to do the best job possible on what he considered to be "one of the most important development jobs in the country," for he was convinced that computers promised rewards to the military as great if not greater than radar. But his attitude toward costs could not fail to be disturbing to those who held the purse strings. Costs that others regarded as expenses, imposing an upper limit of spending, Forrester seemed to consider as productive investments, as means to an end, rather than as determinants of level of effort. His apparently cavalier attitude toward costs was doubly disturbing because of his youth and because he apparently failed to communicate effectively his rationale or philosophy to cost-conscious Navy supervisors compelled to stay within limited, peacetime budgets. They were dismayed, not reassured, by his conviction "that the facilities and funds needed to do a job are subordinate to getting the job done as quickly as technical progress permits."[9]

The rate of progress Forrester claimed for the program did not go unchallenged. His letter of January 1947, carefully composed though it was, nevertheless left the program vulnerable. It compared progress accomplished to goals earlier set, and it permitted critical eyes to find the progress wanting. It suggested that the goals—the time schedule—be modified, but this suggestion brought forward again the impression that progress had not been satisfactory. And indeed, judged strictly by the goals set earlier, the progress had not been satisfactory. So Navy programmers could ask: Was this indeed the case? Had the goals been unrealistic? Or were the capacities of the researchers inadequate? First they were going to build a simulator. Now all that was discussed was a computer, and one that was not even the type of computer that the project had originally set out to build. Were the researchers eager young men who had gone beyond their depth and did not realize it—would not realize it—yet?

Two and a half weeks after Forrester sent in his letter, the head of the Naval Research Advisory Committee, a civilian scientist, spent an hour and a half on an inspection visit. This was but one of several such visits, none of which totally allayed Navy misgivings concerning the project and the young engineers conducting it. Dr. Mina S. Rees, head of the Mathematics Branch of ONR, was of the opinion that the "consensus of visitors to the project is that there is too much talk and not enough machine." To any mathematician who visited the project and who lacked understanding of the engineering problems involved, this comment seemed accurate and only too self-evident. Also, criticisms voiced of Forrester and his project could on occasion be extremely harsh and extreme. One observer referred—as though it were accepted fact—to "the personal animosity which is widespread in the computer development field and especially as regards Mr. Forrester." It is not impossible that such criticisms, even when discounted for their exaggeration, were influential though not sufficient by themselves in shaping Mina Rees's view of Project Whirlwind and its staff.[10]

Without doubt, Forrester and his associates were operating in a very competitive field and one in which the mathematicians exerted a powerful, if not a dominant, influence. Young, inexperienced, and unknown engineers, they were matching skills and abilities with men of known stature and status, such as John von Neumann of the Institute for Advanced Studies, Howard Aiken of Harvard, J. P. Eckert and J. W. Mauchly of the University of Pennsylvania, G. R. Stibitz and S. B. Williams of the Bell Telephone Laboratories, and M. V. Wilkes of Cambridge, England.

The electronic, automatic sequence control machine was in its early conceptual stage. These young engineers were seeking not to refine an already existing device but rather to design, develop, and construct an entirely new one. In short, they were converting a concept into a radically new electronic system that would be embodied in a piece of tangible hardware. If the Whirlwind engineers had not been operating within the protective womb of MIT, it is altogether conceivable that the project would have been terminated by the Navy, particularly after ONR had assumed primary responsibility for Navy research and development. The mathematicians of ONR, enthusiastic about the computer as a scientific instrument of rapid calculation, failed to recognize its potential as a command and control center as early advocated by Forrester and Crawford. The enthusiasm of the mathematicians, however, was shared by Navy policy makers and may even have determined Navy policy views, for computer development had been assigned to the mathematics branch. The engineers of Project Whirlwind and SDC, concerned primarily with application to military needs rather than development of theoretical concepts, saw it as an instrument primarily adapted to facilitate human control of events in the physical world and only secondarily intended as a mathematician's tool.[11]

The misgivings expressed by Dr. Rees were not hers alone, for they were shared by her colleagues within the Mathematics Branch. The mathematicians were concerned because they believed that neither Forrester nor any of his associates actively engaged on the project possessed the "mathematical competence needed in the design of a new type digital computer."[12] Such misgivings were not a recent development, nor had they been allayed by Forrester's semiannual review of January 1947. They led in February to a visit by Warren Weaver, then head of the Naval Research Advisory Committee, to the Servomechanisms Laboratory at MIT to investigate the project. Later Weaver was also to visit SDC at Sands Point. Like Rees, Weaver had been a mathematician who became a capable administrator, too busy to carry on sustained research any longer, but conversant with the substance, the values, and the aims of the profession.

After visiting the institute, Weaver in his comments to Rees expressed no major criticisms, or praise either, of the project or the personnel engaged in it, but he did raise some very penetrating questions about the nature and

◁
The five-digit multiplier was partially constructed in November 1947.

The five-digit multiplier, complete, but without panel doors. Norman Taylor is the engineer in saddle shoes.

▷

purpose of the project. Weaver wondered if the quality of the mathematics matched the "excellent physics and engineering." Subsequently, after visiting SDC and writing with greater retrospection, Weaver observed that neither achievement nor progress could be measured by a single visit. His conversation with Forrester had left him, he observed, with the belief that there was some confusion whether Whirlwind was really "a simulator or a general-purpose computer," since at one point in the conversation Forrester had described it as the latter. But when pressed by Weaver to explain how it would handle certain scientific calculations, Forrester evaded a direct answer by describing Whirlwind as a "fire-control" computer. As Weaver put it, was the project failing to be good biscuits by trying to be cake? Crucial here were the value judgments to be applied; it was easy indeed to make comparisons of engineering simulators and biscuits, on the one hand, with scientific mathematical machines and cake, on the other, and Weaver was wary of rendering such judgments even while phrasing the problem in perhaps suggestive terms. The strongest impression he gained from his visits to MIT and to SDC was that both Forrester and Crawford were extremely competent and able, and that the Whirlwind staff was "well organized, enthusiastic and hard at work."[13]

Weaver's visit to MIT's Servomechanisms Laboratory in Cambridge and his subsequent visit to SDC at Sands Point may have been purely coincidental or part of a general study he was making of the Navy's research and development program, but one coming on the heels of the other strongly suggests that he was investigating Project Whirlwind within its total context, seeking to determine not only the implementation of the program at MIT but also its direction by SDC. Rees and her colleagues were concerned about SDC, its relations with ONR, and the guidance and direction it was providing Project Whirlwind. The Computer Section of SDC, understandably, felt that this concern led to an improper interference in its area of authority; nonetheless the balance of power was shifting to the Mathematics Branch.[14] In the course of a discussion over establishing a "simulation facility" at Sands Point using Whirlwind II (the projected second-generation computer) as its information and control center, Rees expressed approval but had some reservations lest she was "relinquishing some responsibilities that properly belong to the Mathematics Section." In addition, in an aside to Perry Crawford, she questioned if the center were not engaging in "empire building."[15]

If Rees and her colleagues had hoped through Weaver's visits to obtain evidence that would support their efforts to curb Project Whirlwind, they were disappointed. Yet his comments did not still their apprehensions.

It is doubtful that Mina Rees and the Mathematics Branch sought to destroy the project. Certainly, they sought to bring it under firm control, to orient it properly, for they were seriously concerned about the program, which, they believed, had merit but lacked direction. In the fall of 1947 Rees believed that the project possessed tangible possibilities, particularly for "scientific" computation, and even if it failed to attain complete success, "a substantial contribution to the art" would have been made and "the money invested . . . worthwhile." The money was also, one might add, considerable in amount, a fact that seriously disturbed ONR, as events were to prove. Between the inception of the program and the assumption of control by the Mathematics Branch of ONR, the estimated costs had more than doubled and threatened to continue to mount, and the schedule had slipped by some twelve months, yet the original purpose of the program contractually remained the same.[16]

The pot continued to simmer, even if it did not boil, with the discontent of the mathematicians providing a steady source of heat. They continued to be disturbed by the project's lack of that which they regarded as competent mathematical talent essential to a well-ordered, properly organized computer program. For them the ideal electronic digital computer program was the one directed by von Neumann at the Institute for Advanced Study at Princeton, New Jersey. Persistently, they compared the two programs, asking how Whirlwind differed from the IAS computer. If the two devices did not differ significantly, then why was Whirlwind costing so much more? Persistently, also, they asked why Whirlwind was being designed and built as a general-purpose computer if its primary application was to be simulation. These questions were raised at an ONR conference in October 1947, accompanied by the charges that Project Whirlwind lacked sufficient mathematical competence, that no effective analysis of the functions of Whirlwind had been prepared, that the status of the storage-tube program had been exaggerated, and that even within the MIT community, the project was under fire for lack of interdepartmental cooperation and slow progress.[17]

Responding to these questions and charges, which obviously contained the implication that SDC had been remiss in its direction of Project Whirlwind, Crawford recommended that Professor Francis J. Murray of Columbia University be retained to evaluate the "mathematical competence indicated by the work to date" and to make a comparison between Whirlwind I and the computer von Neumann was developing at Princeton. In addition, Project Whirlwind's directors should prepare "detailed information concerning the components designed for Whirlwind I and the design of the Whirlwind I system." Until the information requested was furnished and the decision was reached that the program was indeed valuable, he recommended that no further consideration be given to the financing of Whirlwind II. Crawford's last recommendation may or may not have reflected his own annoyance and misgivings, but certainly it mirrored the opinion of some within the upper echelons of ONR and threatened the use of ONR's ultimate weapon, the power of the purse, to bring the project into line.[18]

To dampen the heat persistently emanating from ONR, Forrester followed two courses. To meet the chronic objections, he prepared with his staff, upon the recommendation of Captain George M. O'Rear of SDC, a twenty-two-volume administrative and technical summary of Project Whirlwind from its inception in 1944, detailing and explaining the changes made in the purpose and nature of the program.[19] This report, he hoped, would explain away ONR's objections and serve as a compendium to provide answers to any future questions the project's critics might ask. The questions and charges aired at the October conference at ONR were answered separately and in detail.

Comparing Whirlwind I to the von Neumann computer, Forrester argued that the former was faster, more applicable to Navy needs, and further advanced in design and construction. Comparative costs could not be determined, he noted, since von Neumann had no cost estimates for his finished device; however, because of "final design refinements and the more finished packaging," Whirlwind's final costs would probably exceed those of the IAS computer by a margin greater than the two-to-one ratio forecast by ONR. His critics, he suggested, showed a real lack of understanding of "the simulation and control field and . . . the meaning of a general purpose computer" when they sought to make Whirlwind one or the other, for the complexities of simulation demanded a flexibility that permitted a wide variety of uses. The storage tube development program was difficult and complex, but one that had always been frankly and candidly discussed without exaggeration.

In denial of the charge that interdepartmental cooperation was lacking, Forrester cited instances in which other departments had cooperated by making either personnel or facilities available. Within his own department, Electrical Engineering, a separate research program—supported by the Rockefeller Foundation—in digital computation had been discontinued to permit consolidation of the two staffs in order to make the total effort more effective. All in all, Forrester argued, because of the immense importance of electronic digital computation, MIT had rendered more aid to the project than the Navy had a reasonable right to expect, and furthermore, this assistance had been given despite heavy teaching and research commitments.[20]

Despite Forrester's disclaimers, supported as they were by examples, there was a continuing feeling that cooperation, if not lacking, was limited. Forrester, belatedly perhaps, had requested assistance from other departments, but the indications were that they had not responded enthusiastically.[21] Beyond the usual obstacles—other commitments, lack of interest, and so on—one significant impediment to cooperation was without doubt the classified nature of the project, a barrier Forrester found to be a continuing problem.[22] Samuel Caldwell, who had been working on the research program supported by the Rockefeller Foundation, refused to work with Project Whirlwind so long as it was subject to military security restrictions.

He would work only "on research concerning electronic computing that will freely serve all science," a view shared by many of his colleagues.[23]

Nevertheless, Forrester did have a measure of assistance and cooperation from the Mathematics Department. Professor Philip Franklin of that department was dividing his time between departmental and Project Whirlwind duties when Crawford called for an inspection visit by Professor Murray of Columbia. Together with two full-time members of the project, Franklin constituted its Mathematics Section. The effort put in by this group and by others working on mathematical problems in the project "would represent a larger staff than available for the entire engineering activity of the Institute for Advanced Study computer" if it included all who performed mathematical functions within the program, Forrester pointed out. Both he and his critics knew that this was an organizational procedure, as well as a legitimate way of interpreting program operations, that was not restricted to the Whirlwind Project.[24]

Although the project was not emphasizing mathematics as much as ONR felt was necessary, it was pursuing research in pure and applied mathematics related to the computer.[25] At the same time, mathematics that was not directly pertinent to the engineering development of the hybrid, practical, general-purpose, science *and* engineering instrument that Forrester and Everett visualized tended to be subordinated. Forrester felt sufficiently vulnerable to ONR's criticisms to be goaded into further defensive action following Murray's visit, which occurred on November 8, 1947. Four days later, Project Whirlwind coincidentally published a memorandum by Franklin surveying in some seven pages of single-spaced typescript the project's mathematical program, both accomplished and planned.[26] In addition, within the month Forrester was planning to enlarge both the mathematics staff and program, subject to Navy approval indicated by adjustment of the contract "to cover continuing basic research programs."[27]

The project's activities were by no means confined to responding to the external pressures generated by ONR's persisting and skeptical scrutiny. Indeed, Forrester shielded his engineers, as far as he was able, from the outside alarms so that they might continue their research with as little interruption as possible. In fall of 1946 he had begun looking actively for space to house the project's preprototype computer.[28] By March the firm of Jackson and Moreland, Engineers, headed by Edward L. Moreland, Frank M. Carbert, and Ralph D. Booth, had estimated that the accommodations specified would cost about $770,000 if incorporated, as proposed, into the projected Navy Supersonic Wind Tunnel Laboratory on the campus by extending the office section of the laboratory "three additional floors, making this building a four-story building in order to house the Servo-Mechanisms Laboratory."[29]

Forrester allowed for a growth factor in a report to SDC in April 1947 on the matter. The Supersonic Laboratory accommodations requested would include enough space, he felt, "for development and operation of the final Whirlwind computer."[30] He could not yet report, he said, on the alternative "purchase or rental of an existing building."

The growth factor assumed more explicit form in a letter to Perry Crawford near the end of April, in which Forrester confirmed earlier verbal discussions, in a manner typical of the degree of cooperation that had become characteristic of relations with SDC and that soon was to disappear as the Mathematics Branch of ONR assumed greater authority. Phase I would be extended to June 1948, because "a reevaluation of progress and time schedules" indicated that more research and development time would be needed "prior to design of Whirlwind I."[31] This was not a "stretch-out" representing reduced effort, however, because "the scope of the Whirlwind I computer is considerably more extensive than originally planned and will require an additional six months' time. Since the computer will be more nearly like Whirlwind II than originally anticipated, the design of Whirlwind I will appreciably ease the design and construction problem of Whirlwind II." Looking ahead, Forrester drew attention to developments that both MIT and SDC viewed at that time as reasonable projections: "It is anticipated that Task II involving the construction of Whirlwind II will overlap somewhat the end of Phase 2 of Task Order 1 covering the system design and that steps will be taken as soon as possible to formulate Task II." As the months passed, it became clear that these projections had failed to anticipate the research and development options available. What happened in practice, in contrast to planning, was that Whirlwind II failed to materialize. Instead, the "preprototype" vanished as well and was transformed into the prototype.

As a matter of policy, Forrester deliberately stopped referring to the "preprototype" in external correspondence that spring; as a matter of custom, "preprototype" yielded to "Whirlwind" in the laboratory as the summer wore on. In the meantime, further investigation by Jackson and Moreland revealed that the earlier estimate of building costs for the Supersonic Laboratory had been too low; an already existing building began to appear more feasible. Before the end of August 1947 the Barta Building, located on Massachusetts Avenue close by the MIT campus, came under serious consideration. It was the Barta Building that finally became the home of the Whirlwind computer.

The technical appraisals undertaken by Forrester, Everett, Fahnestock, Boyd, and other engineers in the project during 1946 had indicated that problems of reducing engineering inceptions to practice were least troublesome in the areas of information input and output and most troublesome in

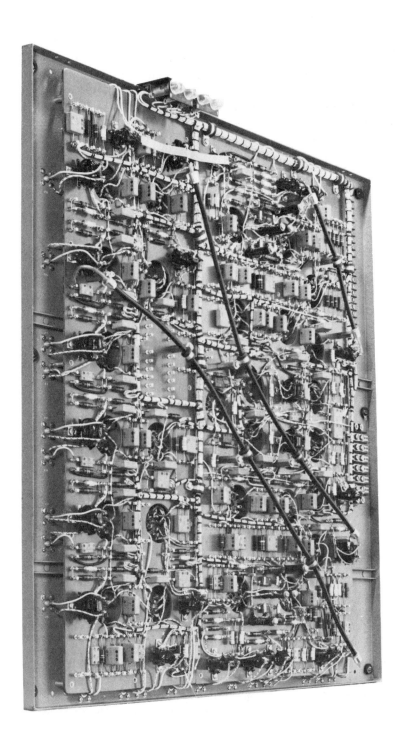

Accumulator prototype.

the area of internal storage. The project leaders had early become convinced that fast internal storage organized in easy-to-add-onto units was essential, and they devoted their efforts particularly to electrostatic storage and the problems of developing reliable electrostatic tubes.[32] Input and output problems they were willing to let the Navy Special Devices Center contract for separately, and by autumn of 1946 Eastman Kodak was involved in providing "equipment for the preparation of input films from a manually operated keyboard as well as output recording devices and mechanisms for reinserting output data into the input of the computer."[33] As matters turned out, the Eastman equipment, using minute clear or opaque spots on 35mm film to represent binary digits to be implanted or read by cathode ray tubes and associated photosensitive tubes, was never perfected for Project Whirlwind, and other input-output techniques brought forward by the industry-wide advancing state of the computer art were employed instead.

During 1947 the quota of graduate students employed as research assistants rose from eight to twelve and then to fifteen. By the end of October, Forrester was requesting twenty for the next year.[34] Most of the assistants carried out or assisted in special investigations that added to the laboratory's pooled knowledge in a modest and detailed way while providing the subject for a master's thesis or occasionally a doctoral dissertation. The practice of bringing students into the laboratory continued as long as it remained on the campus and geographically separate from the MIT subsidiary it later joined, the Lincoln Laboratory located in nearby Lexington. Not only were Forrester and his assistants continuing Gordon Brown's policy with regard to students, but also they found the campus relationship invaluable in providing a small but growing pool of first-class engineering talent, which in later years was to spread out into the growing computer industry. Though these students gave their best efforts to the project, often continuing on the staff after obtaining their degrees, the project gave them in return the experience that put many of them a professional jump ahead of their contemporaries.

While technical work proceeded apace, as Warren Weaver, Professor Murray, and other visitors observed, the project leaders presided over the expanding activity, moving from details to overviews to analysis and back to details. While Everett, for example, spent more of his time on the complex problems of logical circuitry and attended to the details of creating and maintaining an integrated system of working components as research phased into advanced design and design into projected hardware, Forrester occupied himself with internal and external organizational details and with building and maintaining a high-spirited, hard-working organization. Supported by Nat Sage's office, he selected a subcontractor to fabricate the hardware, the racks, the panels—the form and substance itself—of

Whirlwind I. Sylvania Electric Products Company of Boston was chosen during the latter half of 1947 and went to work building the items to the requirements and specifications of the Whirlwind staff.

The Mathematics Branch of ONR endorsed these developments even while preserving its apprehensions over the basic direction and purpose of the project. That there was much activity and increasing amounts of money being spent at Project Whirlwind was no guarantee, after all, that the money was being wisely spent. What was really going on in the Servomechanisms Laboratory? The Mathematics Branch could never share SDC's confidence. The twenty-two volumes of "Summary Report Number 2," for all their impressive and informative detail, were but another manifestation of the peculiar style in which Forrester's operation proceeded to go its own way, *have* its own way, and—for all Mina Rees, C. V. L. Smith, and their associates could tell—be heading for a spectacular fall in its own way.

ONR, consequently, welcomed Crawford's suggestion that Francis J. Murray of Columbia University be asked to look into the situation and deliver a report free of the modulated yet enthusiastic bias to be expected in the project's own summary reports. Murray, as already noted, visited Project Whirlwind on November 8, 1947. He was an associate professor of mathematics who possessed both classroom and laboratory experience in computers.[35] Accompanied by representatives of the Special Devices Center including Perry Crawford, he conferred with Forrester, Everett, and mathematician Philip Franklin. Both professional courtesy and official responsibility required Professor Franklin's attendance at the conference. His presence also served to counter the ONR charge of inadequate attention to mathematics, a consideration Forrester was not likely to overlook. A week later the Cambridge conferees, minus Franklin, traveled to Princeton to meet with John von Neumann and H. H. Goldstine for a discussion of the computer program at the Institute for Advanced Study. Within the following week Murray finished his report and submitted it to the Director of the SDC.[36]

In his report Murray evaluated Whirlwind I in the context of the environment he had seen and had heard Forrester and his associates interpret during the Cambridge conversations. Whirlwind I, they had explained, was to be used primarily for simulation, but since "no single use of the digital computer would justify the development cost," the device would handle two other types of problems: control and scientific computation. Again Forrester, on this occasion supported by Everett, evaded tying Whirlwind to a particular application. To both men the question of application was academic, for Whirlwind was adaptable to a variety of uses, of which ASCA was only one, even if by contract the primary one.

The report contained no direct criticism of the Whirlwind program, but Murray did support the ONR charge of insufficient attention to the mathematical side of the program by noting that no mathematical analysis of the operations of Whirlwind I had yet been made and any existing plans for one were inadequate. Such analysis was essential, he argued, revealing his own professional bias; it should be performed within the Whirlwind program, not by a separate group, and should be treated "as a component of the device." There was no need for the mathematical analysis to await availability of the computer, for it would not interfere with or delay engineering development. The two could and should proceed concurrently.

In comparing the two programs at Cambridge and Princeton, Murray concluded that although they had a "common logical ancestry," they were "distinct to a remarkable degree." The application of digital computation to simulation and control required the "engineering development" of Whirlwind, a requirement not imposed upon the IAS computer, which was at liberty to follow a "direction of interest to its own objectives," namely, the consideration of "purely scientific problems." Hence Project Whirlwind's emphasis upon engineering aspects was proper, for engineering development was "absolutely necessary," and to delay it would "delay the use of digital computers in the type of problem" with which Whirlwind was concerned. He implied that since Whirlwind was being designed as a prototype from which duplicates could be manufactured, it had to follow more rigid engineering standards than did the IAS computer. This was an implication that von Neumann later rejected.[37]

Once the Murray report had made its way from the Special Devices Center to Dr. Rees's office in Washington, a copy was forwarded to von Neumann at the Institute for Advanced Study at Princeton for his comment. Accepting Murray's definition of Whirlwind's purpose as "precise and authentic" and agreeing with the importance of "a thorough mathematical analysis," von Neumann mildly rejected Murray's observations concerning the differences between the two programs. The contrast had been drawn too sharply, von Neumann felt, and he rejected the implication that because Whirlwind had a definite application in mind and was being designed and developed with intent of industrial production, it need be more "reliable and maintainable" than the IAS computer, which was intended for "general scientific purposes."

Von Neumann also questioned Murray's assumption that the difference in objectives had caused the differences in design and plan. These resulted, rather, from the differences in people. If the objectives were exchanged, the courses followed would have remained the same, for "the subject is new and it is the rule rather than the exception that two groups who work independently towards very similar or even identical objectives may come out with rather different conclusions. I need not say that I consider this very desirable. The subject is so new that it is quite reasonable to try a variety of approaches and not to place all bets on the same chance."[38]

Von Neumann's observations and judgments were moderate and restrained and in a vein not unlike Warren Weaver's of ten months earlier. Unfortunately for Forrester, they were not strong enough to allay suspicions in ONR. Instead, the issue was only just beginning to be well joined between MIT and ONR, and it was the sort of issue that many years later was to provide grounds for the remark, "We're *not* going to let it become another Whirlwind!"—a policy view that could be taken as a stout assertion of control by a determined administrator or that, again, could be regarded as a subtle failure of administrative nerve where the vigorous prosecution of research and development might be demanded.

Breaking New Trails

The year 1947 was not solely devoted to administrative and technical surveys by outside experts. Under Robert Everett's leadership during 1947 the operating requirements of the proposed computer had been incorporated into "block diagrams" stipulating the coordinated and systematic operation of the basic functional components of the proposed machine. Using the block diagrams as master plans specifying the performance of the components singly and together, Everett, Forrester, and several of the engineers then proceeded during 1947 and 1948 to lay out and review the design of appropriate electronic circuits. These would carry out the physical operations that would correspond to the mathematical and logical operations associated with binary digital computation and with the storing, retrieving, and evaluating of such digital information.

In general terms, the young MIT graduates in charge of the enterprise faced the task of converting mathematical, logical, abstract concepts into working machinery. The abstract models they conceived and worked up began, for the most part, with theoretical considerations of the arithmetical and logical operations that were to be performed by equipment capable of carrying on *physical* (i.e., electrical) operations corresponding to the abstract models. Until the proper patterns of abstract operations were worked up, no suitable machinery could be devised.

Everett embodied the abstract operations and their patterns in diagrams that set forth the logical functions. Ideally, once a block diagram had been organized, presenting the sequence of steps necessary to accomplish a particular computation, then the engineers could turn to the problem of designing the electronic circuits, including the wiring, the resistors, the condensers, the tubes, and similar elements. These circuits when properly constructed could accomplish, in physical hardware susceptible to differing, controlled, electrical states, the logical steps and computational results desired.

The problem that Everett, Forrester, and their contemporaries faced during the late 1940s was that they had little or no experience working out the precise sequences of controlled electrical states required. ONR, knowing this, had reason to be apprehensive. In lieu of the knowledge of experience, Everett had at his disposal the theoretical insights of the pioneering investigators, among whom were Aiken, Babbage, Bush, Caldwell, Crawford, Eckert, Goldstine, Mauchly, Stibitz, von Neumann, and a handful of others. The practical experience of these pioneers was so limited, in comparison to the challenge the aircraft stability and control analyzer offered, that Everett was compelled to undertake highly complicated system-building of his own, which had no precedent, especially in the realms of reliability of performance and rapidity of operation demanded by the simulator.

It is still premature to rank historically the originality of Everett's and Forrester's contributions in detail with those of their contemporaries and predecessors, other than to point out that Forrester's inventive and managerial talents and Everett's detailed logical designs, together with the resulting embodiment of these properties in the assemblage of electronic hardware called "Whirlwind I," produced a working computer of unprecedented speed and reliability and a complement of engineering personnel possessing unequaled (at the time) design sophistication and engineering know-how. Everett and Forrester, operating as engineering and managerial alter egos and supplements of each other as the years passed, were primarily responsible for the complexion of the project and, consequently, for its failures and successes.

The operating speeds required by the ASCA problem were so great as to be without design precedent. As an early issue of the project's "Summary Report" quietly understated, "additional detailed knowledge" was needed regarding the "timing and synchronization of operations performed by individual circuits when they are integrated into large-scale systems."[1] Accordingly, "operating times for each type of circuit to be used were determined by measurement, and the block diagrams were redrawn in terms of these specific circuits."[2]

The progress of a single electric pulse through various component parts of the computer could be calculated. Consequently, the engineers could ascertain theoretically whether synchronous operation of the components was being obtained, modify their circuit designs to obtain the synchronization they required, and then test the resulting hardware singly and in system hookup to make sure it met their design requirements.

They found that essential computing operations could be performed rapidly enough to be acceptable: "Calculations showed that with present circuits the multiplication process could be safely performed no faster than the rate permitted by a time-pulse repetition frequency of two megacycles per second. This speed is considered adequate for Whirlwind I," Forrester reported at the end of 1947. Although faster speeds were attractive and possible, the engineers realized such modifications would also perpetuate design changes and thereby postpone the operating date. Thus, even though experimental alternating-current flip-flop circuits appeared to be appreciably faster than the direct-current ones the engineers had checked out in detail (fifteen-hundredths of a microsecond, as against twenty-hundredths), because these circuits would be used over and over again as one of the basic types of building block throughout the entire computer and because their general performance characteristics were not well known, the engineers would not risk switching prematurely to the alternating-current design. Besides, conversion could be accomplished "with little difficulty if desired" at a later date.[3]

Realistic engineering policy required compromises to be made between the attractive, untried ideal and the practical, in order to achieve actual machinery. The project was, after all, operating on a schedule, a circumstance that neither the Whirlwind engineers nor the ONR program managers could ignore, in view of the rising costs of the project. The immediate tasks before the Whirlwind engineers included the formulation of component and subsystem parameters that would stand, the preparation of suitable specifications and drawings, and the delivery of these to Sylvania engineers so that physical components and subcomponents could be manufactured and delivered to the Barta Building, to be incorporated into various elements of Whirlwind I.

At the same time that basic circuit diagrams were being completed, laboratory testing equipment was being designed, purchased, and developed so that present and future development of systems could "be facilitated by a line of standardized electronic test equipment for generating, gating, and distributing pulses at desired repetition frequencies." The object was to enable research engineers, "by rapid interconnection of various units, [to] set up and experiment with sections of computer systems."[4]

Professor Murray during his November visit had raised a question with Forrester that pointed up a problem confronting all computer designers. Since one defective vacuum tube, one flawed circuit, could nullify an entire calculational sequence and possibly an entire program, how would Whirlwind be protected from tubes or diodes that were about to go bad, that were becoming marginal in their operation? While this was not a completely new question to Forrester, neither was it one to which he had found an answer, until, as he recalled afterward, in the throes of trying at that moment to formulate a reply that would indicate he and his engineers were masters of the situation, "a solution presented itself. I realized that by deliberately var-

The Barta Building in Cambridge became the home of Project Whirlwind. The computer occupied 2,500 square feet on the second floor.

ying the voltage and thereby changing the loading on any circuit while requiring it to carry out a simple operation, a tube that was losing its capacity to perform would be forced to reveal its identity under the marginal conditions imposed. This was how 'marginal checking' came to be invented."[5]

The formal report to ONR indicating that provisions to accomplish marginal checking would be designed into the machine contained no reference, of course, to the circumstances in which the technique was invented. The report was not couched in terms particularly calculated to reassure those skeptical program managers who, lacking faith in Forrester, were aware that they lacked the "inside" technical view. They also lacked the vision of a Perry Crawford, as well as the familiarity with engineering detail that could be balanced against a mathematical sensitivity such as a Murray might be expected to possess from his own professional experience.

Forrester's official report of his modest innovation was low-keyed and routinely incorporated in a six-paragraph description entitled "Trouble-location" in the project's Summary Report for December. The complete section follows:

Because digital electronic computers contain many thousands of electronic-circuit components, failures may be expected. Such failures almost always cause errors in computation, and temporarily destroy the usefulness of the machine. Rapid trouble-location methods are therefore of great importance.

A scheme which has been proposed for facilitating the location of faults in WWI uses prepared groups of test problems whose answers are known. These problems are of two types:

(1) Check problems, solved periodically, designed to use as much of the machine as possible. Errors in solutions will indicate that some part of the machine is not functioning correctly.

(2) Trouble-location problems, designed to use only small portions of the machine. Errors in the solution of one or more of a series of these problems will provide information on the location of a fault after its existence has been demonstrated by an error in the solution of the check problem.

The machine itself may thus be made to locate faults which would require exorbitant time by manual methods. Simultaneous failure of many elements, or failure of certain critical elements, will result in greater difficulty, but such occurrences should be few relative to the total number of failures.

Although primarily intended as a means for finding steady-state faults due to the complete failure of a component, this scheme will be extended to finding marginal components whose complete failure is imminent, which might be causing random errors. It is expected that such components can be made to give steady-state indications of failure by appropriate variation of circuit supply voltages and of the repetition frequency of applied pulses.

As an example, for certain types of faults, if the voltage of the screen-grid in a marginally operating vacuum tube is lowered slightly, complete failure can be produced, permitting discovery by check problems and subsequent location by trouble-location problems.

Whirlwind I power-supply systems are therefore being designated to permit selective variation of supply voltages in a range above and below normal operating values. The added complexity of cabling and the additional equipment required for this purpose are believed well justified by the expected gain in computing reliability.[6]

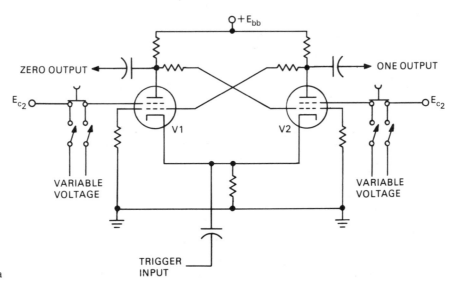

A project diagram: marginal checking of a flip-flop circuit.

By the following spring the basic requirements of a marginal-checking system had been worked out, personnel had been "assigned to design the electrical and mechanical layouts," and preliminary design proposals had been composed.[7] By the end of 1948 marginal-checking features were being incorporated in the five-digit multiplier and tested. If they worked as expected, they would constitute the basic template, so to speak, of the pattern of marginal-checking facilities planned for the entire computer.[8] The five-digit multiplier was the smallest unit of the arithmetic element that Forrester, Everett, and the others felt they could construct as a representative subcomponent that would early tell them whether they had a sound building block of the vital computational portion of Whirlwind.[9]

It was typical, too, of their philosophy and mode of engineering procedure: proceed from the level of system-requirements appraisal to the level of a consequent component; establish the detailed design of the latter and build its parts, assemblies, and subassemblies, testing them singly and together as they come into being, in order to establish preliminary operating characteristics; locate deficiencies in design and material, remedy these, and test the developing component as thoroughly as possible, taking the time to build whatever special test equipment is necessary. This procedure, they were convinced, would produce a soundly functioning building block of operating characteristics that could be depended upon and rendered compatible to the exigencies of systemic (as distinct from isolated) operation.

This philosophy of intimate interplay—that is, proceed from logical and mathematical formulations to design, build, test, integrate, redesign, rebuild, retest, reintegrate—was a major cause of the rising costs associated with Whirlwind that strained relations between ONR and MIT during 1948 and 1949. It was also part of the engineer's dynamic answer to the continuing problem of quality control, and it was a policy position from which the project leaders refused to budge, regardless of the larger and larger percentage of ONR's contract-research budget that they kept calling for. From Forrester's and Everett's point of view, it was the only way to maintain the high performance standards the enterprise required if it was to succeed within a reasonable span of time. Not only did they hold strong personal commitments to a way of doing based on a philosophy of excellence, but in a practical sense they recognized that in the long run to chance errors and mistakes was too costly.

At the beginning of 1948 Forrester had visualized completion of the computer by stages: The arithmetic element of the computer would be ready early, and the five-digit multiplier test portion of this element would be ready even earlier, for the computational speeds were likely to take more time than the information-in, information-out storage speeds or the transfer of information from one part to another of the machine. It is essential that

The empty power ro in the Barta baseme September 1948.

◁
Power supply equip-
ment was partially
installed in November
1948. Whirlwind even-
tually used 150,000
watts of electricity.

Power supply equip-
ment for marginal
checking in operation
in 1950.
▷

they fabricate earlier those parts which would require critical and perhaps extensive testing. Electrostatic storage would come last, not because it required little testing—on the contrary—but because extensive engineering research and development were required. The perfection of these tubes would consume the most time, and Forrester fully realized this. The tubes would provide the essential internal-storage capacity of the machine.

Time schedules were drawn up for the major parts of the computer, and from February 1948 onward, progress toward meeting the schedules was reported monthly to the Navy. These reports, comparing actual progress with scheduled progress, began about the time that ONR embarked on another intensive analysis of the project and its operations in order to acertain how it was proceeding. Von Neumann, presumably at Mina Rees's request, spent three days during February at the project, discussing the operations the machine would be called on to perform, as well as examining the block diagrams, potential uses, and arrangement of the projected machine, and in general familiarizing himself with the project. Rees also brought to the Barta Building John Curtiss and H. D. Huskey from the Bureau of Standards, and they "considered in some detail with Project Whirlwind Staff the nature of engineering problems of computer design and the successive stages of development leading to the final product."[10]

By spring Forrester could say that the building of the computer had begun; the Sylvania Company was fabricating components to the specifications of the Whirlwind engineers. For some units MIT furnished drawings, for others detailed specifications from which the Sylvania engineers could lay out drawings and authorize fabrication. For still others, such as "the prototype of the 28-tube accumulator panel," the project engineers constructed the first unit to serve as a model for the Sylvania engineers to duplicate, and for still others, such as the storage tubes, the project maintained its own in-house research and development enterprise throughout.

By early summer in 1948 tests had revealed that a standard type 6AG7 vacuum tube lacked the reliable life span required. Apparently a silicon concentration in the cathode nickel was raising a barrier to current flow as the tube aged, so the decision was made to switch to a tube manufactured under different techniques, the type 7AD7, which appeared provisionally satisfactory. Many tube sockets in the circuits would have to be changed, but such a prospect was not unusual or dispiriting in the engineering view of Forrester and his associates.

Nevertheless, this was one of the factors that accounted for what had become a five-week lag behind schedule, over the first six months of 1948. Forrester announced at the end of that time that since the regular semiannual revision in the time schedule was at hand, the schedules would be adjusted and the status of work actually existing in July would become the new basis. By this technique Forrester proposed to put his project on a more realistic schedule and thus compensate, in a programming sense, for "procurement delays, necessary design changes, and heavy demands upon personnel time."[11]

Although it might appear at first glance that he was trying to make the project look good by engaging in some sort of scheduling legerdemain, he was in part postponing the completion date and in part recovering some of the time lost by reassessing portions of the program and finding ways to "buy" time by eliminating, shrinking, or clarifying the details of previously scheduled operations that later required modification. Information gained from the experience of the preceding year or more placed him in a position to specify more sharply the delivery sequence of some items and the physical composition of other units. Generally speaking, "actual progress had been made at about three-quarters of the rate as expected in January. The new schedule extends the work by 30 percent in recognition of this fact."[12]

Forrester recalled in later years that the detailed manner in which the monthly Summary Reports kept ONR posted regarding technical problems and slippage of schedules had made such a virtue of frankness that one of the unlooked-for effects was the added fuel they provided to stoke the persisting unease the ONR administrators felt.[13] The same tenor of events reflected by these reports did not disturb Nat Sage, Gordon Brown, and the MIT leadership, however, although it should not be supposed that the latter were directly involved and always informed as to details until the increasingly apprehensive protests from the Navy reached their ears.

During the second half of 1948 the computer itself began to appear, as racks, subassemblies, and assemblies of various component and subcomponent parts began to be installed in the Barta Building. At the same time, the prospective complexities of setting up and then achieving full operation caused Forrester to postpone the final completion date once again, this time from the end of 1949 to the end of 1950.

One of the complexities was the stubborn way in which an efficient, reliable electrostatic storage tube design continued to elude the researchers' grasp, even while encouraging advances continued to be made. Four activities devoted to the storage tube were included in the schedule charts submitted monthly to the Navy during the first half of 1948; the number of such line items jumped to thirteen after June. Yet this could not be taken as a sure sign of trouble, for six months later, at the start of 1949, Forrester had become optimistic that the storage tubes would be ready sooner than he had earlier expected, as a consequence of gains made by the increased emphasis and effort given during recent months. But earlier, in the summer of 1948, it appeared that the storage tube problem was bigger than had been suspected, and the slow rate of progress toward a solution, compared to that which he had expected, caused Forrester to redouble his efforts and consequently to up the ante again, to ONR's dismay.

In spite of such vicissitudes, the research, design, development, fabrication, and testing progress being made on all fronts caused Project Whirlwind in mid-1948 to appear, at least to the MIT administrators, as a healthy engineering project indeed.

7

Problems of Federal Assistance

For Project Whirlwind and the Special Devices Center, 1947 and 1948 were years of increasing difficulties, even while significant progress was being made in the design and fabrication of the physical computer. The joint discharge of the interfingered administrative and fiscal responsibilities that MIT and the Navy bore was complicated by organizational and policy changes occurring within the Navy. In consequence, both Project Whirlwind and the Special Devices Center came under intensified administrative and supervisory pressure as the Office of Naval Research consolidated its responsibility and authority for certain aspects of the Navy's research and development program.

Misunderstandings between SDC and ONR—particularly the latter's Boston branch office—led in October to a division of responsibility for the project between SDC at Sands Point and the Boston branch office: SDC retained technical supervision, but responsibility for "business administration" of the contract was assigned to the branch office.[1] Relations between SDC and ONR continued to deteriorate, nevertheless, until finally technical supervision of the project also was transferred to ONR.[2] The assumption of direct technical responsibility for Project Whirlwind was effected by ONR between September of 1948 and February of 1949. It marked acceptance of the recommendation of the Mathematics Branch that the branch "should have the responsibility of promoting those aspects of the program which involve research, the dissemination of information, and advising the Bureaus on novel applications of computers (in systems or otherwise) which involve research effort." The Special Devices Center, on the other hand, should be concerned only with the "application of machines of proved worth to devices within the scope of their responsibility, as the computing elements of training devices."[3]

The transfer of responsibility within the Navy for Project Whirlwind had been a while in the making, but it was inevitable, for ONR had consistently demonstrated its determination to make itself master in its own house. It could be argued that in formal organizational terms and perhaps in substantial relationships as well, SDC's subordinate position was really not inferior to that which it had held under the Bureau of Aeronautics. However, ONR was created to perform a mission in the realm of research and development for which existing naval bureaus were not to be held responsible. With the centralization of responsibility and authority for naval research and development under ONR, SDC could not continue to enjoy the wide latitude and flexibility of operation it had possessed when, under the aegis of the Navy's Bureau of Aeronautics, it had approved the transition from ASCA to Whirlwind—that is to say, the transition from a flight trainer and analyzer to a general-purpose digital computer.

Instead, a shift occurred in SDC's role that drastically reduced the scope of its activities. Although there was a general cut in military funds for fiscal year 1948, the striking drop in funds made available to SDC by ONR demonstrates what happened to SDC's earlier freedom to select and sponsor research and development projects. From approximately $11 million nominally available to SDC in fiscal year 1947, the amount dropped to slightly more than $5 million for fiscal year 1948.[4]

It was clear by June of 1948 that ONR had lost confidence in SDC's ability to handle the Whirlwind project, and furthermore that ONR was unwilling to follow Perry Crawford's "fearless and imaginative jumps into the future" because of limited funds and because of the belief that "the present job should be under control before bigger areas were staked out."[5] Crawford recognized the trend; in September of 1948 he accepted a temporary assignment with the Research and Development Board of the Department of Defense with the intent, upon completion of the assignment, to return to ONR but not to SDC.[6]

The delay that ensued between the contractual change of September 1948 and the implementing directive of February 1949 transferring technical supervision to ONR probably mirrored both SDC's reluctance to yield completely the traditional freedom of action it had inherited from its predecessor, the Special Devices Division, and MIT's reluctance to accept technical supervision of Project Whirlwind by the Mathematics Branch of ONR. By June of 1948, with the threat of transfer apparently hanging overhead, Nat Sage became sufficiently concerned to discuss the threat with Dr. Alan Waterman, the chief scientist and civilian administrator within ONR. On this occasion Sage expressed the hope that "in making any decisions, the Navy would realize the enormous importance of engineering," including within its "administrative control . . . persons who understood the engineering rather than the scientific attack on a problem."[7]

The empty computer room, September 2, 1948.

Workers began to install wiring for the computer's arithmetic element in the fall of 1948.

By late November most
of the power wiring and
some of the registers for
digits 8-15 were in place.

Waterman, grasping the full import of Sage's comments, assured him that the Mathematics Branch under Mina Rees would not be placed in charge but would represent the Navy only on "the mathematical aspects of the project."[8] Subsequently, in September following, the head of the Mathematics Branch was designated "scientific officer" for Project Whirlwind, the title reflecting possibly ONR's efforts to appease both MIT and SDC.

The Special Devices Center continued to exercise some supervision over the project until the directive of February 8, 1949, which assigned "technical cognizance" to the Mathematics Branch. Thus, between September 1948 and February 1949 SDC had been gradually but completely phased out of the picture. The contractual amendment of September that had made the head of the Mathematics Branch the scientific officer of the project had also contained the last allocation to Project Whirlwind out of SDC funds. The subsequent source of funds became the Physical Sciences Division of ONR, to which the Mathematics Branch was attached.[9]

The lack of harmony that had characterized relations between Project Whirlwind and ONR since 1947 initially stemmed from the apprehensions of the Mathematics Branch over the nature and purpose of the program, the quality of its leadership, and its alleged lack of mathematical competence, on the one hand, and from the inability of MIT personnel to allay these apprehensions, on the other.

An even more profound source of difficulty was involved, however, even though the differing policy views with regard to the proper way to go about developing a computer provided a major source of friction between Project Whirlwind and ONR. This more profound source of difficulty lay on the broadest policy level, from which the federal government through its agencies in the executive and legislative branches appraised the operations of the scientific community and the value of those operations to the nation. The pursuit of scientific research and engineering development to help win the war usually had been sufficient justification in itself for the measures undertaken and the funds spent. But once the security of the nation was no longer in jeopardy, the conduct of peacetime research and development, together with government endorsement especially of such programs, came once more under renewed, careful, and skeptical scrutiny by program managers, fiscal officers, and administrators in the executive branch and by committees in the Congress. Once more the peacetime policies of the institution of government toward the established institution of science and toward the still relatively uninstitutionalized activities of an emerging scientific technology asserted themselves, and there was a resulting impact upon the Navy's relations with Project Whirlwind. Such a turn of events was natural, for these policies had been ambiguous and unsettled at best throughout the nation's history.

reverse side of the
ally completed
metic element
. The large panel
e third rack is an
mulator.

Viewed from this perspective, the gap between ONR and Project Whirlwind was perhaps inevitable, given Forrester's and Sage's insistence upon maintaining the project's level of effort. There resulted finally a fundamental policy confrontation between a powerful member of the private education establishment, MIT, and its less powerful collaborator-adversary in the federal military establishment, ONR. This confrontation occurred at a time when ONR not only was seeking to assert its responsibility for naval research and development but also was striving to gain the confidence of the scientific academic community—a confidence which, by and large, it ultimately succeeded in gaining.

The respective positions of MIT and ONR were, in significant measure, the consequences of the operation of historical trends transcending either institution's private history. These trends established the range of limited freedom of action and the apparent alternatives allowed to MIT and to the Navy where Project Whirlwind was involved. To pause and consider these trends is to render more understandable and natural, and less capricious and "political," the attitudes and actions of the principals. It was not an affair that could be reduced to the appealing, dramatic simplicity of a sparring match carried on between MIT and naval leaders in order to find out who were the more powerful. Rather, it was one of many smaller events characterizing the dynamic, historical distribution and redistribution of judgments and powers continually taking place and operating to bring about further adjustments in the subtle, ponderous, and leisurely process by which human institutions (in this instance those of higher education and the national government) achieve a mutual accommodation over the longer ranges of time.

Considered narrowly, it was Project Whirlwind's relative misfortune to be caught up in this process, but in the wider arena in which national research and development policies and practices were at that time being generated and modified, the stresses to which Project Whirlwind and ONR both were subjected could well be regarded as unexceptional. Indeed, had Forrester, Sage, and the others at MIT bowed without a fight to the pressures that ONR mounted, the affair might well have been transformed into a "business as usual" situation (although not necessarily a pleasant or heartening one for any of the parties involved).

Considered in a wider perspective, the difficulties which beset the relationship between Project Whirlwind and the Office of Naval Research emerge as ramifications of the more fundamental difficulties which accompanied the transition the nation was undergoing as a result of the end of World War II, a transition which was made even more urgent by the Cold War that set in shortly after the end of hostilities. It is generally recognized that World War II and its aftermath had compelled the nation to abandon its foreign policy of isolationism and to commit itself to a role of vigorous participation in world affairs. Less widely appreciated, however, is the fact that the war also had compelled the American people and their leaders to reevaluate the roles of science and technology in the national life and to revise the national posture toward them. In the prewar years that posture had been marked by the absence of any insistence that the federal government should formulate and implement a national policy comprehensively to encourage, coordinate, and sustain science and technology as activities of vital concern to the national welfare.[10]

The wartime mobilization and coordination of the nation's scientific and engineering resources was neither new nor unique, for previous wars had brought similar efforts, although not as successful or on as large and authoritative a scale. The continuation of this pattern in time of peace, however, by the creation of agencies empowered to direct, coordinate, and fund scientific and technological research and development as a substantial and vital part of the national life was without precedent. When President Harry Truman on August 1, 1946, signed into law two bills, one creating the Atomic Energy Commission and the other the Office of Naval Research, the government accepted and was implementing the principle of a continuing and comprehensive responsibility for the advancement of science and technology. The subsequent establishment of similar agencies, such as the Air Research and Development Command of the Air Force, the National Science Foundation, the National Aeronautics and Space Administration, and the Department of Energy gives further evidence of this continuing acceptance.

The statutory creation of the Office of Naval Research marked a victory within the Navy Department for a group of dedicated and perceptive civilians and naval officers who early in the war had seen the need for a central office to direct naval research and development, which in the prewar years had been uncoordinated and routine. Conducted to as great an extent as possible within the laboratories of the various bureaus and the Naval Research Laboratory, it had been concerned primarily with the improvement of existing procedures and equipment.[11] The exception to the routine nature of naval research and development was that conducted under the aegis of the Naval Research Laboratory, where a taste for fundamental work had been developed. The Naval Research Laboratory was, however, "a very small exception to the general lack of research in both Army and Navy."[12]

During the war years as the government's total expenditures for research and development mounted, so did the Navy's. The latter's identified costs rose from $13,566,899 in fiscal year 1940 to $149,887,877 in fiscal year 1944. Total expenditures for this five-year period, including monies transferred to other agencies, approximated $405,000,000, about 22 percent of the government's total expenditures for the period. Of the $405,000,000, the Navy disbursed $348,626,000: $97,853,000 to its own laboratories; $248,834,000 to private industrial laboratories; and $1,939,000 to education and foundation laboratories.[13] The rising trend established during the war years was, with minor and occasional cutbacks, to be carried over into the postwar period.

Throughout the war the Navy's bureaus continued to bear primary responsibility for research and development within their respective areas of responsibility. Coordination of the bureaus' respective programs was attempted, however, by the creation in the Office of the Secretary of the Navy of the Office of the Coordinator of Research and Development. In addition to coordinating internal research and development programs, the Office of the Coordinator represented the Navy on the boards of other research agencies, maintained liaison with the federal Office of Scientific Research and Development (OSRD), and kept the secretary and the various bureaus and offices informed of research and development programs both within and without the Navy.[14]

As the war drew to a close, the coordinator continued to provide whatever central direction there was to the Navy's research and development programs, until the impending peacetime dissolution of OSRD, together with growing complexities of the programs, caused the Secretary of the Navy to establish a central agency, the Office of Research and Inventions (ORI). This agency embodied in itself the Office of the Coordinator of Research and Development, the Office of Patents and Inventions, the Naval Research Laboratory, and the Special Devices Division. The aims of the new ORI were to (1) stimulate research and development throughout the materiel bureaus, (2) assume cognizance where a project was of major interest to more than one bureau, and (3) undertake by contract or within its own laboratories "fundamental work not unique to any single bureau."[15] The creation of the ORI indicated that the Navy was laying plans for the postwar period in recognition of the necessity to coordinate and direct the research and development programs of the respective bureaus and also aggressively to pursue fundamental research in areas pertinent to naval science and technology. Subsequently, these functions of the Office of Research and Inventions were given congressional sanction when the Congress established the Office of Naval Research in 1946.

ONR represented a substantial victory for proponents of the principle of a central departmental authority to coordinate and direct Naval research and development, including basic research as well as engineering development. The establishment of the Office of the Coordinator of Research and Development had been a major step in this direction and one accomplished over the protests of the Navy's General Board. The subsequent creation of ORI had advanced the principle considerably by providing it with presidential as well as secretarial sanction. The legislative establishment of ONR added congressional acceptance of the principle to the presidential and secretarial. Most importantly, congressional approval guaranteed appropriation of the funds necessary to fulfillment of the principle—a guarantee not implied in the sanctioning of ORI by executive order. Indeed, the Navy had been compelled to request of Congress the passage of legislation establishing the Office of Naval Research, because the House Appropriations Committee had refused to consider monies for ORI until the approval of the Congress had been given.[16]

Congressional resistance to ORI did not imply objections to the principle of centralization; rather it reflected the resistance of Chairman Carl Vinson of the House Committee on Naval Affairs to continuing executive "use of war powers in peacetime." Such use, Vinson had warned, "could seriously impair the relations of the Navy Department with the Congress." In fact, Vinson's committee had strengthened the office by writing into the bill changes giving the office "control of all naval research," including—subject to the secretary of the Navy's approval—authority to control the research programs of the bureaus. Thus, if the secretary approved, the newly created ONR presumably would exercise authority over the total spectrum of naval research and development.[17]

The Vinson bill creating the Office of Naval Research became law on August 1, 1946, thus antedating by some four years the creation of the altered peacetime successor to the wartime Office of Scientific Research and Development, the National Science Foundation. Consequently, the Navy was one of the first government agencies to fill, at least partly, the void created by the phasing out at the war's end of the Office of Scientific Research and Development. In fact, the imminent end of the war had hastened the administrative and legislative steps that culminated in the establishment of the ORI and its successor, ONR.[18]

From the beginning the primary task of ONR, theoretically, was sponsorship of basic research. Development was to remain with the respective bureaus. The first Chief of Naval Research, Vice Admiral Harold G. Bowen, implemented this policy by supporting fundamental research, and by 1947 the office had planned a research program that would cost about $20 million annually. Toward the end of 1948 ONR had in its employ some 1,000 scientists distributed among three in-house laboratories and six branch offices. It had contracted for some 1,131 projects at 200 institutions, a program according to one estimate accounting for approximately 40 percent of the nation's total program in basic research. The value of contracts in which ONR was involved approximated $43 million, of which $20 million came from the office's own funds; $9 million came from other federal agencies—principally the Atomic Energy Commission—but was distributed by ONR; and $14 million came from various universities, again according to one tally. Thus, during the crucial postwar years while the Congress was debating the kind of organization that should be created at the national level to sponsor basic research, the Office of Naval Research was actively preempting the field and continuing a program that many considered vital to the national security.[19]

The founders of ONR had assumed that, once established, it would mount a comprehensive and sustained program in basic research, and one not restricted to areas of naval pertinence only. The proponents of a peacetime national agency for scientific research and development, however, had assumed that Navy responsibility for a comprehensive program would be temporary, pending congressional authorization of such a federal agency to sponsor basic research in its broadest sense. Vannevar Bush, one of the most forceful advocates of a comprehensive national agency, had supported the Navy undertaking while voicing the reservation that it was "entered into with the full understanding on the part of everyone that it was to a considerable extent a temporary program, and that if the Congress saw fit to establish a Foundation for the purpose, the principal burden of that work would be transferred to the Foundation."

Although the Navy would continue to sponsor some projects, Bush thought the bulk of basic research would be the responsibility of the foundation, where it could be managed "by a group which can combine the military and the civilian points of view and which can judge the thing from a somewhat broader basis than the services, by their very nature, can hope to judge it." Despite Bush's reference to an initial "full understanding," ONR did not share his opinion. While it was willing to transfer some Navy projects of broad interest to the proposed agency, it intended to continue its own program at the fiscal level already attained, expanding in areas of immediate pertinence.[20]

These efforts to organize a coherent, peacetime, federal policy toward the conduct of scientific research and engineering development were far more intricate and involved than has been indicated here. They were caught up in the strong currents of political power that are generated, in the American tradition, whenever economic wealth is being created and allocated on a large scale. In this perspective, MIT, ONR, and Project Whirlwind were little more than pawns in a larger game that would impel President Dwight Eisenhower in his farewell address in 1961 to warn the nation to keep a firm, restraining hand upon its growing "military-industrial complex," which showed signs of being more interested in its own welfare than in that of the nation at large.

Whatever the merit of Forrester's and Everett's technical dreams for Whirlwind and whatever the merit of this or that managerial arrangement for carrying on the research and development that Whirlwind required, the larger forces at work redistributing political power and funding authority and responsibility were generally heedless of any research and development criteria, as distinct from economic or managerial criteria, for judging the prosecution of research and development projects. The special relationship between ASCA-Whirlwind and the SDD in the project's early years was far more fragile, because of its wartime basis, than Forrester at the time was perhaps willing to realize.

The trend generated by the larger forces was toward more conventional administration and control, and ONR followed this trend. In consequence, Forrester's and Everett's philosophy that funds and facilities needed to carry on research and development should be subordinated "to getting the job done as quickly as technical progress permits," had to be judged a mistake if the trend was to be encouraged. Besides, to admit the rightness of their view meant giving them more money than ONR was able to give and more discretion than it was inclined to give. ONR did not subscribe to the philosophy that Gordon Brown had applied to his wartime Servomechanisms Laboratory; by conventional standards that philosophy was risky, expensive, and imprudent.

The expansive powers granted the Office of Naval Research by the Congress implied the eventual centralization of Navy-sponsored research under the new office. As ONR sought to implement the authority inherent within its enabling legislation, it took steps that had profound consequences for the Special Devices Division and for Project Whirlwind. Within a span of two years, as has been noted, the Special Devices Division was subordinated as the Special Devices Center, and Project Whirlwind was transferred to the jurisdiction of the Mathematics Branch of the Office of Naval Research. For Project Whirlwind this meant that the understanding fiscal supervision and program encouragement of the engineers of the Special Devices Center were replaced by the skeptical, less-than-enthusiastic supervision of the mathematicians of the Mathematics Branch. It did not help matters that the latter were more interested in the computer as a tool for scientific computation than as the "brain" of a command-and-control center for tactical and logistical operations, as envisioned by Forrester and Everett with Perry Crawford and other SDD staff members who became familiar with the two MIT engineers' "L" reports, L-1 and L-2 on antisubmarine warfare.[21]

Another complicating factor in the relations between the two groups was the rising cost of carrying forward Project Whirlwind at the very time the nation was undergoing postwar military retrenchment, with its impact upon military budgets. Funding, if a problem, had been a very minor one until the fall of 1948. From then the question of money was to overshadow all others and continue as a chronic source of irritation and difficulty.

The initial amount of money—$1,194,420—committed to the project by the Navy in June 1945 under the terms of Task Order No. 1 of Contract N5ori-60 had been increased two years later by an additional $100,000 and again in January of 1948 by $520,000.[22] The first increase was apparently required to meet the extra costs incurred by extension of the contract's terminal date for one year to June 30, 1949. The second increase was intended to defray the costs of program acceleration requested early in 1947 by

SDC.[23] In addition, part of the work was subcontracted to the Sylvania Electric Company at an estimated cost of $319,576.75. Sylvania was to "conduct studies and experimental investigations in connection with: final packaging design and construction of the Whirlwind I electronic digital computer."[24]

The cost of the Sylvania subcontract was included in the MIT request for additional funds for fiscal year 1948, which was forwarded to SDC in August 1947, totaling some $441,520.75. These requested funds, it was noted, would not cover the costs "for photographic input-output devices" to be purchased from Eastman Kodak or for "aircraft simulation components," which ONR would have to fund separately.[25] The amount finally allocated by the Navy in January 1948 was, as noted earlier, $520,000, approximately $80,000 above the MIT request, but between the time of the request and final Navy action, Project Whirlwind had entered into a subcontract with Eastman Kodak in the amount of $70,000 for "photographic storage equipment . . . necessary to the completed simulator."[26]

Neither MIT's request nor the Navy's final allocation caused any furor in either organization. Jay Forrester did comment to Nat Sage that the estimated cost contained in Amendment Number 4, which officially allocated the additional funds, was some $500,000 short, but there for the time being the question died.[27] The "blow up" came in the fall of 1948, following a letter from Nat Sage to SDC in which he requested $1,831,583 for the project funds for the fifteen-month period between July 1, 1948, and September 30, 1949. This amount, when added to an unexpended balance of $385,260, produced a total of $2,216,843 or a monthly expenditure rate of approximately $148,000. Sage's request for more than $1.8 million raised havoc with ONR's budget and brought into the problem both the Chief of Naval Research and MIT's top administration.

Earlier, in the winter and early spring of 1948, MIT's administrators had become concerned about the friction that had developed between Project Whirlwind and ONR and presumably felt a trifle dubious either about their ignorance of the project in detail or about the project itself and its management. To determine the quality of the program and its leaders, MIT's leadership through Dr. James R. Killian, Jr., then vice president, asked Ralph Booth, of the Jackson and Moreland engineering firm and a member of the MIT Corporation's Electrical Engineering Committee, to review the status of the project. Booth, questioning his own competence to "pass on the theoretical and technical merits" of the electrostatic storage tube under development, retained as a consultant Dr. J. Curry Street of the Harvard physics faculty and formerly a member of the MIT Radiation Laboratory.

Booth, and presumably Street, had visited the project in May, July, and August of 1948 to study its operations and obtain the information and impressions necessary for an appraisal of its worth. Booth submitted his report to Killian in a letter dated August 26. He stated that the purpose of his review had been "to determine whether the accomplishments to date and the organization and procedure of the work currently in hand insured a successful completion of the project approximately in accordance with the present schedule." His report was very favorable. Booth observed that the project's "accomplishments . . . give every promise of providing within the scheduled date a successful computer at speeds hithertofore unrealized." With the exception of the electrostatic storage tube, the program in all its phases had reached that point, he noted, "where the remaining work can be classified as design engineering or development of refinements." The storage tube, he anticipated, would be successful; however, if not, the other components of the computer could be adapted to other types of memories with no greater penalty than some loss of speed in computation.

Booth and Street were enthusiastic about the potential of the storage tube and strongly urged that the "Navy be asked to acquaint itself with the high promise of this development, since it is entirely possible that this tube may supplant mechanisms which hold less promise and which are in an earlier stage of development and on which appreciable sums of Navy research money are currently being expended." All in all, Booth reported the project to be "well-organized, staffed by efficient, capable people, and . . . conducted in proper accord with the timetable."[28] Booth's favorable report, when added to the support rendered the project by Nat Sage and Gordon Brown, convinced MIT's leading administrators that Project Whirlwind was worthy of their support. So they came to its rescue in the funding crisis of 1948.

Nat Sage's request on August 4 for $1.831 million to cover costs for fifteen months through fiscal year 1949 and the first three months of fiscal year 1950, may not have caught the Navy totally unawares, but it was nevertheless an irritating if not downright disturbing request. Not only did it ask ONR to double the amount ONR had already committed to the project, but it was submitted some thirty days after the 1949 fiscal year to which it was to apply had begun. To the Navy it must have been a splendid example of the continuing, erratic, and unpredictable pattern of behavior followed by Forrester and his colleagues, who, between the spring of 1947 and the fall of 1948, had raised their estimates of financial requirements for FY1949 by some $1.3 million. Here was a pattern particularly disturbing to administrators whose policies were controlled more by financial considerations than by technical ones.[29]

Looking back, one could see that in the spring of 1947 both MIT and SDC had agreed that costs for FY1949 might equal $500,000. But by October 1947 MIT foresaw FY1949 costs of $940,000, and in December it raised the estimate again to $1.2 million. Since FY1949 would begin July 1, 1948, it was then only six months in the offing.

ONR, in the meantime, had been raising its estimates at a different pace. Although ONR's subordinate, SDC, had agreed on the $500,000 figure in the spring of 1947, its reaction to MIT's $940,000 estimate was to go up only to $600,000. But during the spring of 1948, SDC once again came into agreement with MIT, now at the higher level of $1.2 million. Then in June of 1948, just before FY1949 was to begin, Admiral Paul F. Lee, chief of naval research, cut ONR's support back to $900,000.[30] In August, *after* the beginning of FY1949, Forrester and Sage proposed to raise the ante once again, as though Admiral Lee's action meant nothing. This time the MIT figure rose from the earlier $1.2 million to $1.831 million and covered fifteen months instead of twelve. The FY1949 portion would be $1.465 million. ONR's response by Admiral Lee's successor, Admiral T. A. Solberg, was a courteous but firm "no"; the sum of $900,000 would remain ONR's commitment for FY1949.

Admiral Lee's reasons underlying his decision to reduce Project Whirlwind's FY1949 allocation to $900,000 were presumably many and complex, but a lack of funds was not included among them. It is reasonable to assume that at the time Lee made his decision he must have had a fairly good idea of what the amount of unexpended ONR monies to be carried over from the previous year would be, for at the time the FY1949 budget was under consideration, such monies were estimated to approximate $32 million.

Other considerations had to provide his guidelines, therefore. In view of the pattern of events involving the transfer of technical responsibility for Whirlwind from SDC to the Mathematics Branch, which was to take place during the winter of 1948 then approaching, one likely consideration was the intent to bring SDC into its proper relationship with the rest of the ONR structure—in this case by diminishing SDC's role in computer research. The decision had been made only after a careful review of SDC's programs for fiscal year 1949,[31] and the $900,000 that SDC was permitted to allocate to Project Whirlwind represented the last monies SDC was to receive for this purpose. Future funds were to be allocated and controlled first by the Physical Sciences Division, to which the Mathematics Branch was attached, and subsequently by a newly formed Mathematical Sciences Division of ONR.

That was not all. The amendment that announced the allocation also announced the appointment of the head of the Mathematics Branch as scientific officer of the project,[32] and within six months Lee's successor was to eliminate SDC from the program completely by giving direct control of the project to the Mathematics Branch.[33]

Another primary reason for reducing the Whirlwind allocation, presumably, was Lee's intent to bring the project under firm control. There is no sign that he was discouraged in this by the Mathematics Branch. On the contrary, that unit had been concerned about the project ever since ONR had become responsible for it. The project by its own behavior had provided some substance to feed the fears of the Mathematics Branch. Within a period of eighteen months, at most, Forrester's estimates of the additional financial needs for FY1949 had escalated from $500,000 to $940,000 to $1 million, and then to $1.465 million. Sage's August letter, requesting $1.831 million for fifteen months, exceeded by a magnitude of three the combined allocations for the two previous fiscal years.

Not only did Sage's request exceed by some $700,000 the original monies obligated under the terms of the contract when first negotiated, it also almost matched the $1.850 million that Admiral Lee, in his testimony supporting the proposed Navy budget for FY1949, had estimated ONR would need to support the entire general area of mathematical research, nationwide, in that year. The Whirlwind request not only would have used approximately 10 percent of ONR's total funds for contract research in FY1949; it threatened to consume almost the total amount designated by ONR for all research in mathematics.[34]

It is to be hoped that Admiral Lee understood his job well enough to have considered both the impact of his reduction upon MIT alone and its reverberatory fiscal effect upon the rest of the academic community with which ONR dealt. The Navy, through other bureaus as well as ONR, was maintaining active research and development programs in the nation's universities, spending some $25 million in fiscal year 1948 alone.[35] In this connection it is doubtful that the 1948 funding crisis over the $1.831 million requested by MIT would have had a drastic financial effect upon university relations in general. However, the psychological impact might have been considerable, particularly upon the fragile, newly established relations between ONR and the universities; in this respect the matter had to be handled with the greatest finesse and diplomacy.

Whatever Lee's reasons, he was proposing to cut Project Whirlwind's requested allocation for FY1949 ($1.465 million) by $565,000. If the project were to stay within these financial limits, planned monthly expenditures would have to be reduced from $122,000 to $75,000, or over 38 percent.[36]

The consequences for Project Whirlwind were serious, and they were so regarded by MIT. The program's rate of progress as planned by the MIT group and accepted in the main by SDC, although not by ONR, would be severely curtailed, and at a time when Forrester and his colleagues were quite sanguine in their belief they were on the edge of success. The reaction of Forrester and Sage to the threat of inadequate funds to meet the planned schedule provoked a major disagreement that was then carried to the highest administrative levels of both ONR and MIT.

On September 2, 1948, the new Chief of Naval Research, Admiral Solberg, responded to Sage's letter by approaching the president of MIT, Dr. Karl T. Compton, with the suggestion that in light of the wide discrepancy between the funds requested by Project Whirlwind and the allocation made by ONR for fiscal year 1949, "future commitments and rate of expenditure be scaled down," pending an evaluation "of both the technical and financial requirements of the project." Such an evaluation, he implied, might result from a study of all computer programs then being conducted by a Department of Defense committee, the Computer Subpanel of the Research and Development Board. In the meantime, Admiral Solberg proposed a conference between MIT and ONR to "reexamine both the technical and financial scope of the project" in order to clarify "future policy and . . . establish a firm basis upon which Project WHIRLWIND should operate in the future."[37]

Solberg's letter to Compton brought the MIT president directly into the matter and precipitated within Project Whirlwind a flurry of activity aimed toward indoctrinating Compton and winning his support. Within a few days after receipt of the letter Compton conferred on the matter with James R. Killian, Jr., the vice president who would shortly become president when Compton moved on to the chairmanship of the Research and Development Board, and also with Nat Sage, F. L. Foster, Sage's assistant in the Division of Industrial Cooperation, and Jay Forrester. Forrester presented to the group his appraisal of "the size of the total digital computer program . . . the United States was facing." He estimated that costs would run some $100 million per year for ten years "if the apparatus that people counted on getting was to be made available." In his comments Forrester included the opinion that some estimates of time and cost tended "to be hundreds of times too low." The subsequent history of the computer would demonstrate that Forrester was right, but his visionary assessment was not widely shared at the time, nor was it obvious how acute his evaluation would prove to be.

Nevertheless, the MIT president was apparently enough impressed by Forrester's presentation to ask that it be suitably prepared for him to take to Washington for distribution within influential official circles. This informal request was followed on the same day by a formal request to Sage from Compton, in his capacity as president of MIT (and hence ultimately responsible for Project Whirlwind) and also in his capacity as an adviser to the armed services: prepare a report that would clearly present the "potentialities for useful applications inherent" in the digital computer and give some estimate regarding the "time, money and staff" needed to "carry digital computing equipment to the point of use by the Armed Services."

Such a report, Compton noted, would not only be of immense help to him as he sought to grasp fully the potential use and cost of digital computer programs in general and Whirlwind in particular, but would be also of great benefit to ONR and to any other organizations that might be considering the use of the digital computer. It obviously would provide Forrester with an excellent opportunity to arrange his thoughts and to gain access for them through Compton to higher command levels within the government, an important factor in the struggle with ONR that was looming on the horizon.[38]

The decision was also taken at the internal MIT conference to press Ralph Booth of the MIT Corporation for his formal evaluation of the project. (The conferees could be sure it would be favorable in light of his complimentary report to Killian the previous August.) It was further decided to ask Booth to serve as a representative of MIT in the forthcoming meeting with the chief of naval research and his staff. Apparently their own background knowledge, Booth's letter of endorsement, Forrester's presentation, and Sage's judgment and confidence in the project persuaded Compton and Killian that the project was in competent hands and had a significant contribution to make.

Although the record does not show it, MIT's leaders may also have perceived that here was a test case which afforded them the opportunity to induce officers of the federal government to recognize principles and guidelines that should be invoked if military-sponsored research by private universities was to prosper. It is not unreasonable to suppose that those responsible for the institute's policies were astute enough to realize that three years had passed since the war had ended; that the shakedown period into peacetime procedures was drawing to a close, causing these procedures to lose the plastic flexibility they had possessed when new; that the tenor of international affairs was becoming increasingly discordant as a consequence of Stalin's vigorous intransigence; and that the computer technology then dawning offered prospects and applications in war and peace that quite transcended those afforded by the usual military project. MIT administrators and some of the faculty were already involved in an emerging, loose, but effective organization of civilian scientists (known informally among scientists two decades later as the Eastern Establishment), the aim of which was to maintain the intelligent prosecution of private scientific and engineering research funded by federal interests.

In any event, whether they were moved or not by such explicit long-range considerations in addition to their informed faith in the competence of Project Whirlwind, the MIT leadership made elaborate preparations that beggared those undertaken in ONR.

The confidence and the support engendered at the institute were displayed not only by Compton's request to Sage for the report he wished to circulate in Washington, but also by Sage's observation that "these reports must be gotten into various people's hands fairly promptly." Even more emphatically, it was demonstrated by the men Compton appointed to represent MIT in the forthcoming meeting with ONR. Once the institute's position had been determined and Solberg's proposal accepted, Compton nominated Jay Forrester and Nat Sage, along with Ralph Booth, to argue Project

Whirlwind's cause—three men whose views were known, whose biases and commitments in the matter were shared, and whose policy views were in close accord with those of MIT's administration.[39] The institute leadership had heard the case, had rendered judgment, and had not found the project wanting. Thus prepared, Project Whirlwind and its supporters were ready to meet with ONR.

Collision Course

Whirlwind had long since passed the stage at which its likelihood of success or failure could readily be judged, and this circumstance became one of the reasons why the project was so difficult for the Navy program managers to either bring to a stop or place under tighter rein. The most experienced and sophisticated of administrators and analysts, possessing the highest authority and influence—whether a von Neumann or a Solberg or a Weaver or a Sage or a Compton—were not at all inclined to take drastic action in either direction. They knew instinctively that evaluative judgments, whether to give more rein or pull in the harness, were too personal, too intuitive, too complex and obscure in their rationale to be explained easily and convincingly to another. To justify or condemn Project Whirlwind on its intrinsic merit, then, was impossible.

From the point of view of basic ONR policy and the responsibility for enforcement of that policy that Mina Rees and subsequently Admiral Solberg shared, the high standards the young MIT engineers were determined to maintain became standards too high and too costly to be long endured. It was inevitable that a difference of opinion should arise between Project Whirlwind and ONR as to whether ONR was trying simply to bring roject Whirlwind into line or to kill it off.

In any event, as the budget disagreement sharpened during 1948 and brought MIT's top management into direct involvement with Forrester's and Rees's policy dispute, the MIT leaders became aware they had a partly finished, well-begun computer of unique design on their hands. They realized also that they could not expect Project Whirlwind to be judged on its own merits alone by all the parties concerned. Since the prospects and perspectives concerning the future applicability of digital computers that Sage and Forrester had offered opened up singularly powerful channels of persuasion, MIT must undertake at the federal level an appropriate educational and thoroughly legitimate propaganda and informational campaign. In addition, MIT would reserve the "muscle" and power of its national prestige and reputation for any confrontation that might arise.

Accordingly, Project Whirlwind provided further detailed information. President Compton's September request to Nat Sage for a report on the uses and costs of digital computers led, as has been said, to a flurry of activity within the project. Between September 14 and October 15 four reports—defenses of the project, although not labeled as such—were prepared and published. Two versions of the first report were prepared; one was submitted to President Compton on September 14, apparently in response to his request of September 8, and the second was completed and published on September 17. The second version discussed the same subjects but in more detail, providing more explanatory and illustrative argument and material. It is the one that will be described here. It set forth the possible military applications of digital computers and included an approximate estimate of the "time and cost to bring such information systems to useful military realization." The authors—Jay Forrester, Hugh Boyd, Robert Everett, Harris Fahnestock, and Robert Nelson—estimated the time required would be about fifteen years and the cost about $2 billion. They were concerned not with the digital computer solely, but rather with the complete system of which the computer would be but a part, so that the programs envisioned included "auxiliary equipment, applications studies, field tests, and training

Some of Whirlwind's console equipment was in place in December 1948.

of staff required to do research and to produce and operate the equipment."
The areas of application that could be foreseen included "air traffic control,
integrated fire control and combat information centers, interception networks, scientific and engineering research, guided missile offense and defense, and data processing in logistics." The report reflected the most
advanced thinking of the young MIT engineers and the SDC engineers at
Sands Point.[1]

Although it was primarily concerned with the application of digital computation systems to military needs in a general sense, it provided a defense
for Project Whirlwind by implication. Without referring to any specific
computer development program, it pointed out the advantages to be gained
once successful development of digital computation systems made possible
"the better integration and more effective use of other military equipment."
In this manner it justified "the diversion of men and resources to digital
information-system development."[2] Forrester and his coauthors were reit-
erating their thesis that the potential of the digital computer was so great
and the benefits to be derived from its use so immense that the costs involved, no matter how great, were warranted. To them a national computer
development program was as important to the well-being of the nation as
had been those programs which had led to the development and use of radar
and the harnessing of nuclear energy.

Their analysis of the research and development program essential to the
achievement of digital computing systems reflected the experience Forrester

The console room in
1950. Jay Forrester and
Robert Everett stand
behind Stephen Dodd.
At the left are the
marginal checking and
toggle-switch test
control panels.

and his colleagues had gained since they had embarked upon their own program in 1945. They noted, perhaps ruefully, that the costs of making equipment for military application appeared sometimes to have been "underestimated because of linear extrapolation of past laboratory programs." Instead, they argued, similar development programs had "grown exponentially," and they cited the development of radar as the "nearest parallel."[3] This observation, although reflecting their own errors as to the time and costs, countered the charges made by Project Whirlwind's opponents that it was too expensive in money, time, and manpower for the benefits it would provide. The cumulative costs of such programs, the authors argued, would be more than repaid by the benefits the nation would derive from the application of digital computers to national needs. It was a prophecy subsequently borne out.

The second report, also quite detailed and extensive, pertained directly to Project Whirlwind, outlining three possible "levels" of operation for the period 1949 to 1953. This report was completed on September 21, 1948, one day prior to the conference of the MIT group with the Chief of Naval Research, and was designed to serve as a basis of the presentation that the MIT group intended to make to Admiral Solberg. Plan 1 indicated the extent of "the research, development and limited experimental computer operation" possible under the proposed budget of $1.4 million per year. Plan 2 was based upon an annual operating budget of $3.8 million, which would allow the addition of "a substantial operating force for the efficient solution of engineering and scientific problems." Plan 3, which proposed an annual budget of $5.8 million, would further permit the inclusion of a research program into "the application of digital computers to the field of control and military uses."[4] To some extent, the second report complemented the first by noting how Project Whirlwind's program could be organized to permit the realization of the military applications outlined in the report of September 17.

It is interesting to note that the September 21 report contained no discussion of any program that could be conducted under the minimal figure proposed by ONR. The minimal rate considered was that proposed by Sage in his letter of August 4 concerning the allocation for fiscal year 1949 and had been based upon an anticipated average monthly expenditure of $148,000. There seems to be no doubt that the directors of Project Whirlwind were determined not to strike their flag, if strike it they must, without a battle. Forrester recalled in after years that the Whirlwind group had by this time become so deeply committed to the idea of doing the technical job right or not at all ("Do it on our terms, or let it be shut off!"), that the arbitrary, unilateral nature of the view they took was not readily apparent to them. Instead, they were aware that there were other worthwhile projects to which they might apply their talents, should the Navy find itself unable to supply the proper funds.[5] Their high-spirited mixture of determination and bra-vado was not put to the test on this occasion, however.

September 22, 1948, had been agreed upon as the day for the Navy and the MIT representatives to meet in Washington to discuss the financial and technical ramifications of Project Whirlwind. ONR was sufficiently im-pressed with the importance of the conference to hold a "rehearsal confer-ence" on September 21, a rehearsal that lasted all day but which, when compared to MIT's preparation, was barely minimal. The purpose was to acquaint the Chief of Naval Research with the program, but more im-portantly, perhaps, "to establish a common understanding within the Office of Naval Research and to solidify the thinking of all individuals within the Office of Naval Research on the Navy's position relative to Project Whirl-wind."[6] Thus ONR was establishing its "party line" even as MIT, through the conference called by President Compton on September 8, had estab-lished its "party line." Each organization had taken a tentative position for the first round of discussions, but each, as events were to prove, had also remained sufficiently flexible to permit compromise.

The general conference of September 22 served in many ways as a forum for the reiteration of previous questions and explanations. Forrester ex-plained the reasons underlying the transition of emphasis from an aircraft simulator to the digital computer, covering the same ground he had covered many times before. Mina Rees once again raised the question of com-parative costs between Whirlwind and the computer von Neumann was de-veloping at the Institute for Advanced Study. Captain J. R. Ruhsenberger, director of SDC, "presented an emotional plea for the aircraft analyzer and the benefits that would accrue from it." Perry Crawford, to Forrester's dis-may and irritation, was strangely quiet about the many conversations he and others from SDC had held with Forrester and his associates concerning the course Project Whirlwind was following and the varied and diverse ap-plications open to it, leaving the "erroneous impression," Forrester later noted, that SDC "had been steadily interested in the aircraft analyzer prob-lem to the exclusion of other applications."[7]

What Forrester perhaps did not know or recognize at the time was how greatly the visionary spirit with which SDC had infected Project Whirlwind had waned within the Navy. SDC had lost its fight against ONR, and Craw-ford's silence was in part the silence of dejection and in part the contin-uation of a policy that de Florez had adopted at the start. For although de Florez's experience with aircraft simulators and the insights he had picked up from Hunsaker, whom he had known since college fraternity days, all led him to place greater emphasis in his own mind upon the design aid that a simulator run by a computer could render and less emphasis on its un-doubted virtues as a training aid, he had nevertheless always led from strength when appealing for support from within the Navy by stressing the trainer application. Crawford in later years reflected that probably by early 1948 de Florez had given up seeking a broader mission for SDC.[8] The aggressive, visionary spirit infecting Special Devices personnel in 1947 and responsible for encouraging Forrester and Everett, in frequent meetings at Sands Point, to see more ambitious prospects of the sort that had stimulated the forward-looking systems-control views represented by their L-1 and L-2 reports, had all but disappeared from SDC by the time of the ONR/MIT meeting in September of 1948.

The important point made by ONR in the course of the September discussions was its inability to meet the financial requirements of the project as set forth by its directors. Indeed, the question was raised if the project as envisioned by the institute was not too large for ONR to handle and, possibly, too large even for the Navy. The ceiling of $900,000 already established was at the maximum for ONR, and the MIT representatives were asked to determine "how the program could be continued for the fiscal 1949 period for that amount." The reply, made by Nat Sage, was that "no immediate or tentative solution was foreseeable." Nevertheless, the monthly expenditure rate would be reviewed in the hope a reduction could be effected. Then Sage left the door open by volunteering the observation that an allocation of $1.2 million rather than $900,000 "would probably be sufficient to finance Project Whirlwind to the end of Fiscal 1949 (30 June 1949)."[9] Sage was coming down from the $1.465 million-per-year base he had proposed in his August 4 letter that had precipitated the current crisis.

The $1.2 million figure that Sage volunteered would permit the program to continue without drastic cutbacks, although the rate of acceleration would be less than Forrester could have preferred. If the additional monies were allowed by ONR—and eventually they were—then the total funds available to Project Whirlwind for fiscal 1949 would be approximately a quarter of a million less than the original request.

Despite the adamant stand the ONR representatives took regarding the $900,000 ceiling, the conference concluded with the formulation of an agreement signed by the representatives of ONR and MIT, which strongly implied that additional monies would be forthcoming, provided MIT would strive to hold costs to the minimum by a "reasonable diminution of effort." The $900,000 would be formally allocated. The project's estimated date of completion would be extended to April 1, 1949; however, every effort would be made by Forrester to stretch the allocation to cover as much as possible of the three months between April 1 and the end of the fiscal year, June 30, 1949.

MIT had been granted the $900,000 for a nine-month period upon the understanding frugality would be practiced. Meanwhile, evaluation of the project would be continued, to determine what would be the "best reasonable rate of effort on a scaled-down basis for future operation."[10] A week later to the day, Amendment No. 6 to Task Order No. 1 of Contract N5ori-60 extended the date of completion and confirmed the allocation of $900,000.

The conference ended in a compromise, leaving for future discussion the final resolution of the rate at which the project would be conducted. MIT had received assurances of continued support, even if not to the extent desired. ONR had received assurances that measures would be taken to limit the project's rate of acceleration. The Navy had apparently succeeded in reducing its allocation without seriously offending the institute. This latter point was without doubt a very sensitive consideration for ONR, as it sought to establish and retain the growing confidence of the academic community in ONR's ability to mount sustained, consistently managed and funded research programs.

The agreement that ended the conference was temporary and expedient. Subsequently Admiral Solberg emphasized this view in a commmunication to President Compton; he had concluded that the project was a "long-range one," to be evaluated within the context of the total national computer development effort as well as within the context of ONR's total research program. Solberg was striving to be fair. He was willing to accept temporary continuation of the program at a rate that approached 10 percent of ONR's university research program funds and even to consider the allocation of more funds if absolutely necessary. He was not willing, however, to grant unlimited funds and freedom of direction, at least not until a thorough investigation of the project had provided a sound appraisal of Whirlwind's genuine importance and position within the total national computer effort.[11]

Compton, in an "off-the-record" reply to Solberg, explained that future discussions on Project Whirlwind would be conducted for MIT by James R. Killian, who, upon Compton's resignation to succeed Vannevar Bush as chairman of the national Research and Development Board, would become president of MIT. Observing that in light of his new appointment he could not properly be "an intermediary in these discussions," Compton nevertheless did informally convey to the Chief of Naval Research some thoughts that he believed Killian would later express concerning the institute's stand in the matter. In general he concurred with Solberg's opinion that the government computer development program was so important and costly that it deserved "the most expert possible evaluation"; meanwhile he pledged MIT to respect the agreement reached at the Washington conference.

Turning to Project Whirlwind, Compton explained that "our group"—the term was his—was preparing a memorandum for the chief of naval research that would "add considerable clarification of the issues" for Solberg as it had for Compton. The memorandum would explain the "philosophy" of approach taken by Project Whirlwind. As Compton saw it, this

Panel selection rack
with cross-bar switch for
marginal checking dial.

approach appeared to differ in three respects from other computer development programs, "especially the one at Princeton." He was convinced, he wrote Solberg, that the IAS and MIT programs were "essentially non-competitive in the sense that one may prove to be a useful research tool and the other a useful operational tool." Through his informal reply Compton permitted Solberg to infer not only the institute's position but also, and perhaps more importantly, the position that the chairman-designate of the Research and Development Board would probably take. In a sense, Solberg was being forewarned by Compton.[12]

The memorandum to which President Compton referred in his letter to Admiral Solberg emerged in definitive form as two reports—the third and fourth in the series of four generated by Compton's desire that the nature and purpose of Project Whirlwind be clearly articulated. Bearing the dateline October 11, 1948, both reports sought to emphasize the importance of the project by explaining its unique characteristics and the contribution it had to make to contemporary computer technology. The third report, "Memorandum L-5," set forth the general philosophy and plan of attack the project sought to follow.[13] The fourth report, "Memorandum L-6," offered a comparison between MIT's Project Whirlwind and the computer program at the Institute for Advanced Study in Princeton.[14]

Close-up of the marginal-checking control panel. The telephone dial was used to select elements for checking.

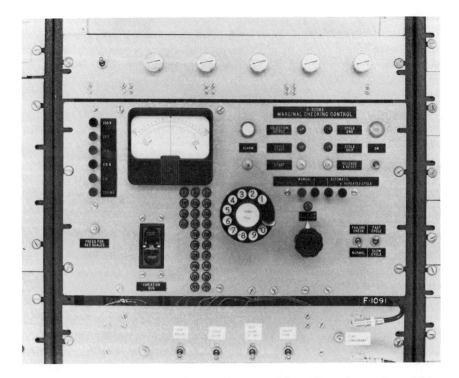

The third report, prepared by Jay Forrester himself, set the project within the context of the policies and procedures of the Servomechanisms Laboratory in an effort to show how the program that Project Whirlwind was following reflected the purposes and procedures of the laboratory and, by implication, the very principles that MIT itself followed. Noting the preference of the laboratory for projects that combined "engineering research and development with systems consideration," Forrester sought to point up the design, development, and construction of Whirlwind as but one element of a system that was, in this instance, by contractual agreement an aircraft analyzer. At the same time he reiterated a favorite argument: "The scope of the project might not be justified by this application alone, were it not for the benefits which will accrue to all other digital computer applications." These applications, Forrester felt, could be so important that the Navy might even decide to "redirect future work." To Forrester this meant the natural development of sophisticated "control systems" for practical military use in the future.

Time was of the essence, he argued. It could not be wasted by following the usual sequential procedures of "research, development, and design." These three steps had to overlap, even run concurrently when possible, in order to obtain a "reliable operating" computer at the earliest possible moment. Herein lay the singular strength (and costliness, it should be admitted) of Project Whirlwind, for even as the staff conducted research, building and testing were taking place. In addition, through the project's use of graduate students in the tradition of the Servomechanisms Laboratory, it produced trained and experienced personnel for "a development of national value."[15]

Forrester and Everett jointly prepared the fourth report as a rebuttal to the charges of those who had persistently implied that the digital computer project at MIT was inferior to the von Neumann project at the Institute for Advanced Study. The two authors argued that the two programs had been established for different purposes and consequently followed different procedures. About the only thing they possessed in common was the intent to design and construct a "parallel-type digital computer"; otherwise, the two groups held "very few common views on the methods for specifically achieving working equipment."

As von Neumann wisely had done before them, in his remarks to Mina Rees regarding Professor Murray's report on Whirlwind, Forrester and Everett made no attempt to demonstrate the superiority of their program by denigrating the IAS program. Rather, they recognized the differences between the projects to be quite valid, for their origins lay in different purposes and projected uses. Von Neumann and his associates at the Institute for Advanced Study were "engaged in scientific research the goal of which is the study of high-speed computing techniques"; Forrester, Everett, and their associates at MIT were "engaged in engineering development the goal of which is to produce and use computers." While the IAS group was building a machine that would "apparently be for their own laboratory studies and mathematical problems," the young MIT engineers were seeking to design and construct a computer that they intended to be part of a larger *system* employing a digital computer as an integral element.

Speed and reliability were of greater importance to the MIT program, since the digital computer within the system had to operate "in real time" and with minimal error. The IAS program, on the other hand, since it was to be used primarily for mathematical computation, did not need to meet the same standards of speed and reliability. These differences in purposes and goals made necessary a difference in procedures that in turn led to a difference in costs. Project Whirlwind was building a "prototype," and although the approach followed was "less efficient and more expensive," it was faster, and this was a consideration of primary importance under contemporary conditions.[16]

While Solberg and Compton were exchanging views and Forrester and his associates were preparing reports, the press for additional funds from ONR continued. Forrester had accepted, albeit reluctantly, the $1.2 million ceiling proposed by Sage and agreed to by ONR, and with his staff he had planned a program conforming to an allocation in that amount. He aggressively sought to prevent any further reduction in what he already considered an inadequate budget. In addition to forestalling further cuts, however, he had to convince ONR that additional funds were mandatory if a minimal rate of progress was to be maintained. To this end, Forrester and members of his staff prepared in massive detail position papers that explained, on the one hand, the financial needs of the project for the balance of fiscal year 1949 and, on the other hand, the disastrous impact upon program goals that would follow if the Navy failed to meet those needs.[17]

Forrester also became more active and more personally involved in "selling" his project to his more influential and recognized colleagues within the institute. Early in November he spent a morning with Dean Thomas K. Sherwood of the School of Engineering, Nat Sage of the Division of Industrial Cooperation, and professors Harold L. Hazen, Jerome B. Wiesner, Samuel Caldwell, and Gordon Brown, "discussing applications of Whirlwind I, particularly to scientific problems and to control applications."

With the exception of Caldwell, those present at this meeting were to participate in a subsequent conference in December with representatives from ONR. Meetings of this kind not only reflected Forrester's desire to win the support of the more influential members of MIT's academic community, but also Compton's intent to have the institute's leading scholars in areas directly pertinent to the work of Project Whirlwind become more familiar with its nature and purpose and with its director.

Three days before the meeting with ONR, Forrester had lunch with Professor Hazen and used the occasion to explain that the "lack of mutual understanding" between ONR and Project Whirlwind originated in the different approaches each took to computer research and development, approaches based upon their respective views concerning the ultimate use of the computer. Dr. Rees and her associates approached the matter from the viewpoint of the mathematician, whereas Forrester and his associates approached it from the viewpoint of the engineer. Since Hazen was planning to have lunch with Rees and E. R. "Manny" Piore, the ONR deputy for natural sciences, Forrester apparently hoped Hazen would become an intermediary and try to make clear the validity of the engineering approach and possibly clear up some of the misunderstanding. Forrester entered in his record of the lunch the cryptic comment that the two men had also "covered . . . the current political situation."[18]

The persistent pressure for more funds, Solberg's desire to gain a greater insight into the nature and purpose of Project Whirlwind, and the mutual intent to resolve the differences between ONR and MIT stemming from the conduct of the project led to another conference between representatives of the two organizations at Cambridge on December 9, 1948. Both organizations sent their top staff to the meeting. ONR was represented by the Chief of Naval Research, Admiral Solberg, Deputy Chief of Naval Research and Chief Scientist Alan Waterman; Science Director T. J. Killian; Head of the Mathematics Branch Mina Rees; and several others, among whom was Perry Crawford, then on temporary duty with the Research and Development Board.

MIT was represented by its president-designate, Dr. James Killian; Dean Sherwood of Engineering; Nat Sage, director of the Division of Industrial Cooperation; Gordon Brown, Director of the Servomechanisms Laboratory; Harold Hazen, head of the Department of Electrical Engineering; Jerome Wiesner, assistant director of the Research Laboratory of Electronics; and Forrester and other members of Project Whirlwind's staff. The official positions of the representatives alone indicated the importance both ONR and MIT attached to the meeting and to the matter under discussion.

The meeting was chaired by Dean Sherwood, who also acted as chief spokesman for MIT. After a few remarks by Forrester on the program and its rate of progress, the group from Washington toured the partially completed computer installations in the Barta Building. Then the two groups settled down to a serious discussion of the matters at issue. The exchange of views was quite blunt. Sherwood, in order to counter rumors to the contrary, "stressed the united MIT support of the Project," and noted the "desirability of having good communication among all groups concerned to prevent the spread of rumor, and especially of the need of having some technically competent person in Washington designated to follow the Project." The very presence of MIT's scholars and administrators gave substance to Sherwood's point.

The conferees acknowledged that "confusion" had been created and "some appreciation of background lost" with the transfer of supervisory authority from SDC to the Mathematics Branch of ONR. Mina Rees acknowledged that her ignorance of engineering made her incapable of comparing the Whirlwind program and its emphasis upon an engineering approach with other computer projects that sought different goals and followed different procedures. Consequently, she expressed her intention to have the project "evaluated by independent experts."

When the discussion turned to financial requirements, Nat Sage estimated the additional funds necessary from fiscal year 1949 funds to approximate $275,000. Sherwood, in his comments on funding, left the ONR representatives with a thinly veiled warning by explaining that it was MIT's policy to give three months' notice when releasing staff members. Since there then remained sufficient funds to continue operations for only four months, he suggested that ONR render a "prompt decision" concerning the allocation of additional monies. Bending to this pressure, the ONR group intimated that more funds would be made available and requested a statement on the amount necessary to get the project through fiscal year 1949. In light of the blunt exchange of views and ONR's acceptance of the need for more funds, it is small wonder that Forrester expressed the conclusion that the "general result of the meeting seemed to be quite satisfactory."[19] Perhaps in some ways he was a bit optimistic, for although the December conference brought out the full strength of MIT, it also marked the apogee of the support that the institute's directors were to give Project Whirlwind's appetite for Navy funds.

The following day Nat Sage submitted to ONR a request for additional funds in the amount of $378,186 to carry the project to June 30, 1949. The Navy ultimately made available $300,000,[20] providing thereby a total of $1.2 million, the amount that Sage upon several occasions had suggested would be acceptable. In a letter informally notifying Sage of the additional funds and the extension of the contract to June 30, 1949, Mina Rees added that budgetary considerations indicated ONR would be unable to allocate to Project Whirlwind more than $750,000 for fiscal year 1950. Consequently, she advised, it was essential the project "eliminate . . . any long range activity, supported by ONR, which does not contribute in a direct way to the completion of Whirlwind I." That this could be done, she explained, had already been determined in conversations with Forrester in Washington in early January 1949.

In his conversations with Rees, Forrester had acknowledged that research could be terminated if necesary to "conserve funds for the completion" of the computer, but his point of practical reference was the continuation of the $100,000-per-month rate of expenditure that he and his colleagues had accepted as the minimum amount for the maintenance of a dynamic and active program. This was the amount required to underwrite the anticipated program outlined in the draft of Memorandum L-10, which Forrester and Rees had before them. He predicted that if this rate were continued, the computer could be completed, using a test storage component by October 1, 1949, and an electrostatic storage component by December or January. Rees asked if it were not possible to continue this rate of expenditure for six or eight months and then taper off; this Forrester acknowledged as a possibility. Rees and C. V. L. Smith of ONR, who joined the conversations, were both of the opinion that $1 million was the maximum that could be anticipated for fiscal year 1950. They recommended that the program be planned on that basis. Forrester was left with the impression that the Chief of Naval Research was unwilling to approve a larger amount; for that matter, the figure mentioned did not yet have his approval.[21]

It seems clear, from the discussion between Jay Forrester and Mina Rees and the subsequent allocation of $750,000 for Project Whirlwind, that the directors of ONR had determined to reduce the costs of the project to a level that would place the allocations more in line with the monies available to

ONR for research and development in computers. Whether this was a general goal or Solberg's alone cannot be determined, but certainly Forrester's comments following his discussion with Rees convey the impression that the Chief of Naval Research was exercising a strong influence in this direction.

Apparently Solberg had become convinced that the time had arrived to terminate research and push the project to completion at minimal cost. Political as well as technical considerations made necessary a more gradual reduction than perhaps he preferred, but the evidence suggests he had no intention of underwriting the project at the level proposed by Forrester. Subsequent actions by the leaders of MIT suggest that, fully recognizing the problems besetting ONR, they were more amenable to a compromise than was Forrester, with the result that he found himself being placed under greater pressure within the institute itself. The creation of a computer center at MIT appeared to be an instance of this pressure, but it was an operational development that Forrester himself suggested in order to facilitate the efficient operation of the Whirlwind project.

Neither position papers nor oral argument were successful in moving the Navy, however. ONR allocated to Project Whirlwind for fiscal year 1950 not the $1 million that Rees and Forrester had talked about early in 1949, but $750,000, and Forrester had to prepare to tailor his program accordingly. Fortunately, his luck, or that of the project, was still running strong. Since July of 1949 conversations had been taking place between Forrester and his associates and representatives of the Air Force over the possibility of applying the digital computer they were developing at MIT to air traffic control. These conversations led eventually to the negotiation of a contract in the amount of $122,400 for research in this area during the period from March 1, 1949, to April 30, 1950.[22] Although the amount of money involved was not relatively large, it did help ameliorate the situation, if only by providing a means whereby key professionals could be kept on salary. More importantly, however, it was to lead to the creation of a pool of technical experience that proved of immeasurable value later.

R&D Policies and Practices

With the funds available to him for fiscal years 1949 and 1950 Forrester was able to push the project steadily on toward completion. Most of the people on the staff became aware of the pressure that the Mathematics Branch of ONR was applying, but few besides Forrester, Everett, Boyd, Fahnestock, and others who had been there since 1946 realized how far the Navy had shifted from its once enthusiastic support of ASCA to its grudging funding of Whirlwind. To the old hands the crisis of the fall of 1948, the recurring inspection visits by different outside experts, and the attitude of ONR and its Boston branch office personnel made it clear that the old happy days were gone. The project was being put on its mettle.

There was much to be done inside the laboratory. The problems were so new and so challenging and the signs of design progress so encouraging that the staff's philosophy, attitudes, and morale remained for the most part optimistic, confident, and constructive. In one respect the engineers, the graduate assistants, and the technicians were surrounded by nothing but technical problems; but they saw these, variously, as easy to solve or as challenging and ultimately soluble or as so stubborn and unyielding as to require alternative appraisal and a shifting of the line of attack in order to alter the problem to soluble form.

Forrester was sufficiently optimistic about the progress they were making to draft a memorandum to Sage in January of 1949, declaring that the research phase of the project was virtually complete and that "only a small amount of design, a fair amount of construction, and installation remain to be finished."[1] The subassemblies of the computational heart of the computer, the arithmetic element, had been completed and tested separately and were being linked together to form the element itself.[2] Marginal checking techniques were being tested on circuits of the five-digit multiplier and were yielding promising results. Only three of the four electrostatic storage tubes fabricated in December functioned well enough to submit to circuit and life tests,[3] but such incidents in engineering development operations were to be expected, especially since the fabrication techniques for these special, giant cathode ray tubes were as experimental as the very tube designs themselves.

Multiplication and shifting operations were attempted first in the arithmetic element, and toward summer, further testing indicated that the speed, versatility, and reliability sought in the design phase were being approached in preliminary operational phases.[4] In the meantime the type 7AD7 vacuum tubes used in the multiplier and elsewhere were found to be deteriorating more rapidly than expected. The problem warranted investigation by Sylvania and MIT engineers. Since the 7AD7 pentodes, together with 7AK7 gate tubes, comprised about two-thirds of the 4,000 tubes Whirlwind I was expected to require, project engineers began to ride the problem especially closely. They had already shifted from type 6AG7 tubes earlier, in an attempt to eliminate this problem. Impurities in the coating materials applied to the cathodes were again the target of their studies, and the fabrication of various batches of these tubes came under close scrutiny.[5]

Limited advance was made toward the solution of tube deterioration when by the end of 1949 the engineers working on the problem were able to point to certain alloys used in tube manufacture that persistently supported the possibility that silicon impurities were the cause. However, the sources of the silicon traces were not always easy to determine. In addition, it was by no means clear just how tubes should be fashioned to guarantee a reliable life span running into the thousands of hours. The theoretical knowledge of the causes of tube failure seemed to be sound, but engineering fabrication and the "reduction to practice" of that knowledge provided challenging problems to which only continuing analysis and controlled life-testing would provide long-run, practical answers. Such problems, with their preliminary solutions and long-term resolutions, were characteristic during 1948, 1949, and 1950. This tenor of technical events remained unaffected by the funding adventures generated by changes in national (as well as naval) policies.

The momentum that Project Whirlwind had generated by 1949 largely determined the character of its operations during the rest of the time that the Navy remained the principal program manager and during the first years after the Air Force stepped into the picture. It was not until the mid-1950s that the larger momentum of continental-defense policy needs, which caused MIT to create Project Lincoln and the Lincoln Laboratory, presented a superior force. To this force the project stubbornly bent, then yielded, modified its operational character in the transformation, and lost first control over its own destiny and then its original leader.

But in 1949 the individuality and the dynamic character of the project as a group of young men organized to carry on specialized electronics research and development were in full strength, and the sources of this vitality were to be found not only in the personal qualities of the leadership Forrester, Everett, and their group leaders provided, essential though these were, but also in the technical procedures and policies that project personnel followed in carrying out the technical tasks and resolving the technical problems that arose. These procedures and policies sought to construct a research and development enterprise of outstanding efficiency and excellence of performance. But it was not easy to select and combine elements of the research and development process to accomplish this goal, and the actions that Forrester and Everett took were unconventional, unsettling, and difficult to appraise. The project and its mode of operation exhibited both virtues and deficiencies that are worth examining.

As has been indicated, there was a persistent search for talented and intelligent personnel. Continuing efforts to keep standards high were matched by continuing efforts to supply whatever materials were needed. The project was kept operating in an atmosphere as free as possible from the exasperations arising from delays caused by lack of materials or by inadequate performance of inferior substitutes. Preliminary design and testing obviously could not avoid every exigency that might unexpectedly appear, and some unplanned-for delays were to be expected while an elaborate piece of test equipment, for example, was being ordered or built to cope with a new technical requirement. Shortages of standard supplies, however, were considered inexcusable, because they could have been avoided; the project placed a premium on foresight and careful anticipation of needs. To encourage these it provided a working climate of planned yet (by its standards) prudent plenty, in which efficiency, morale, and productivity prospered. It was not a "business as usual" operation, and all the project engineers took pride in the fact.

Along with the philosophy of plenty ("hot and cold running secretaries," as one critic sarcastically put it), went a philosophy of genuine prudence and accountability. Office walls were to be kept clean and bare of cartoons and frivolous pictures. Verbal and written reports in quantity were insisted upon, and since the immediate availability of these was considered imperative because of the need to circulate the technical information they contained, the project soon had its own print shop and photo lab. Friday afternoon workbench cleanup resulted in incidental inventory and thus kept work space from degenerating into storage space. One never knew when Everett or Forrester would stop by a workbench or a test rig to see what was going on; there was no question they were keeping in touch, nor was there any reason to doubt their ability to grasp the essentials of a problem and see promising avenues of attack.

F·793

"Their approaches were very different," reminisced one engineer. "Bob Everett was relaxed, friendly, understanding—and I have never seen anyone who could go right to the heart of a problem so fast! Jay was as fast, maybe faster, but he was always more formal, more remote somehow, and you weren't always sure how dumb he thought you were, or how smart. That kept us on our toes, I suppose. It was difficult to know what he was going to do next, but he was so terribly capable, it didn't matter if you couldn't follow his reasoning. He was always thinking with seven-league-boots on. It made him a pretty formidable guy to work for—partly because he and Bob always made sure you understood the problem you were working on, by finding out what you *didn't* know as well as what you did know, if you get what I mean. I never resented Jay's obvious ability, but he wasn't the sort I'd call easy to work for. He definitely never was 'one of the boys.' He was the Chief, cool, distant, and personally remote in a way that kept him in control without ever diminishing our loyalty and pride in the project."

"Forrester would come into the lab and tear everything apart," recalled another with a smile, "and Bob would come along and put it back together again."

"Tear you apart, you mean," said a third.

Norman Taylor (behind panel), Robert Everett, and J. A. O'Brien discuss the control matrix.
▷

"Well, maybe so . . . There was absolutely nothing personal about it, though. He was not an easy guy to know. No small talk, or if there was, it was such an obvious preamble to getting down to business! The chances were, your problem was one he'd run into before somewhere and found the answer to, and I never could see how he could be so patient. There was no question who was boss. You took it for granted he could design anything you could faster and better, but then, I was a graduate student privileged to work in a hush-hush classified project—that was before Korea changed everything—and to my eyes at that time he had an awfully impressive amount of experience, from World War II days on. Bob had, too, but somehow I was never in awe of him the way I was with Jay."

"There were Jay's Friday afternoon teas," recalled the third. "I remember feeling I'd really arrived when I was asked to attend. That was later on, and he kept the group manageably small, so that whoever was reporting was talking about something of use or relevance to your work. Like everything Jay did, it was run very efficiently—very high signal-to-noise ratio!"[6]

Nearly a third of the technical workers (as distinct from supporting and clerical personnel) were graduate students, seeking or working on thesis topics. Their participation produced highly motivated, rather than perfunctory activity, and as each achieved a level of competence sufficient to handle the short-wave, video-pulse phenomena around which the brand-new type of machine (Whirlwind I) was being built, he was set to work on a particular problem.

The lines of investigation were many, relative to the number of staff, and Forrester and Everett keenly realized that the cessation or interruption of any individual's work could bring to an abrupt end one of many concurrent courses of inquiry that were essential to the continuing progress of the project. Moreover, if the investigator were to leave because of a cutback in funds, his work could not readily be picked up by another, because it was not routine.

Since the fundamental business of the project was probing the engineering unknown, research to obtain engineering specifications and parameters was regarded as an essential preliminary to design, and wherever possible, design was to incorporate advance provisions for testing. It was an idealized principle in Professor Gordon Brown's Servomechanisms Laboratory that the gamut should range from research and creative design through bench-test models to a practical, working prototype. Project Whirlwind held tenaciously to the belief that "experimental equipment, merely for demonstration of principle and without the inherent possibility of transformation to designs of value to others, does not meet the principle of systems engineering."[7]

Systems engineering required the "reduction of equipment to accurate drawings, and results to well-written reports."[8] The goal was dual and sounded simpler than it was: "to produce and use computers."[9] Systems engineering, Forrester explained in a report prepared at President Compton's request, involved "the knitting together of important and valuable new systems from old and new components" in order to demonstrate "the useful application of the research results."[10] In this assertion he was a trifle wide of Whirlwind's mark, as a consequence of the spectacular lack of old components and the hazy prospect of nothing but relatively formless and untried mechanisms. It could be argued that vacuum tubes and crystal diodes and circuits of all sorts were really just "old components," but to those interested in the prospects of electronic computers these were not the interesting or the vital components, except to the engineer. The impressive components were the computational "heart" of the machine and its internal "memory," for with these—properly designed, integrated, controlled, and tied to information input and output devices—a computer really became a computer worth thinking about.

While Project Whirlwind sought a "systems approach" to the building of computers, major interest elsewhere in the nation continued to center upon questions of what *performance* one might expect from a finished machine. From performance prowess could be estimated; the kind of performance in view was calculational, the kind of prowess esteemed was logical and mathematical. Project Whirlwind, on the other hand, was spending all its energies—and all those ONR dollars—on prior questions of physical structure and electronic performance, rather than on calculational performance. This was a consequence of the fact that attention at MIT focused on em-

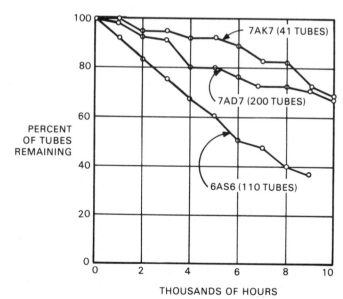

Vacuum tube life experience in computer circuits, 1950.

pirical considerations, which the young engineers in the Barta Building considered inescapable. To them it was at once a truism and a serious fact of engineering life that "in many systems the greatest difficulties lie in achieving the required reliability."[11] The 7AD7 pentode tubes were a case in point.

Project Whirlwind's leaders sharply appreciated and shared the view that "producing a satisfactory working system often requires greater technical contribution than producing the basic components of that system."[12] Engineering research and development *must* be combined with system considerations; this was a policy commitment ingrained in the very name of the Servomechanisms Laboratory, and it was a policy commitment the abrogation of which the project leaders found unthinkable when trying to design and build the Whirlwind computer.

As the authority of Special Devices Center personnel faded and that of Mathematics Branch personnel grew, so the visible respect that ONR felt for the IAS computer project at Princeton became more significant. Aware of this trend, Forrester and Everett sought to show how different was MIT's systems-engineering approach from that pursued by von Neumann, Goldstine, and their associates. The MIT engineers realized, as did von Neumann, that the two philosophies of research and development in question started from different postulates and followed different routes in reaching their common goal, a working computer. The MIT engineers realized, as had von Neumann in his remarks after Murray's inspection visit of November 1947, that any comparison based on adoption of either of these philosophies as a standard could only judge one project at the expense of the other and produce invidious comparisons while hopelessly confusing and intermixing the differing means and ends of the two projects. If the MIT project were selected as the norm, then the IAS project must be considered inadequate and unacceptable. If the IAS approach were to provide the cri-

TYPE TUBE	NUMBER IN USE	FAILURES		LOCATED BY MARGINAL CHECKING	
		NUMBER	PERCENT	NUMBER	PERCENT
7AK7	1412	18	1	2	11
7AD7	1622	243	15	168	70
OTHERS	1187	92	8	20	22
TOTAL	4221	353	8	190	54

Vacuum tube failures in Whirlwind during 1950 (3,054 filament hours).

teria, then the MIT procedures must be rejected as wasteful and inappropriate.

Since von Neumann and Goldstine had made it abundantly clear in 1946 how profound was their understanding of the potential value of the automatic sequence-controlled calculator mode of attacking hitherto prodigious and unassailable problems by mechanical (including electronic) means, the two unheralded young MIT engineers were at a disadvantage from the start. Nevertheless, they hammered away at the differences between the IAS and the MIT research and development procedures. "IAS," they pointed out in their analysis to Compton in October 1948, "is presently engaged in constructing what is essentially a breadboard model of a computer." MIT, on the other hand, "is building what can more correctly be called a prototype and not an experiment or a breadboard."[13] This analysis of their differences in 1948 was equally descriptive and to the point in 1949 and 1950.

Fellow engineers, as well as basic-research scientists and mathematicians pure and applied, could be expected to perceive the distinction: IAS was committed to making one of a kind, while MIT was fabricating the parent of a subsequent line of computers. Obviously, the latter effort was the more ambitious, since not a half-dozen computers had yet been put into successful operation.

The experience to date was so limited and the field of development was so wide and so full of unknown pitfalls that there was no way in the world of guaranteeing in advance that the MIT venture would not fail. If what Everett and Forrester were saying was true, then the enormity of the risks they ran was obvious to anyone who had any acquaintance with the problems of developing elaborate new machines that must work when built. In this respect the apprehensions of ONR personnel that they might well be pouring money down a bottomless though chromium-plated drain appeared well-

TYPE CRYSTAL	NUMBER IN USE	FAILURES		LOCATED BY MARGINAL CHECKING	
		NUMBER	PERCENT	NUMBER	PERCENT
D-357	7,500	64	0.09	32	50
D-358	3,500	278	8	197	70
D-359	400	2	0.05	0	
TOTAL	11,400	344	3	229	64

Crystal failures in Whirlwind during 1950 (3,054 operating hours).

grounded indeed; only after the fact could they reliably take the measure of the MIT enterprise. There was no way of knowing whether the Whirlwind approach was catastrophically premature or a dramatic leap forward. If the lessons of all past research and development experience were worth anything, they suggested that Project Whirlwind would most likely turn out to be neither of these alternatives. It would become instead an attenuated fizzle, discreetly squelched, from which useful gleanings might be garnered in such salvage operations as would prove practical before the whole business was quietly swept under the rug.

Obviously, the Whirlwind group stoutly rejected such a dismal prospect. After all, they knew what they were doing, and in the fullness of this knowledge they explained that "on the basis of considerable study, MIT has reached a fairly firm conclusion as to the nature of the computer needed." What was "fairly firm" supposed to mean? Was it to become another funnel down which MIT would ask the Navy to pour another million dollars, when even a quarter of a million would be risky and hard to come by?

Certainly there was no disagreement regarding the aptness of Forrester's and Everett's admission that "much is still to be learned that can only be learned from this machine itself."[14] At least, later investigators might prosper from their mistakes made possible by de Florez's original enthusiasm for the aircraft analyzer and ONR's subsequent reluctant expenditures. So might one reflect gloomily.

The MIT engineers went into amplifying detail, to indicate how they hoped to avoid large mistakes (including the production of a machine that would be obsolescent before it was finished). But these amplifications, designated to support MIT's case, could as easily be read and as reasonably be

COMPONENT	AVERAGE NUMBER IN USE	NUMBER OF FAILURES
CAPACITORS	21,107	4
CHOKES	3,989	0
RESISTORS	26,210	16
PULSE TRANSFORMERS	3,425	7
DELAY LINES	143	2
POWER CONNECTORS	991	3
TOTAL	55,865	32

Other component failures in Whirlwind during 1950 (3,054 operating hours).

interpreted to raise new specters for ONR, because the fundamental issue, undemonstrated by a thousand or a million words, lay in the question of whether the talent to reduce to practice in the manner in which they were proceeding was a talent the young engineers—men not even of Ph.D. rank—really possessed or not. Consequently, when they declared that their prototype was being built "as near to the presently foreseen needed characteristics as possible, with the following differences," the effects of these remarks could be to reassure those, such as Nat Sage, who remained confident of their abilities and to redouble the misgivings of those, such as Mina Rees, who were uneasy yet expected to be held to account.

Subsequent events demonstrated a curious feature of these statements by Everett and Forrester: They proved to be apt descriptions and accurate forecasts of the procedures by which Project Whirlwind actually carried forward its research and development investigations. As descriptions and forecasts they were idealistic in tone and generally reassuring in the manner of corporate annual reports to stockholders. To the degree that they represented the untroubled tenor of events in the world of the ideal, they naturally glossed over those rough edges of reality that give the world of experience its relatively scratchy character. The MIT engineers happened, however, to employ usable ideals that proved to be convertible to practical action in the particular forging of events that constitutes the research and development process. Had the young men failed, then ipso facto they would have lacked the talent required. Since they succeeded beyond even their own first dream (although not later ones that came with greater knowledge and experience), then equally obviously they possessed the needed talent, and the estimates and judgments they employed in gauging future general needs were indeed appropriate.

"Great flexibility is being built in," they pointed out:

Every facility for easy study, maintenance, and modification is being provided. Wherever compromise on specifications has been necessary it has been made only with provision for later improvement and without relaxing the specifications for other elements. Where necessary to meet specifications, special component research has been undertaken. Elaborate and sometimes redundant trouble-location and prevention equipment has been designed. The intention is that the prototype should embody as many as possible of the desired features and characteristics, and to insure this the prototype will probably include many which are not needed.[15]

This was how they expected to carry on the research and development program they had long since begun. Furthermore, they had adopted a strategy of research, design, build, and test sharply different from that which von Neumann, Goldstine, and their associates employed: The IAS approach to the problem of building a machine unlike any yet built was experimental. To call this approach trial-and-error was to distort its true character, for there was no blind casting about, no "let's see what happens if . . ." It was a plan of attack that shifted back and forth from the realm of the ideal to that of the practical, in order to see how close an approximation could be obtained between the performance of physical equipment and the execution of logical procedures.

The IAS builders would be willing to go back to the drawing boards more times than would the MIT builders in order to achieve a given degree of technical improvement. The IAS approach, said Forrester and Everett, was "to attain the desired goal by an iterative procedure, the first step of which is a single attack aimed in the estimated direction."[16] This attack would produce a bench-test, or "breadboard," device, the subsequent performance of which would tell them whether it needed refinement or whether it would suffice until such time as connecting it up with other elements in a system would reveal deficiencies—a frankly and honestly linear and experimental procedure.

Project Whirlwind's approach was more ambitious: "to estimate the goal more exactly and then to flood or saturate the area surrounding that estimate in a complex attack."[17] Although subsequent fiscal, administrative, and programming events were to show that these words fell on deaf ears and that even ears at MIT seemed to grow slightly hard of hearing at times, this description of the research and development approach the project was following was honest and accurate. Theirs was a strategy that the engineers had deliberately adopted and adhered to, not fallen into, as a consequence of their World War II engineering experience in Gordon Brown's Servomechanisms Laboratory.

Unfortunately, the virtues of this approach were not apparent, even though it was a technique superbly fitted to cope with certain problems inherent in the engineering analyses of systems of machinery. It was expensive. It was elaborate. It was not widely used, partly because it was so expensive, partly because it placed such unremitting emphasis upon premium-quality performance, and partly because it required a rare measure of engineering sophistication, experience, and insight. In addition, those most interested in the new computers and most influential were not versed in such engineering modes of procedure; they were interested in scientific problems, in the tantalizing, potential applicability of the computer, in mathematical problems, or in information-retrieval problems. Because these interests were nonengineering in their direction and did not join issue either on the policy level or on the shop-practice level with the problems of design, fabrication, and performance, they failed to appreciate the power, the virtue, and the relative, long-run cheapness of such a formidable, unorthodox, and in a sense, daring research and development procedure as the MIT engineers had adopted.

So Project Whirlwind and its way of doing things were vulnerable not only because of the relatively small funds made available by ONR for fiscal year 1950—three-quarters of a million dollars—but also because of the peculiar, if not unique, and costly nature of the research and development procedures that the MIT engineers insisted on adhering to, so different from traditional and prevailing modes accepted by Navy administrators during the late forties.

10

Crisis and Resolution

When the Office of Naval Research in the spring of 1949 made its conservative allocation of funds to Project Whirlwind for fiscal year 1950, a skirmish or even a battle may have been lost, but Forrester had not yielded the field. In December 1949, responding to a request from the deputy director of ONR, Captain J. B. Pearson, Forrester projected into fiscal years 1951 and 1952 a program for digital computer work at MIT that would have cost $1,150,000 and $943,000, respectively. The program he envisaged was quite expensive, including a "normal continuation" of the existing program and an expanded program for research in the area of application. Again Forrester warned against "the over-optimism and unfounded promises which have been so apparent in much of the digital computer planning and publicity." The programs would be long, and sponsors could not immediately expect "hardware for the complete solutions of their own problems."[1]

Forrester's response to Captain Pearson brought forth some rather strong opposition from various members of ONR. R. J. Bergemann, physical scientist for the Boston branch office, severely attacked Forrester for not containing his program within the limits established by ONR. Instead of planning to complete the computer at minimum cost, he charged, Forrester was directing his thinking "towards the great possibilities that lie in computer application." Herein lay Forrester's sin, for he had clearly been instructed, according to Bergemann, to eliminate "long range planning." Bergemann directly attacked Project Whirlwind for producing "less for the money than might be obtained elsewhere," and he unfavorably compared it to the "Hurricane" computer under development at Raytheon.

The Raytheon project, Bergemann argued, was technically superior and cost less, primarily because the men engaged in it possessed greater experience and competence. Whirlwind personnel on the other hand, he noted, had had no "previous digital computer experience," and few of the project's engineers had had "any engineering experience other than under OSRD-NDRC contracts where cost was no object." Bergemann's recommendation was that "ONR reemphasize the necessity for lower expenditures in Project Whirlwind by concentration of effort on completion of the computer in its simplest useful form." Forrester, he explained, must be made aware of the difficulty of justifying the spending of "one twentieth of the ONR budget on his project, when Raytheon has done so much more on a smaller expenditure."[2] To Bergemann, Whirlwind's sin was its refusal to recognize the return to peacetime budgets and practices.

Unfortunately for Bergemann, the project to which he so unfavorably compared Whirlwind did not measure up to expectations. Within the year Navy program managers recommended that the Raytheon contract be terminated, upon the grounds the company could not meet its "contractual obligations . . . with their existing organization, on their presently estimated schedule and at the estimated cost."[3]

C. V. L. Smith, head of the Computer Branch, was another who seriously attacked Forrester and his project, referring to the latter's estimates in his letter to Captain Pearson as "fantastic." He found "appalling" Forrester's refusal to recognize "that funds simply are not available to support such an extensive program." Smith also found the program projected for Whirlwind "excessive" and the staff not sufficiently qualified "to justify this expenditure." He did not, however, repeat Bergemann's unfortunate mistake of comparing it unfavorably to the project under development at Raytheon. He summed up his argument by recommending that Whirlwind be made operational during 1951 and that Forrester be convinced of the necessity to drastically reduce expenditures and to stop thinking "in terms of a million or so per year."

In response to a proposal, apparently advanced by Pearson, that a conference be called to discuss the financing of Project Whirlwind, Smith's attitude was negative. He believed that Whirlwind had been "oversold," that "a very considerable skepticism" had arisen. It would be "a great mistake" to call a meeting before it was "possible to demonstrate a fully operable machine." He suggested the machine be tested by running several diverse problems on it to permit "a really convincing demonstration" of its potential. "Anything short of this would not only be futile, but probably harmful in its total effect."[4]

It is interesting to note that during the course of a visit to Project Whirlwind on January 12 and 13, neither Bergemann nor Smith was, understandably, as caustic in his comments to Forrester and his colleagues as each permitted himself to be in memoranda intended only for Navy eyes. At least the trip reports prepared by the two men give no evidence of such blunt and candid exchange. Smith did, however, upon this occasion review with Forrester the latter's proposed budget for fiscal year 1951, explaining that it was impossible for ONR to raise the $1.15 million proposed and that at best the office was planning to allocate $250,000 to $300,000.[5]

Once again Forrester's proposals on program and budget for Project Whirlwind raised the matter to the highest levels within both MIT and ONR; once again the decision was taken to discuss the matter in a general conference, to be hosted this time by MIT; and once again Forrester, in preparation for the exchange of views, sought to win the institute's administration to his side. In a letter to the provost, Dr. Julius A. Stratton, Forrester explained in great detail the capabilities of the computer, which, he wrote, would be assembled by the fall of 1950 and ready "to start research into 'real-time' applications." He predicted the computer would be capable of "preliminary work" in at least 80 percent of the applications listed in his letter to Pearson, including fire-control studies, logistics studies, centralized

Forrester, Youtz, and Dodd check a storage installation. The magnetic shield has been removed from the electrostatic tube on the right.

digital computer service, weapon evaluation, engineering and scientific applications, antisubmarine-control studies, air-intercept combat-information-center research, simulation, and air traffic control research.[6]

This time, however, Forrester was less successful in persuading his superiors to give him full support. Had the Navy, or more particularly, ONR, finally executed an end run around Forrester and Sage and reached MIT's top administration without effective interference? Or was Forrester unable any longer to convince his superiors that he recognized the peacetime funding realities of life that prevailed in the conduct of research and development during that uneventful spring of 1950? Ironically, that was the spring of the year the Korean War suddenly broke out and impelled the United States unexpectedly to send fighting men abroad once more, and military leaders found themselves facing the prospect that the nation might come under actual aerial attack. But these events still lay in the future when Project Whirlwind took on ONR once more.

Perhaps the project's vulnerability this time around was greater because it had eliminated the cockpit program. Whirlwind had become a computer without a practical, specified mission as a consequence of Forrester and Everett's commitment to an avowedly general-purpose instrument and of their single-minded concern to bring such a computer into being. The research and development process itself had for years demonstrated the practical worth of Benjamin Franklin's shrewd rhetorical query (uttered in reply to a critic of the first balloon flights)—"Of what use is a new-born

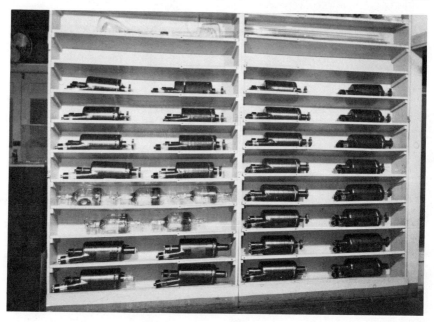

Electrostatic storage tubes for Whirlwind cost approximately $1,500 each.

◁
An electrostatic storage
rack with panel covers
removed to show tubes
in place.

Electrostatic storage
rack viewed from
console room doorway.
▷

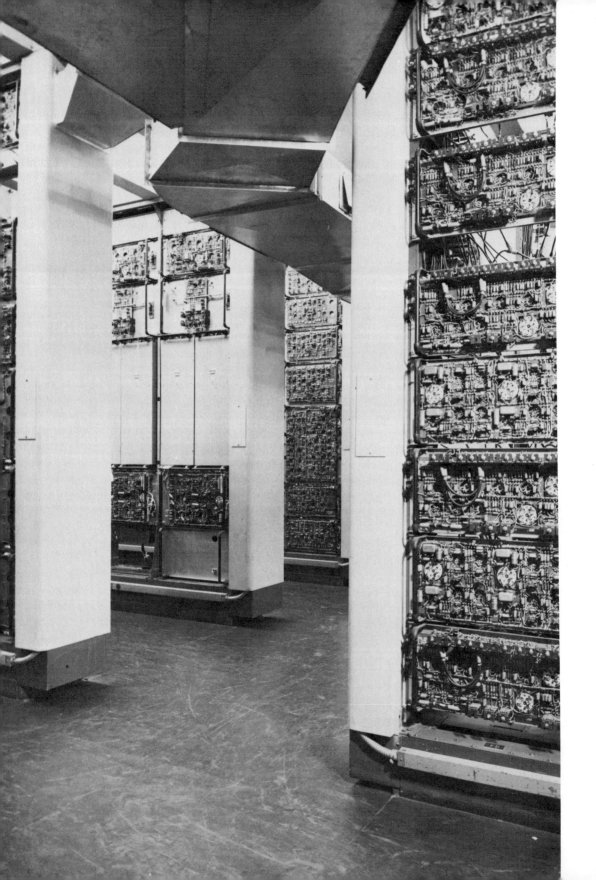

baby?"—but this general wisdom did not automatically justify, in the particular instance of the Whirlwind project, the torrential outpouring of ONR dollars that Forrester sought.

The traditional philosophy of government peacetime funding of research and development indicated that the Navy could not afford to gestate so costly a baby of so uncertain pedigree when more promising purebreds of superior pedigree, such as the IAS machine, were costing so much less. Nor did it simplify the problem to have some of the Navy program managers feel that Forrester's reiteration of his demands was bordering on the arrogant. Forrester recalled in later years that he had shared the apprehensions of Special Devices Center personnel regarding confidential projections of a Russian atomic strike capability by 1953.[7] These concerns were less central in the minds of the mathematics- and science-oriented programmers in ONR who were now responsible for liaison with Project Whirlwind.

It is quite possible that the series of investigations and inspection visits instituted by MIT and by the Navy over the previous three years were by this time exerting an appreciable cumulative effect. In any event, these investigations and their findings did not improve—if they did not actually harm—Project Whirlwind's chances of gaining and maintaining the degree of financial support Forrester so unremittingly and unrepentantly sought.

The determined efforts made by ONR to reduce the costs of Project Whirlwind and to restrain Forrester indicated that the early apprehensions of those directly responsible for the administration of the project had not been allayed. Instead, their concern eventually had reached even the highest levels of ONR and MIT. Both Warren Weaver and Francis J. Murray in 1947 had been relatively mild in their respective evaluations, neither one finding any major flaws in the Whirlwind program. Yet both had confirmed, if only mildly, the fears of the Mathematics Branch of ONR that the project was weak in mathematical competence and direction. The only evaluation which had been outspoken in its praise was that prepared by Ralph Booth of the MIT Corporation, assisted by J. Curry Street. To some extent this investigation could be discounted, on the grounds that it had been conducted by sympathetic investigators.

Other evaluations, however, were more sharply critical if not outright condemnatory of the project, its cost, and the absence of a definite purpose. One of these evaluations was prepared sometime during 1948 for Mina Rees and by someone in whom she apparently had considerable confidence. The criticisms were so strong that even sixteen years later Rees declined to reveal her informant's identity. This anonymous critic sharply challenged the project, finding it completely "unsound on the mathematical side" and "grossly over-complicated technically." It was a program without purpose, one that had become "one of the most ambitious in the country . . . notable for the lavishness of its staff and building." Apparently, there was little about the program and its directors that this critic could praise, although perhaps grudgingly, the critic did approve Forrester's "ideas about great reliability and the necessity of convenient and complete provisions for checking and for locating trouble."[8]

Continuingly aware of the controversy revolving around Project Whirlwind, of her own lack of understanding of the engineer's approach, and of the necessity for a valid, competent, and objective evaluation if her recommendations concerning the program were to possess substance, Mina Rees had undertaken in late 1948 and early 1949 to organize another inquiry that would familiarize her with the program and provide the critical analysis she needed. The organization of a team for this purpose was not easy, for although she could appoint members from the ONR staff, it was exceedingly difficult for her to find an impartial expert acceptable to her and also to the administrators of MIT and the project.[9]

Eventually, Dr. Harry Nyquist of the Bell Telephone Laboratories in New Jersey was settled upon. The committee—composed of Dr. Nyquist as the impartial expert, Rees, C. V. L. Smith, and Dr. Karl Spangenburg, head of ONR's Electronics Branch—visited the project in the spring of 1949. The group reviewed and analyzed the program, finding apparently no major weaknesses. Some technical questions were raised regarding "the means of communicating with the machine," the "means of auxiliary storage," the computer's word-length, and the storage-tube development program, but all in all the group, according to Smith, "was favorably impressed by the thoroughness of the engineering effort displayed by the Whirlwind staff, and by the energy, enthusiasm and directness of approach with which the numerous difficult problems encountered have been attacked."[10]

In response, Forrester expressed his appreciation. At the same time, he noted that in an earlier communication he had anticipated the committee's recommendations by suggesting new task orders to cover the proposed work.[11] This was not exactly what the committee had had in mind, for new task orders meant additional funds.

The evaluation that truly hurt came at the end of 1949, and it brought a sharp and irritated rejoinder from Forrester. This was the investigation that the Chief of Naval Research had been anticipating, conducted by the Ad Hoc Panel on Electronic Digital Computers of the Committee on Basic Physical Sciences of the Research and Development Board of the federal Department of Defense.

The Ad Hoc Panel was created on July 29, 1949, to provide scientific and engineering policy advice to administrators in the new Department of Defense. It was composed of Dr. Lyman R. Fink, chairman; Dr. Gervais W. Trichel; and Dr. Harry Nyquist. Fink had received his Ph.D. in electrical engineering at the University of California (Berkeley) in 1937 and at the time he served on the panel was employed by the General Electric Company. Trichel had obtained an M.S. in engineering at MIT, a Ph.D. in electrical engineering at the University of California in 1938, and was then serving as a staff assistant to the General Manager, Chrysler Corporation. Nyquist had taken his Ph.D. in physics at Yale in 1917, had worked in Vannevar Bush's Office of Scientific Research and Development during World War II, and had been associated with the Bell Telephone Laboratories since 1934. It was, of course, his second visit of inspection to the project. The panel members proposed "to look critically at the several projects comprising the program on digital computing devices in the Department of Defense, with emphasis on the objectives, management, engineering planning, current status, and probability of successful completion of each project."

After visiting various contemporary digital computer projects, holding hearings, attending the Second Symposium on Large-scale Digital Calculating Machinery at Harvard University, and studying contemporary progress and engineering reports, the panel issued a tentative report of its findings and recommendations on December 1, 1949. Jay Forrester, it is interesting to note, was not included in the distribution list; John von Neumann was.

The report was circulated for "information and comment." It discussed broadly the need for high-speed digital computers, the requirements that should be met for a rational, overall program, and the status of the contemporary program. The panel found the overall program to lack coordination, organization, and centralization and noted that it failed to realize "optimum" return from the effort and money expended. The panel did not ascribe these flaws to any particular agency or cause; indeed, it conceded that the projects appraised antedated the establishment of the Department of Defense. The military services should in fact be "commended rather than criticised for the degree of voluntary cooperation" that had taken place. These words were probably the kindest the panel wrote into the report.

Critically, the panel observed that "no specific procedure" had been established "for the review, coordination and control of high speed digital computer development." There was no central agency to collect and distribute information or evaluate performance in order to provide new users with "reliable sources for advice and assistance in technical procurement in an unfamiliar field." Further, the technical guidance and supervision provided the individual projects by their respective sponsoring agencies were insufficient. In several instances technical reporting was poor and not kept current; technical directors were not always aware of the contemporary state of the art; the exchange of information was often poor. Contractors were not always given proper direction; in some instances contractors had made "important changes in the operating characteristics of systems" without approval; estimated dates of completion were not realistic; and some devices were being "built as part of contracts for other devices or incident to service contracts."

To cope with and eliminate these fundamental weaknesses, the panel recommended that the Research and Development Board create a centralizing agency in the form of a new panel, subsumed not under a mission-oriented engineering committee but under a committee that would regard the computer as the scientific engine the Ad Hoc Panel knew it to be. This central panel should then be placed under the Committee on Basic Physical Sciences and coordinate the Department of Defense digital computer programs. Any project not approved by the proposed panel would be denied budgetary support. Existing projects, however, should be left "substantially intact," since this would serve the "best interests" of the department.

In its treatment of specific projects the Ad Hoc Panel was no more charitable than it had been in its treatment of the overall Department of Defense program; even the program at the Institute for Advanced Study received its fair share of critical comment. Project Whirlwind, although commended for its "excellent job training" of graduate students, for the excellence of its engineering and scientific staff, and for the quality and quantity of its engineering reports, was held to be lacking a "suitable end use." If the Navy could not find one, the panel recommended, "further expenditure for the completion of the machine should be stopped." However, the panel did suggest that consideration be given to using MIT's excellent staff "on system studies and on the development of specific computing components," especially the storage tube.[12]

Forrester and his colleagues were distressed and angered by the panel's findings and recommendations. Acknowledging many of the panel's general recommendations to be excellent, they found the portions of the report that dealt with specific projects to be incomplete, based upon inaccurate information, and superficial. The panel had stressed the flaws and weaknesses disclosed by the investigation to such an extent, Forrester charged, that it had raised the "real danger" of "shaking confidence in the field" and destroying thereby the efficacy of the general recommendations offered "for strengthening the digital computer program."[13]

Without doubt, a good portion of Forrester's irritation and that of his associates found its genesis in the panel's comments on Project Whirlwind itself. This is understandable, for the Whirlwind staff had prepared long and detailed explanatory memoranda describing the purpose and nature of the program, its historical background, and the contribution the project was making and would continue to make to computer technology—all apparently for nought.[14]

The Ad Hoc Panel had concerned itself with the total computer program supported by agencies within the Department of Defense. Yet, as Forrester observed, the panel had overlooked the United States Naval Computing Laboratory operated in St. Paul, Minnesota, by Engineering Research Associates on a budget and staff level three times that of Project Whirlwind. This was, perhaps, his retort to the panel's conclusion that the "scale of effort" on Project Whirlwind was "out of all proportion to the effort being expended on other projects having better specified objectives." If the panel's figures were even approximately accurate, Whirlwind's estimated completion costs, made by the project staff at about the same time the panel was conducting its inquiry, were about 27 percent of the total amount the panel estimated would be the cost of the entire Department of Defense computer program. This overall program, comprising some thirteen machines under development by eight suppliers, would cost, the panel estimated, some $10 million.

In addition, many of the panel's criticisms and recommendations either reflected or were modified versions of the very points Forrester had been advancing over the course of the preceding years. Without doubt, the engineers and scientists of Project Whirlwind felt let down over what to them must have been the panel's failure to recognize their contribution to the state of the art and angered by the panel's recommendation that the program to which they had dedicated themselves be eliminated unless a specific and positive use for Whirlwind was found.[15]

The cries of anguish and anger were not Project Whirlwind's alone. The charges made by the panel were sufficiently penetrating to compel the acting head of the Computer Branch of ONR, A. E. Smith, to prepare a rebuttal that in essence defended not only ONR, but Project Whirlwind as well. Replying to the specific charge that ONR had no purpose in view for Whirlwind, Smith noted that when completed, the computer would be "useful . . . to point the way to the solutions of the numerous control and real time simulation problems of importance to the Department of Defense." Listing the various areas of application that had been considered or were under study at the time of writing, Smith argued that each would require "voluminous arithmetic experimentation . . . before goals can be set with any precision or efficiency." This, coupled with the "interest of the many different activities in Whirlwind," provided justification enough to proceed with the program. As far as Smith was concerned, Whirlwind's completion was mandatory, in order to realize "the original goal of the project" and also the proposals made by the panel itself concerning the use of the MIT group for system studies and the development of components.[16]

It was in such an atmosphere of investigation, criticism, complaint, and countercomplaint, or in the climate influenced in part by such developments, that Forrester late in February and early in March 1950 was unable to persuade his superiors at MIT to give him the full support he desired. One might argue that the common cause allying ONR and MIT against a common, hostile critic, the Research and Development Board and its Ad Hoc Panel, caused the two organizations under attack to submerge their smaller differences, such as how much funding support to give Project Whirlwind, and expediently to close ranks to deal with the greater issue at hand. Whatever the combination of causes, Forrester found himself corralled as never before.

Three days after Forrester wrote his letter to Stratton, ONR representatives came to Cambridge to discuss Project Whirlwind and its place in the overall ONR computer program. Two conferences took place on March 6, 1950, one in the morning and one in the afternoon. At the morning conference, a policy meeting, were Provost Stratton, Dean Harrison, and Dean Sherwood of MIT, and Dr. Alan T. Waterman, Dr. Mina Rees, and Dr. C. F. Muckenhaupt of ONR. The fact that Forrester did not attend suggests that the MIT administration recognized that some of the Navy criticism of Project Whirlwind was strongly colored by ONR's reaction to Forrester's way of conducting his affairs. Perhaps the MIT authorities recognized the wisdom of maintaining ONR support in common cause against such Defense Department criticisms as the Ad Hoc Panel had leveled. It was to the advantage of both parties to resolve existing differences as unemotionally as possible.

In any event, Forrester did not attend the morning meeting. It appeared that the MIT leadership had decided to formulate, with ONR representatives, broad guidance principles to which Forrester and his associates would have to conform. But the MIT leaders could afford to pursue their course tactfully and magnanimously, for they had an ace up their sleeve, and of this circumstance Forrester was reassuringly aware, especially since the project had assisted in placing it there.

The morning conferees discussed MIT's thoughts concerning the "advisability" of combining the institute's computer programs under a single head while permitting the individual programs to continue within the departmental structure. The representatives of ONR welcomed the proposed reorganization, provided a "suitable head of the program . . . be chosen." Forrester was not among those considered for the appointment. The conference ended with MIT's agreeing to see that Project Whirlwind lived within a $250,000 budget for the following year, the maximum amount ONR could allocate to the program.[17] Thus Forrester's hopes appeared to be frustrated without any possibility of an appeal to a sympathetic MIT administration.

Mention has been made that MIT had an ace up its sleeve. Events suggest the Navy knew it was there and was equally good-humored about it. For during the preceding month Whirlwind had found a practical mission and a new backer with a purse larger than ONR's. A new ball game was opening, but the old one had still to be played out. The afternoon meeting was attended by all the morning conferees except Dean Harrison; present also were Jay Forrester, C. V. L. Smith, and a new figure, Dr. George Valley of the MIT Physics Department. Valley was chairman of an Air Force committee that had been created to investigate the state of contemporary air defense and recommend improvements and changes. It was Valley's presence that altered the whole financial picture for Project Whirlwind, for he proposed at the afternoon conference that Whirlwind be applied to experiments in air defense. To this purpose, he believed, the Air Force would be willing to allocate some $500,000. All agreed that this would be an excellent solution to the situation, for it would assist the Air Force in a problem of great national importance yet leave the computer available for scientific use and for use on Navy problems also.[18]

The following day, March 7, another meeting was held to discuss in greater detail the financing of Project Whirlwind and the program suggested in Forrester's letter to Captain Pearson. The financial basis for the discussion was $300,000 from the Computer Branch of ONR plus another $30,000 from the Armament Branch for a fire-control study. Monies over and above this total of $330,000 would have to come from sources other than ONR.

The two-day conference did demonstrate that neither MIT nor ONR was inclined to permit Project Whirlwind to become an operation resembling in size or cost such efforts as the wartime radar program or the Manhattan Project, as Forrester had occasionally suggested.[19] If it had not been for the Air Force and its search for an adequate air defense system, Project Whirlwind might well have been limited to scientific calculations and such modest Navy projects as might have arisen. The program underwritten by ONR alone would never have met Forrester's desires or expectations. In the imposition of limitations upon ONR's funding support, ONR had finally won the cooperation of MIT, aided by the fortuitous cooperation of the Air Force.[20]

By early May Forrester was planning the project's program for fiscal year 1951 on a partial, base allocation of $780,000—$280,000 from ONR and $500,000 from the Air Force. He submitted a memorandum to this effect to Nat Sage, who in turn forwarded it to ONR in May 1950 as an enclosure to the institute's official request for funds for fiscal year 1951. In addition to the $280,000 from ONR and the $500,000 from the Air Force, Forrester anticipated $120,000 from the Air Force for the air traffic control study and approximately $32,000 for an additional Navy study in the application of digital computers to fire control: a total of $932,000.[21]

The following month C. V. L. Smith, head of the Computer Branch, replied that scientific approval of the proposed budget had been granted and that MIT would shortly hear from ONR's Contract Division. Smith remarked that it was planned by ONR that the $280,000 would carry the project for about four and one-half months; meanwhile, the Air Force, he anticipated, would transfer to ONR $500,000 of Air Force funds for fiscal 1951 to carry the project to June 30, 1951.[22] On June 29, 1950, the amendment officially confirming the ONR allocation and extending the time of the contract to June 30, 1951, was issued.

In a comment to Nat Sage in July, Forrester observed that the ONR allocation was for a period of four and one-half months, and it was his intention to implement his program on the assumption an additional $500,000 would be forthcoming from the Air Force to finance the program for the balance of the fiscal year. Sage's brief reply on July 11 that Smith's letter of June 26 provided the answer to Forrester's implied question suggests that Sage had either accepted the impossibility of obtaining more funds from ONR or had become convinced that the Air Force would accept the recommendations of George Valley and his committee and underwrite the proposed experimental program in air defense.[23]

The Air Force was slow in making its funds available, however, perhaps in part because of the indecision and confusion resulting from intensified concern over the adequacy of the nation's defenses against air attack. This concern was a product of the Cold War, which had become more ominous with Russia's detonation of an atomic bomb in August 1949, and also a product of the outbreak of active fighting following the North Korean invasion of the United States-supported Republic of Korea in June of 1950. Finally, in mid-November 1950, the Air Force transferred to ONR $480,000, to which the Navy added $20,000 to provide the anticipated $500,000 for the air defense study.[24]

The entry of the Air Force into Project Whirlwind's affairs, together with reorganizations carried out by MIT to centralize and coordinate computer-development projects in which members of its faculty were engaged, resulted in a broadening of the institute's involvement with digital computers and furnished a not uncommon instance of the growing importance of the computer on the American technical scene at that time. In an action that left the Whirlwind project freer to pursue its air defense investigations and carried out in part at Forrester's suggestion, MIT ultimately established a Center for Machine Computation under the direction of Professor Philip M. Morse of the Physics Department. It became Morse's responsibility to "combine and coordinate the use of existing computing machines at the Institute," both MIT and government owned, including Whirlwind, but Morse's center was not concerned with air defense problems.[25] Formally, the Whirlwind staff that originated in the old Servomechanisms Laboratory of the World War II era became the Digital Computer Laboratory in September 1951, under the direction of Jay W. Forrester, with Professor Gordon Brown as faculty adviser, Robert Everett as associate director, Harris Fahnestock as executive officer, and J. C. Proctor as personnel and security officer. They remained housed in the Barta Building, where they had been located since September 1947.[26]

Beginning with fiscal year 1951 allocations from ONR, although still carried under the original contract, were designated for use not by Project Whirlwind but rather by the Center for Machine Computation, for research in applied mathematics and for research that would lead to improvements in computers and advance the state of the art. To this end the center was allocated $600,000 in June of 1951, and an additional and final allocation of $50,000 was granted for studies in the application of the digital computer to air defense.[27] In March of 1952 $250,000 was made available; a year later $285,000. Although subsequent allocations were made, they were much less; these apparently were the final allocations of substance to be made by ONR under Contract N5ori-60.[28]

The success by March 1950 of ONR's policy to reduce the dollar cost of Project Whirlwind to the Navy does not appear to have been contingent upon Air Force willingness to follow Professor Valley's judgment and "pick up the tab," nor was it made possible by the fact that Whirlwind I (having long ago given up the aircraft simulator) finally appeared to have found the practical reason for being that the Ad Hoc Panel had criticized it for lacking. The principal reason may have been the Navy's willingness to write off to experience the unacceptably high cost of maintaining Project Whirlwind's lavish standards of operation. But the situation was probably not that simple, even though ONR never did endorse Forrester's mode of operation, nor did the Air Force or the Department of Defense.

It could be argued that, in a sense, even MIT found it necessary to repudiate Forrester's way of doing things, as Nat Sage's letter of July 11, 1950, implied. It could be argued further that Forrester's style could not be MIT's style, under the circumstances of limited federal funding that prevailed before the Korean War broke out in June. Even then, there was a delay while government echelons convulsively executed about-faces. So, one might conclude, it was not the essential merit of the project's research and development record and performance that moved the Air Force to follow Valley's lead, but rather it was the emergency, "crash program" nature of the need imposed by the nation's vulnerability to aerial attack from beyond the continent that furnished Forrester his reprieve and restored, at least in part, the sense of urgency that had marked World War II.

There remains to be taken into account the behavior of the Navy and its ONR program managers. As Forrester himself recalled, in spite of their repeated protests the Navy managers *did* continue to support the program financially during the crucial development years of 1947, 1948, and 1949.[29] When their misgivings grew sufficiently intense or an investigating committee made a dubious or negative report, managerial apprehensions would generate the appointment of still another investigating committee. In short, if the Navy did not dare—or did not care—to support wholeheartedly the Whirlwind project and its insatiable funding demands, apparently neither could it shut it off.

By 1950 ONR's growing reputation with the scientific community was not likely to be shattered or even seriously sullied by a simple decision to stop funding an unorthodox engineering venture preoccupied with a scientific machine of untried capacity and directed by young men who were still scarcely more than graduate students and considerably less than professional faculty. What about pressures within the Navy, then? Dr. Rees received pressures and counterpressures from within her own organization, as technical promise was measured against practical doubt and limited funds by different advisers who reached contrary conclusions. The situation that resulted could as well have made it awkward as have made it easy for ONR to drop Whirlwind. On balance, it appears to have been awkward rather than easy.

The research and development momentum that the project built up over the years became a factor contributing to its survival. Ironically, the technical, visionary, command-and-control projections that Forrester and Everett had committed to paper in their early L-1 and L-2 reports on antisubmarine warfare techniques failed to impress the Navy with the obviousness of their anticipation of things to come, yet the mounting dollar costs of the project did not cause Admiral Solberg, Alan Waterman, Manny Piore, Mina Rees, C. V. L. Smith, and their associates to agree to "pull the plug."

The reticent character of the recollections of some of the Navy administrators in after years may prompt the disinterested observer to infer that they had the well-known bear by the tail, were unable to let go, and would rather not remember it, but the fact remains that in those pioneering days in the history of computers they were extending continuing financial support with the palm of one hand while extending continuing technical skepticism with the back of the other. Perhaps the soundest lesson to be offered here is the *typical* character of the research and development situation in which the MIT engineers and the ONR program managers found themselves. Although the particular events were of course unique, the pattern of relations between buyer and seller was customary. Those familiar with the conduct of research and development will recognize that Project Whirlwind was not staggering along the precipice brink, as in some melodrama, but was following, as the events set forth here suggest, a defensible course in its pursuit of research and development.

The ambivalence of the Department of Defense with regard to Project Whirlwind's situation has already been indicated in the account of the preliminary report of the Ad Hoc Panel to the Research and Development

Board. Reaffirmation of this dissatisfaction, slightly muted, is to be seen in the panel's final report of June 15, 1950, even though by this time the status of Whirlwind had been considerably altered by the Air Force's decision to employ Whirlwind to test the feasibility of establishing a centrally controlled air defense system.[30] Jay Forrester did not neglect to bring this decision to the attention of the Research and Development Board. The board had authorized further hearings and discussions in order to air the various criticisms of the tentative report of December 1, 1949, and to incorporate corrections and modifications.[31]

The Ad Hoc Panel's parent Committee on Basic Physical Sciences met on February 9, 1950, to consider the panel's earlier report of the preceding December and to hear objections to it from "interested persons . . . invited to be present . . ."[32] The criticisms heard fell into three categories, according to the panel: (1) inaccuracies and omissions, (2) defects in suggested means of implementing certain panel recommendations, and (3) errors in findings and recommendations related to particular computer projects. The committee took due note of all evidence, accepted the panel's report, and discharged the panel, thereby putting it out of existence.[33]

In institutional affairs, the power to destroy implies the power to create, and the following May the chairman of the Research and Development Board "invited the members of the . . . Panel to act as consultants" in order to modify the report they had given the Basic Physical Sciences committee and produce thereby a final report that the Research and Development Board might consider. Former panelists Fink, Nyquist, and Trichel met on May 11 and 12 in Washington. "Acting in their capacity as consultants" to the chairman of the Research and Development Board, they made "minor revisions . . . to meet pertinent objection," eliminated certain criticisms for which corrective action in the intervening nine months had been taken, corrected errors that had been brought to light, and heard verbal reports from project representatives in order to bring their information up to date.

The May sessions convinced the former panel members that "no serious criticisms" of their earlier report had been found, that original objectives had been sound, and that the "broad purpose" to which their study was devoted remained unchanged.[34] These conclusions put the best face on the panel's discharge of its function but by no means reflected the actual state of affairs. The first report had provoked sharp counterattacks from industry, government, and university representatives on two counts: the panel urged reforms in the way in which the public and private sectors of the national economy had been collaborating to carry on research and development; and the panel criticized specific projects, their aims, and the way in which they were being conducted.

The fact that the projects were vulnerable and offered themselves as fair targets for such reforms and criticisms did not strengthen the panel's essential weakness, however. Neither the panel members nor the Research and Development Board possessed the leverage to accomplish the coordination and control that the panel and presumably its parent board sought. The broad purpose had been to survey existing computer projects being sponsored by agencies in the Department of Defense and see what sort of integrated program should be developed to meet "the over-all needs and objectives of all three Services." As the panel saw it, coordination among existing programs was lacking; they felt that limitations must be placed on the laissez-faire practices presently and in the recent past exercised by different federal agencies. They also felt that the appropriate organization to determine those limitations should be the Research and Development Board.

These recommendations ran counter to deeply ingrained habits of carrying on highly technical industrial and engineering affairs in the American economy. According to these habits, the freedom of industrial and engineering enterprises to enter into research and development projects with interested federal agencies was a traditional and respected practice. If the coordinative management policies the panel recommended were followed, they would restrict the freedom of action of business, of universities, and of individual government agencies. Such a consequence was as unthinkable as it was insufferable in its implications for the extension of government control. The major recommendations of the panel were not implemented.

The panel created further difficulties for itself by its inability to practice what it preached or remain consistent in its preaching. Thus, a specific recommendation in the preliminary report against building and leaving with the builder a computer over which the Department of Defense would retain no rights of priority, title, or recapture was deleted from the final report.[35] But in both the preliminary and the final versions of the report the information appeared elsewhere that the IAS machine would "remain at the Institute and be its property, with the Department of Defense holding no title to the machine or its use."[36] This kind of preferential treatment was not being recommended for Whirlwind or the other computers the government was financing.

Again, the panel had recommended that a "study project be initiated on the subject of standardization of input and output language of future machines." Apparently this suggestion was considered premature, ill-advised, and impractical at the time by some of the experts, for it too was deleted from the final report.[37] Similarly, the panel's objections to "a program for copying a non-existent machine or a machine with an indefinite completion date" and to a program "without a well defined objective of value to the Department of Defense" were stricken from the final report.[38]

Hindsight permits perhaps too facile criticism to be made of the Ad Hoc Panel's efforts to provide the Research and Development Board with information and insights that it might use. Their aim was to bring the progress of

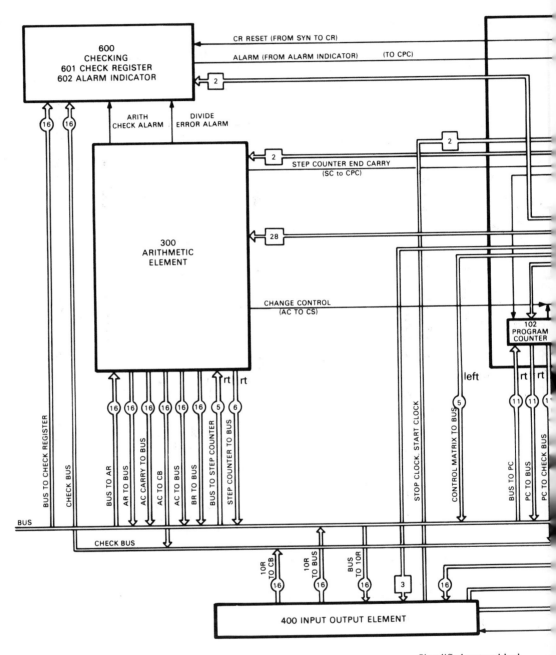

Simplified system block
diagram of Whirlwind
from Report R-221

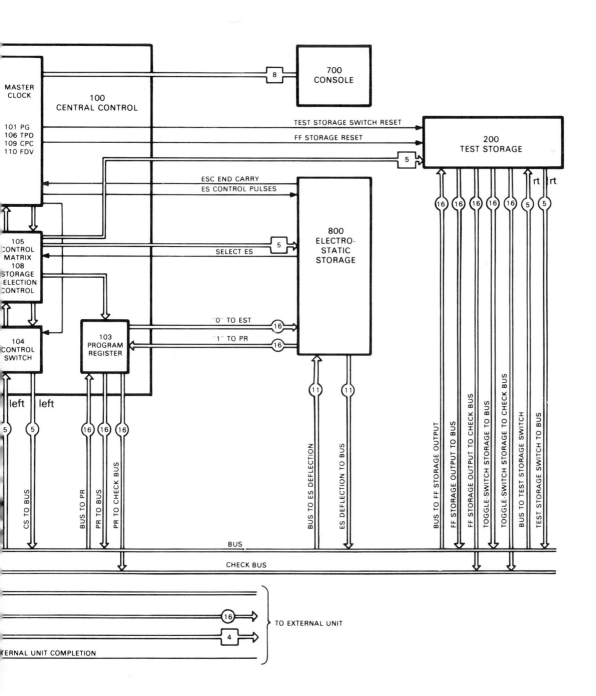

computer research and development under more efficient control, and history shows that these efforts failed. It shows also how great was the difficulty, even for accredited experts, to appraise the activities then going forward in the newborn computer technology.

The panel also ran into trouble when it attempted to evaluate the technical competence of individual projects and ascertain whether they were carrying on effective research and development operations. Instead, it only entangled itself in inconsistencies of judgment of which it was not always aware. Neither its superior, the Committee on Basic Physical Sciences, nor the Research and Development Board itself, detected these inconsistencies, so far as the record shows. Yet to fault the experts who belonged to these groups for such a failure is to overlook the fundamental problem confronting all those engaged in computer research and development. The problem was—and is—that of entertaining policy judgments about the conduct of research and development that can be applied to the practices being carried on and that provide effective control of those practices.

On the one hand were the policy ideals; on the other hand were the daily, monthly, annual operations. The task of integrating these operations generated formidable problems to which Forrester and Everett were sensitive, to which Perry Crawford was sensitive, to which Luis de Florez and Nat Sage and Gordon Brown were sensitive, to which Mina Rees and Warren Weaver and John von Neumann were sensitive, to which Compton of MIT and Solberg of ONR were sensitive. Such problems, of course, are not restricted to computers but permeate all scientific technology. In the case of Project Whirlwind there was, as has been shown, conspicuous divergence of opinion regarding the correspondence that should be maintained between policy and practice, and Forrester's opinions were sufficiently extreme to cause ONR continuing trouble because of the more orthodox views its programmers tended to hold.

The Ad Hoc Panel's struggles to co-estimate policy and practice are significant because they were so typical of the resistances that Project Whirlwind encountered when contemporary experts, handicapped by the fact that the expert is always also the measure of contemporary ignorance, sought to appraise its unorthodox procedures. For example, the panel criticized Project Whirlwind in its earlier report for being without a specific, practical end use. It was frank enough to admit it was unable to find such a use, and said so with such blunt candor that a reader might well infer there really was none, and that the fault here lay principally with the machine and with the conduct of the project.[39]

At the same time, the panel in both versions of the report criticized the general conduct of computer research and development because it did "not include sufficient emphasis on real-time computation."[40] Presumably Whirlwind did not qualify. "We may remark, in passing," said the panel in its first report and in its final report, "that there are at present no real-time electronic digital computers in operation."[41] And they were right; there were no such machines in full operation. Was the panel supposed to be prescient enough to realize that Whirlwind soon would qualify? In 1949 they found Whirlwind I "as presently envisioned . . . a very large machine with but five decimal digits capacity, extremely limited memory capacity, and with as yet indefinite plans for input and output equipment."[42] Assuming these views to be the ones the panel developed from its visit to the laboratory on May 26, 1949, they were in error and out of date a year later, in part as a consequence of the progress of the project. So they were replaced by more accurate and more optimistic information in the final report. There Whirlwind was described as "somewhat limited in its application due to its short word length (16 binary digits) and limited internal storage (256 words). Progress is being made toward 2048 word storage, however, and certain applications for the machine have been set forth in which the short word length is not a severe handicap."[43]

From the panel's point of view, the fact still remained in 1950 that there were no real-time computers in operation. True, "a large portion of the [MIT] computer has been operating as a system since the fall of 1949," admitted the consultants, and "it is planned that the machine will be available for useful computation in the fall of 1950."[44] Yet following its survey, the panel could conclude reasonably that these prospects still did not invalidate their judgment that too little effort was being devoted nationally to providing real-time computers. The machine farthest along was the unorthodox, untried Whirlwind, and the panel did not appear to find this very reassuring.

The panel knew that Whirlwind had indeed come far in one respect: it had found a mission since the Research and Development Board had learned of its predicament in 1949. "Equipment currently is being connected," the consultants were happy to point out in their "confidential" final report, "for using the machine in real-time air defense research for the Air Force, and plans for the first year of machine use have been crystallized recently."[45]

The striking feature of the Ad Hoc Panel's predicament in assessing the state of the art stands forth when one asks why the panel could not earlier find a practical use for Whirlwind at the same time it was bemoaning the lack of work in the real-time area of computer applications. The answer would seem to be that the panel could not free itself from the conventional attitudes that prevailed. Instead of seeing Whirlwind as a possible answer to the real-time problem, it had pointed out sharply in its preliminary report that the project's scale of effort was "out of all proportion" to that of other projects with "better specified objectives."[46]

Decades later the panel's vision of how research and development should be conducted appears conspicuously clouded in several respects. They followed the prevailing opinion among scientists that mathematical criteria of computer design and operation were more crucial than engineering criteria. They thought common-sense managerial rules of thumb that had been found valuable to guide and guard traditional institutional affairs should also apply to innovative research and development. They considered centralization of program control a greater virtue in exploring the terra incognita of a new field than an unintegrated diversity of research projects. Their notions of level of effort and of acceptable cost-benefit ratios were routine, cautious, and conventional.

The Ad Hoc Panel's honest statements make it plain that their policy views, though appearing to reflect and appraise the existing situation, were not well adapted to describe or to cope with the research and development practices the situation called for. In the final report the panel softened its earlier criticism of the way in which Project Whirlwind had operated (and was continuing to operate). Said the panel in June of 1950, after the Air Force and Valley's committee had come to the project's rescue:

The technical direction of WHIRLWIND seems to have suffered seriously by frequent changes in objective and transfer of the project from one division of the Naval Establishment to another. Although the machine now has a definite objective, which seems to us suitable and of enough importance to justify the scale of expenditure contemplated, the current objectives have only recently been assigned. During much of the time this project has been in existence, the scale of effort has been out of proportion to that being expended on other projects having more definite objectives.[47]

Was the panel being realistic? Practical? Consider the evidence in the realm of costs. The Raytheon "Hurricane" prototype computer would cost an estimated $460,000; the IAS computer $650,000; the Eckert-Mauchly UNIVAC $400,000 to $500,000; the National Bureau of Standards "Interim Computer" $188,000; the UCLA Institute for Numerical Analysis "Zephyr" Computer $170,000; the ONR-supported CALDIC computer at the University of California $95,000; the famous ENIAC $600,000 (three years old); its successor EDVAC $470,000; ORDVAC at the University of Illinois $250,000; and the Harvard Mark III (just finished) $695,000.[48]

The maximum order of magnitude of cost appeared to be one-half to two-thirds of a million dollars. Whirlwind, however, according to current estimates would cost $3 million, and if all research costs were thrown in since the beginning of the project, another three-quarters of a million dollars should be added on top of that. To say that Project Whirlwind was out of step is to put it mildly. Whirlwind was costing as much as Forrester had estimated it should two or three years earlier. Over a span of five or six years the total would round off at about $5 million. Whatever satisfaction this correspondence of action to prediction gave Forrester was irrelevant in the light of the panel's criticisms of "excessive cost."

The policy judgment called for was clear to the panel: no computer should cost so much, and all other research and development experience with computers supported this policy view. Whirlwind was far, far out of line. It appeared that Forrester somehow had induced both MIT and ONR to carry on research and development at a fantastically inflated scale and cost. Again one is reminded of the heated remark uttered years later by a veteran engineer and project manager, "We are *not* going to have another Whirlwind!" Seen from this perspective, the criticisms of the Research and Development Board's panel were temperate indeed. No wonder its members had urged in 1949 that if no practical end-use could be found, the project should be closed out!

Reflecting philosophically on these events a decade and a half later, Mina Rees had remarked of the success of Project Whirlwind's leaders in acquiring Air Force funding, "They were lucky." They were lucky in the sense that for one set of reasons Forrester and his associates had designed, developed, and built a high-speed, parallel digital computer that happened to be becoming operational at a time when, for a different set of reasons, a serious national need had become evident. Without doubt, the need of the Air Force had converged with the need of Project Whirlwind at a time that was opportune to both.

It is possible that other major uses could have been found for Whirlwind. Forrester's search for applications had been persistent and extensive and had become more intensive as Whirlwind approached operational status. The curious historical feature, nevertheless, is that dedication, persistence, and industry—political as well as technical—had produced a device at a time when there became apparent a crisis in the national defense that it might help meet. Whirlwind thus became a splendid example in support of the novel and not-well-tested argument that research and development should be supported for its own sake, because the use will always be found. If this *was* a sound moral to be learned from the Whirlwind experience, the lesson was not subsequently applied. Instead, the story of Project Whirlwind became submerged in the larger drama of Lincoln Laboratory's crash program, and basic policy judgments about the conduct of research and development on a national scale remained as conventional and clouded as before.

11

ADSEC and Whirlwind

The Air Force phase—the "Valley Committee," Project Lincoln, and SAGE—was the beginning of the triumphant end for Project Whirlwind, for its greatest successes and the vindication of Forrester's and Everett's research and development policies occurred during this period, which began in 1950 and extended into the middle years of the decade. None of the principals was in a position to perceive in 1950 that the end was coming into sight, nor did they realize that the end would take the form of subtle transformation of the project as a consequence of gradual alteration of the research and development environment in which the project had achieved its identity and begun to flourish. This transformation produced an assurance and a sophisticated maturity of operation as the project began to live with its own successes, along with intimations that the frontier in which the project had come to life was passing on and that a more settled way of life was approaching.

That the Air Force should have become involved in 1950 in determining Project Whirlwind's ultimate fate, rather than the Navy, was the circumstance of a current of events generated quite independently from those which had brought Whirlwind into existence. These events are worth looking at because they created the conditions in which Whirlwind was to succeed and because they were not anticipated by the Navy and the MIT managers who were bringing Whirlwind along or by the Research and Development Board and its Ad Hoc Panel. These events were central in setting in motion the changes in the research and development climate that were subsequently to transform the project.

Significant antecedent events began to take form during World War II, when the technology of aerial warfare advanced far enough to pose the threat of aerial attack upon the United States. The American people, their government, and their military leaders, all sustained by a confidence derived from geographical isolation and continental dominance, had not during the years preceding the war seen a need to plan, research, and build a continental air defense system.

In the immediate postwar period the American people, residing in a homeland unscathed by the war and basking in the warmth and fellowship of the Allied victory and the birth of the United Nations, did not foresee the dangers inherent within the changed international balance of power. Increasing difficulties with Russia, however, coupled with the advances made in military technology during World War II, aroused American leaders from the euphoria of victory and compelled them to give serious consideration to the nation's vulnerability to attack from the air in the new age of long-range bombers, missiles, and atomic warheads.

This growing awareness was reflected in the United States Air Force in December 1947 when Vice Chief of Staff General Hoyt S. Vandenberg, in a letter to Dr. Vannevar Bush, chairman of the Research and Development Board, expressed anxiety over the lack of an adequate national air defense system. The vice chief of staff discussed a plan that might use obsolescent radar of World War II design to increase by the end of 1952 the nation's protection. Modernization with postwar developed and manufactured equipment would follow. It was this last proposal, however, that seriously worried General Vandenberg, for he was of the belief that the existing state of electronics research and development in air defense and guided missiles would not produce advanced designs available for production until after 1953.[1] This was particularly critical, since the mid-fifties were estimated to be a period of special danger for the nation.[2] With these fears in mind, Vandenberg put three questions to Dr. Bush: Were new developments coming along at the most rapid rate possible? Was the Army–Navy–Air Force program properly balanced? Were there serious technical deficiencies in the military programs that required immediate correction?[3]

Reacting to the seriousness of the problems raised by the general, Bush asked the Subpanel on Early Warning of the Radar Panel of the Committee on Electronics of the Research and Development Board to investigate the existing state of national air defense and to prepare a careful analysis of the system or systems-in-being and contemporary programs seeking improvement in the national air defense posture. The subpanel concluded that while existing research and development programs were ample, maximum progress could be made only if funding restrictions were lifted from long-range plans and programs. An improved air defense system could be effected even earlier than the vice chief of staff had predicted, the subpanel concluded, provided existing research and development programs were given immediate priority and were accelerated by increased funding. Otherwise, a new system would still be years off.[4]

The existing system was inadequate and decentralized. It comprised separate defense areas, each with its own radar and each responsible for locating, identifying, and intercepting hostile aircraft that had penetrated the area. The radar was automatic, but accumulation, analysis, and interpretation of the data received, whether from radar or other sources, had to be performed by men; hence the defense of any single area was dependent upon the speed, competence, and efficiency of the forces responsible for it, and these were not unlimited.[5]

Weaknesses within the system were numerous. The radar could easily be saturated. There were communication difficulties between machines and operators. Serious gaps existed in low-altitude coverage, and the employment of smaller radars to fill such gaps was not considered feasible, since additional data would impose a heavier burden upon already overtaxed control centers. Voice-radio communications between stations and control centers were not reliable. Along the eastern and western sea frontiers, arrangements for early warning of approaching aircraft were inadequate. The primary weakness, however, was the limited ability of the system to process, organize, and use the information it gathered.[6]

Air Force interest in the condition of the nation's air defense system was boosted in March of 1948 when the Joint Chiefs of Staff gave it primary responsibility for defense against air attack. This assignment of primary responsibility, coupled with the Air Force's definition of air defense as "all measures designed to nullify or reduce the effectiveness of the attack of hostile aircraft or guided missiles" after they had become airborne, left the

Air Force with almost exclusive responsibility for continental air defense. The only exception, antiaircraft artillery, continued a functional assignment of the United States Army.[7]

In September 1949 Americans heard the alarming news that in the preceding month Soviet Russia had successfully detonated an atomic bomb. This broke the American monopoly several years earlier than had been anticipated. Shortly thereafter intelligence sources suggested that Russia possessed enough air carriers to penetrate existing American air defenses and might soon match the United States in both the number and size of nuclear weapons and the quality and quantity of jet bombers. This increased Russian military power in the midst of Cold War tensions transformed a threat into a clear and present danger and compelled the Air Force to reappraise the state of the nation's air defenses. The reappraisal was carried out by several study groups, each of which analyzed existing systems and equipment with a view to determining their weaknesses and recommending corrective measures.

The Air Force was not alone in its fears. The Department of Defense, reflecting similar apprehensions, also established a study group under the aegis of the Weapon Systems Evaluation Group. A new sense of urgency regarding air defense spread throughout the federal military establishment. Two ad hoc programs were mounted by the Air Force. One, conducted under contract by the Bell Telephone Laboratories, was concerned with immediate improvements of the existing system and its equipment.[8] The other studied new approaches and new systems. It came into being as the result of actions generated simultaneously in the military and scientific communities. General Vandenberg was the military proponent and George E. Valley of the Massachusetts Institute of Technology was the scientific proponent.

General Vandenberg, now Air Force chief of staff, became increasingly apprehensive after the Russian atomic success of August 1949. He urged upon his colleagues the desperate need to act immediately to develop and construct a continental air defense system that could cope with the offensive potential of jet bombers and missiles. The vice chief of staff, General Muir S. Fairchild, relayed these fears to a civilian consultative body, the Air Force Scientific Advisory Board (SAB), and added his superior's request that the board undertake "a continuous study of the technical aspects of the air defense of the Continental United States."[9]

Concurrently, Professor Valley, a physicist and a member of the SAB, was involved as both observer and participant in testing and discussing the existing national defense system. Disturbed by the confusion and poor technical understanding that seemed to him to surround the problem, Valley proposed in November 1949 that the SAB create an Air Defense Committee

The computer room in 1952.

to conduct a technical investigation of the existing system and to determine "the best solution of the problem of Air Defense."[10]

In response to Vandenberg's and Valley's urging, the Air Defense System Engineering Committee (ADSEC) came into existence to examine the apprehensions of military and scientific planners, assess the vulnerability of the nation to aerial attack, and propose appropriate solutions. The chairman of ADSEC was Professor Valley, whence the frequent informal references to ADSEC as the "Valley Committee." Its members included George Comstock, Allen F. Donovan, Charles S. Draper, Henry G. Houghton, John Marchetti, and H. Guyford Stever.

All of the committee's members save two—George Comstock and John Marchetti—were members of the SAB, and all came from the northeast section of the country. The geographical concentration was deliberate, intended to permit easy consultation and recourse to the facilities of the Air Materiel Command and the Continental Air Command at the Air Force Cambridge Research Laboratories (later, Center) in Cambridge, Massachusetts. Valley had recommended this arrangement because he assumed that the members of the committee would be able to serve only on a part-time basis, that solution of the problem would be difficult and long, and that experiments would be undertaken that would require the use of radar and aircraft. Conditions on the West Coast, he thought, might be different enough to require a special investigatory group for that region.[11]

Events following the creation of ADSEC proceeded on at least two levels significant to the story of Project Whirlwind: One was the level of long-range, institutional policy development; the other was the level of unfolding scientific, technical, and military insights into practices that might achieve a working defense system that would constitute a defensive force-in-being. Against aerial attack over the North Pole no standing army, no navy at battle stations could provide such a force. Aerial attackers would have to be detected in the air and defeated in the air before they released the bombs and rockets they carried. The first problem thus became one of scientific technology, even before appropriate military and naval operations could be instituted. ADSEC indeed had its work cut out for it, nor was there sure warrant in advance that ADSEC or any other responsible agency could effect a practical solution before time ran out.

In January 1950 ADSEC submitted its first report, and the conclusions that ADSEC reached were reinforced by a separate Department of Defense investigation that its Weapon Systems Evaluation Group (WSEG) had carried out. Both confirmed Air Force fears about the inadequacy of the nation's air defenses. In extremely strong language the SAB subcommittee compared the existing system "to an animal that was at once 'lame, purblind, and idiot-like,'" insisting that "of these comparatives, idiotic is the strongest. It makes little sense for us to strengthen the muscles if there is no

Lincoln Laboratory, Lexington, Massachusetts. The square building on the left housed the air defense computer modeled after Whirlwind.

brain; and given a brain, it needs good eyesight."[12] Translated into technical language, this meant that an adequate air defense system needed not just improved interceptors, ground-to-air missiles, and antiaircraft artillery, but improved radar and advanced command and control centers.

ADSEC submitted a fuller, formal report in October 1950, and the cumulative impact of the ADSEC and WSEG studies and their separate but reinforcing conclusions produced a request from the Air Force in December of 1950 to the Massachusetts Institute of Technology, asking the institute to create a laboratory dedicated exclusively to research and development leading to the design and construction of an adequate national air defense system. Early in the next month the SAB added its voice to the Air Force request and in addition asked MIT to undertake a more intensive study of the technical problems connected with continental air defense. From this latter request evolved Project Charles, an investigation conducted between February and August of 1951.[13]

Upon the approval of its board of governors, MIT acceded to the request of the Air Force and established Project Lincoln, subsequently better known as Lincoln Laboratory. Physical facilities to house the laboratory were shortly constructed at Hanscom Air Force Base in the nearby Bedford-Lexington area. The laboratory's immediate task was to implement the defense concepts formulated by the Air Defense Systems Engineering Committee and Project Charles. This immediate task plus its own researches led, in the months and years that followed, to the Lincoln Transition System and then to the Semiautomatic Ground Environment (SAGE) system, a total continental air defense system that was at the same time "a real-time management system," using "digital computing systems to process nation-wide air-defense data."[14]

Project Whirlwind—to return to the technological level of events—had become involved with ADSEC immediately after the formation of the committee. Perry Crawford, visiting Project Whirlwind on January 20, 1950, had informed Jay Forrester of the creation of the committee.[15] Within a week by coincidence there occurred a chance meeting on the MIT campus of two of its faculty members, George Valley and Jerome Wiesner.[16] As Valley recalled it years later, Wiesner asked him conversationally how things were going, one remark led to another, and soon he was indicating to Wiesner his need for an information-gathering and information-correlating center that could organize with extreme rapidity great numbers of diverse pieces of information. Wiesner suggested he take a look at Jay Forrester's operation to see if it would have anything of value to offer. Shortly thereafter Valley followed up this lead and visited the Digital Computer Laboratory in the Barta Building.

Valley found a machine so promising that he and his fellow ADSEC members immediately investigated the prospects of applying it to air defense. They decided to support a test harnessing of Whirlwind in order to determine whether geographical information received by radar scouting stations could be transformed into tactical information and directions that would enable a fighter to intercept a bomber long before the latter reached its target. It would be a test under "real time" conditions. The computer would have to keep up with and even anticipate the airplane's movements.

For Forrester the involvement of Whirlwind in ADSEC affairs came to pass within a few days after Crawford told him the committee had been formed. On Friday, January 27, he was having lunch with Professor Wiesner. At the lunch table, as Forrester wrote in his notebook later with customary attention to recording developing events, "we were joined by George Valley to discuss his committee work on Air Defense System Engineering."[17] As yet, Forrester had no special reason to believe that decisions of particular consequence would follow. This was but another of several "leads" he was pursuing as part of his probing operation to find a use for Whirlwind and incidentally either relieve or justify (or both) his heavy dependence on ONR for funds.

Wiesner's role appears to have been that of the unobtrusive broker who, having been deliberately instrumental in setting events in operation, fades gracefully into the background and equally deliberately passes on to the principals involved the responsibility of carrying affairs forward. During the course of their lunch Valley explained the purpose of his committee, outlined the weaknesses of the existing air defense and early warning system, and discussed "his plans for a research project involving the Cambridge Field Station, Draper's group, and possibly the Digital Computer Laboratory." After lunch he accompanied Forrester to the laboratory. There, after observing Whirlwind operating with test storage, the two men discussed the possibility of the computer project's participation in the work of the Valley Committee. Valley expressed his intention to pursue the matter further, and Forrester gave him copies of Reports L-1 and L-2, the reports he and Everett had written in the early autumn of 1947, detailing how computers might be employed to handle interception problems in antisubmarine warfare. Although Valley's interest was in airplanes, the problem was the same.

Forrester and Valley arranged to get together the following week with certain of Valley's ADSEC associates, and Valley spoke of using this situation to help him prepare the inevitable proposal to Washington. "He seemed quite interested in possible use of Whirlwind I for analyzing data from a chain of doppler radar stations which would give range rate only," Forrester noted at the time.[18]

Three days later, on Monday, January 30, Valley returned to the laboratory, bringing with him three other members of the committee, John Marchetti of the Air Force Cambridge Research Laboratory and H. Guyford Stever and Charles S. Draper, both of MIT's aeronautical engineering faculty. Accompanying the group was Eugene Grant, a colleague of Marchetti but not a member of the committee. The visitors reviewed some of the material Forrester and Valley had discussed at their earlier meeting, observed the computer and the "storage tube television display," and discussed the use of Whirlwind I in some of the "trial systems" the committee was considering.[19]

The trend of the discussion revealed that Valley's initial interest, which had been heightened by his reading of the L-reports and had brought him back to the laboratory, was shared by his colleagues. To Forrester, his visitors seemed "very enthusiastic about the prospect" of making use of Whirlwind, and this opinion was given substance by the group's discussion of the question of funding. "Valley and the other men," wrote Forrester that same day, "seemed well aware of the fact that they would be called upon to share some of the basic $600,000 a year budget for the laboratory, plus additional charges for special work on their own project . . . The Committee is apparently meeting in Washington in the next few days to crystallize the matter further."[20]

Forrester's observation was quite accurate. ADSEC became committed almost immediately to the use of Whirlwind. Its meeting of February 17 was attended by project leaders Forrester, Fahnestock, and Everett. The discussion focused on the possibility of attempting some trial interceptions, using the Bedford Missile Early Warning radar to track the aircraft involved and feed the data to Whirlwind I to process. The committee's enthusiasm induced Forrester to enter in his record of the meeting the cautionary observation that "we shall have to be careful not to be driven into a situation demanding more than we can deliver."[21]

Of greater significance to Forrester and his colleagues was the information Valley had given Forrester just a few days before the meeting. When informing Forrester that formal approval for ADSEC to go ahead with its work was anticipated by March 1, Valley had confidentially disclosed that the Air Force, if required, might assume the entire cost of the project.[22]

As a consequence of this groundwork, laid early in 1950, Valley was in a position formally to offer the dollar support that neither ONR's nor MIT's executives considered feasible to continue under the long-standing relationship that had begun with de Florez's office and since passed through many Navy hands. The apparent withdrawal of a measure of MIT support from Forrester on this occasion, as it may have appeared from ONR's vantage point, was tempered by the awareness in Provost Stratton's office of what Valley was prepared to do in the cause of continental defense. Project Whirlwind now would have an opportunity to prove itself and relieve itself of the onus cast upon it by the Ad Hoc Panel.

Forrester was able to go into the March 1950 meetings with ONR with reasonable assurance of Air Force financial support and, moreover, with the

Left to right, Forrester, Secretary of the Air Force Thomas K. Finletter, Professor Wheeler Loomis, and General J. F. Phillips.

confidence that at long last he was to be given the opportunity to demonstrate the concept he, Everett, and Perry Crawford had consistently advanced: the usefulness of the high-speed digital computer to a command and control center.

Actually, the ease with which Project Whirlwind became incorporated into the program of the Valley Committee was understandable and logical. In several different ways the project was uniquely qualified to serve the committee's needs. It was conviently located geographically. It had brought to the edge of operational status a high-speed digital computer that was not only appropriate but even essential to some of the tests the committee envisaged. It possessed a pool of scientists and engineers trained and experienced in digital-computer research and development. Lastly, there was its long-standing commitment to practical problems. This commitment had caused Warren Weaver in February 1947 to ask probingly whether the project was trying to produce "biscuits" or "cake." The same commitment had impelled Forrester and Everett several months later to write those first L-reports on naval warfare, and later still had involved the project in investigations for the Air Force into air traffic control.

This commitment to practical problems ever since the ASCA days had given the project a unique expertise. In naval warfare problems and in the "application of digital computers to the long-term Common System of military and civil air traffic control" lay applications "in many ways similar to air defense."[23] The problem common to all was the processing and organizing of information to provide "the ability to see a complex situation as a whole." Possessing computation speeds immeasurably greater than man's, the computer could "scan the component pieces of information which make up the system so rapidly that it is able to approximate a continuous grasp of the whole situation."[24] Therein lay its value to naval and air defense as well as to air traffic control, for these represented the obverse and reverse of the same problem.

Of greater significance and importance to the air defense phase of Project Whirlwind was the recognition gained from the air traffic control study that the approach to such problems had to be systems oriented rather than component oriented. When in March of 1949 Project Whirlwind had contracted with the Air Force to undertake the air traffic control study, "there was little or no background in the use of a digital computer as the control element of a physical system and very few people . . . experienced in this sort of work." The investigators were working in virgin territory, and as they gained experience and understanding, it became more and more evident that the application of the digital computer to air traffic control was "as much a systems problem as a computational problem." Totally "new concepts of the whole system" were required if maximum results were to be derived from using the computer.[25] The insights into systems engineering gained from the air traffic control study were of great benefit to the engineers of Project Whirlwind who later, as a part of Lincoln Laboratory, were to contribute vitally to the development of the SAGE air defense system.

12

Phasing into Operation

When ADSEC came on the scene during the winter of 1949–1950, the Whirlwind computer was still unfinished and unproven. Its hardware was in no condition to accept yet the performance responsibilities that Valley's committee wanted to thrust upon it. All the parties concerned understood this, and they understood there was much to be done, not only to Whirlwind but to the staggering, larger project of designing, testing, building, and putting into operation the first continent-wide early warning system against air attack. The engineers and technicians in Project Whirlwind were involved that winter in fabrication, assembly, and testing operations that kept them too busy to draw any conclusions other than the pragmatic day-to-day and week-to-week conclusions that genuine progress (as well as apparent physical progress) was being made in all areas—with the possible exception of the electrostatic storage tubes, and even the latest designs of these were performing impressively.

Nevertheless, Project Whirlwind was beginning to run out of time, including the planning time Forrester had allotted to himself two years earlier. In the summer of 1948, in his August "Summary Report" to the Navy, he had published a "Long Term Whirlwind Schedule." As of that date Forrester had spent thirteen months, by his own reckoning, on the analog-computer phase of the aircraft stability and control analyzer before abandoning that line of inquiry at the end of 1945. Between October 1945 and February 1946 he and the engineers he gathered around him became committed to the digital computer as the most practical alternative.

Digital design studies occupied the project for the following ten months of 1946, and during the eighth and ninth months specifications of the speed and storage requirements of the ASCA had been settled upon. Speed and efficiency considerations during the ninth, tenth, and eleventh months led to the decision to undertake parallel, or simultaneous, digit transmission, and by the end of 1946 it was clear to the Project Whirlwind engineers that they were talking about a machine that could cope with far more than aircraft analyzer problems. They were undertaking to develop a practical general-purpose machine, or at least the prototype of one.

During the first half of 1947 the block diagrams detailing the basic logical (though not electronic) functions for a parallel arithmetic element and central control had been worked through by Everett, and in the spring of that year the design of the Whirlwind prototype had begun to be laid down. Since the proper operation of the arithmetic element was essential to the success of the machine, the five-digit multiplier was conceived as a preliminary test component and committed to construction during the subsequent months of 1947.

Sixteen months after they had begun to design Whirlwind itself, the project began to receive electronic panels from the Sylvania company, and by November of 1948 the basic racks were up, the arithmetic element of the computer was going in, and power sources were being installed. So in 1948 the physical computer began to emerge. It acquired the physical equipment of the central control element during the first half of 1949 and received minimum input and output equipment after mid-1949.

During the third quarter of 1949, "after nearly two years of research, design, construction, and tests," Forrester was happy to report, "the computing section of WWI, has just passed a most significant milestone: solving an equation and displaying its solution" on an oscilloscope, showing values for x, x^2, and x^3. Previous test problems had called for only "single-point solutions," whereas the progressive display required by this problem, "no matter how simple, can result only when all the basic parts of the computer act in harmony."[1]

Only the internal-storage element was left, and the state of completion of the rest of the computer, as 1949 passed into 1950, made it mandatory that electrostatic tubes be incorporated in order that testing, maintenance, checking, and trouble-location procedures might continue. These procedures had begun to be applied to the emerging machine at the start of 1949 and were prerequisites to a fully tested and operable machine.

But the incorporation of the storage element depended upon the progress of the storage-tube research and development that had been carried forward since 1946, especially after parallel transmission of digits had been decided upon late in that year.

Forrester found it entirely reasonable to assert a decade and a half later that World War II electronic-circuit development experience had left a fairly straightforward prospect for computer design, but that satisfactory internal-storage elements had posed an entirely different problem.[2] The mercury delay line proposed for EDVAC, as well as the rotating magnetic drum developed by Engineering Research Associates in St. Paul, were both too slow for Whirlwind's real-time response needs—those needs which had been dictated originally by the aircraft simulator and then held to by Forrester, Everett, and their associates as an essential feature of the high-speed, general-purpose machine they visualized. From 1947 to 1950, one could argue, they and Perry Crawford appeared to be about the only ones who could see actual, attainable applications for such a computer; yet their radical position gave them no cause to depart from their conviction. To others in the growing computer business their stubborn conviction was part of the irregularity their project exhibited, part of the youthful and immature enthusiasm that "tainted" them.

Their early analysis of "moving-target indicator" tube designs generated out of the British invention of radar led them to conclude that this type of internal-storage system, which initially looked promising, suffered from limitations that became prohibitive when examined in greater detail. This was the Williams storage tube in its basic concept, and when Forrester considered its prospects for further development and refinement as a digital-computer internal-storage element, he concluded, rightly or wrongly, that it "inherently lacked the high signal levels, the high signal-to-noise ratio, the ability to give good signals from the noise, that we would require for our high-reliability application." In consequence, recalled Forrester, "we did not stay with the Williams tube idea for very long."[3]

In this state of the art of the key storage elements of the computer, Forrester and his associates had early come to recognize the "serious disadvantages" of any device, even the MIT Radiation Laboratory tube, similar in some respects to the Williams tube, which the project finally settled upon for further development work. Forrester's chariness from the beginning to state when Whirlwind would incorporate reliable storage tubes indicates how serious he felt the contemporary lack of a developed high-speed, reliable, internal-storage element to be; it vitally affected the reliability, the speed of operation, and the usefulness of the entire computer.

In 1947 Forrester even had briefly considered using interconnected "gas glow discharge cells" in three-dimensional array as an alternative, for these offered such advantages, at least theoretically, as "high initial breakdown voltage," "low holding voltage, and low forward impedence after breakdown." But investigations were "soon dropped because of the variability of the individual cells with time and from sample to sample."[4]

Once Forrester had committed his project to electrostatic storage-tube research and development, he publicly buried his earlier misgivings in order to get on with the courses of action that to him appeared to be least impractical as far as an internal-storage device was concerned. During 1947, 1948, and 1949, as the electrostatic tubes began to be developed, he remained apprehensive, for new problems continually were emerging, were being overcome, and were being replaced by other problems. Forrester, and later Everett, closely watched the design progress from the earliest research-demonstration tube forms, through versions in 1948 that Forrester cautiously but accurately called "experimental research tubes," to a more compact form of late 1948 and early 1949, which possessed a shorter beam-throw from the writing and reading electron "gun" and from the holding "gun" to the storage surface. The first gun was "an ordinary type cathode-ray gun." The second operated at a low voltage to furnish "a uniform flood of electrons over the entire surface," thereby keeping the different charges on the mosaic points, or "spots," of the storage surface from fading away. These charges, depending on their value, were the "bits" of binary-code "information" the tube was expected to store, relinquish, or alter on demand.[5] Access to a tube's information (including obtaining a "read-out" of a single charge, or bit) should have been six microseconds, but the tubes available early in 1949 performed at ten to twenty-five microseconds.[6]

The work was proceeding perhaps about as well as might be expected, but within Forrester's own thoughts, out of sight and knowledge of the project's staff, except for perhaps Everett, was disquiet and a continuing watchfulness. The electrostatic storage tube was analogous to a patient making reasonable—or perhaps not quite reasonable—progress, yet by no means out of danger of a relapse.

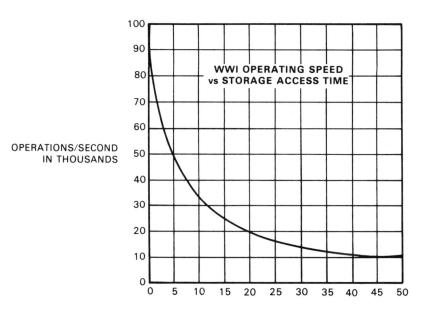

Operating speed versus storage access time, 1950.

Forrester had early recognized that rapid access time was essential to a vast storage capacity, hence he saw the advantages of the geometry of arrangement suggested by three-dimensional coincident-excitation storage, such as the gas-glow discharge cells had seemed at one time to offer. When, in the spring of 1949, he saw an advertisement announcing the industrial availability of a magnetic material "Deltamax," there recurred to him the possibility of reviving his three-dimensional, coincident-current system, employing reversibly magnetizable intersections.[7] In June he began to make entries in his computation book that indicate he was at work on this problem in the lab again.

"Shortly before the Air Force came into the picture, from where we sat," recalled a former graduate student in the laboratory, "Jay took a bunch of stuff and went off in a corner of the lab by himself. Nobody knew what he was doing, and he showed no inclination to tell us. All we knew was that for about five or six months or so, he was spending a lot of time off by himself working on something. The first inkling I got was when he 'came out of retirement' and put Bill Papian to work on his little metallic and ceramic doughnuts. That was in the fall and winter of 1949–1950."

Forrester at the end of June 1949 had begun to test rings, or cores, of the Deltamax magnetic material he had seen advertised by the Arnold Engineering Company, a subsidiary of the Allegheny Ludlum Company.

He could see advantages in certain theoretical prospects. The question was, would the magnetic materials behave *every* time the way they should in principle, or, like the electrostatic tube, would they prove delicate, operable at a peak (and essential) level of performance for only a relatively brief time, and difficult to produce and maintain at the quality and reliability levels required? In principle, a magnetic core should be capable of holding either of two electromagnetized states and should require sharp differences of energy to change from one state to the other. This property, describable in more technical terms as a rectangular hysteresis loop effect, would provide the binary "bits"—the "yes" and "no" information—required. Such information could be tapped ("read") or altered ("written"), depending on the kinds and strengths of pulses fed to the magnetic core.

Everett recollected it was early in the summer of 1949 that Forrester had brought the possibilities to his attention in the form of a plan for a planar array of cores. Shortly, he showed Everett a three-dimensional plan, and by early August he had satisfied himself that tiny cores an inch or less in diameter ought to perform well if composed of suitable magnetic materials. The hunt for proper materials and sizes had begun.[8]

On August 1 Forrester talked over the telephone with Dr. Eberhard Both, a specialist in magnetic materials working at Fort Monmouth, New Jersey, about the composition of Deltamax and other materials, and during August and September he was carrying on conversations with Allegheny Ludlum and its subsidiary, Arnold Engineering, regarding his need. In the fall Forrester selected William N. Papian, a graduate student looking for a thesis topic in the laboratory, to go to work testing individual cores by the dozen in order to ascertain ranges of performance and to pick out cores exhibiting exceptionally good properties.

To a visitor to the laboratory it might have appeared that young Papian was engaged in a routine chore of sorting and testing the tiny rings, but both Papian and Forrester regarded it as a development project committed to converting an attractive theoretical principle to reliable practice by testing various types of materials. "He set me to work developing magnetic-core storage," recalled Papian, "and he treated me in that way anybody in the lab would recognize, supporting and guiding the effort to success with very little detailed nagging."[9] During October new cores received from Allegheny Ludlum proved to be some 300 times faster in their switching interval from one state to the other: down from 10,000 microseconds to about 30 microseconds. Electrostatic tubes were still faster, however.

Following his practice of keeping in touch with the work of the laboratory engineers and carrying out his responsibility for the graduate assistants as they pursued their thesis investigations, Everett made it a policy to get around the laboratory every couple of weeks, stopping to review and discuss the work in progress. Thus he was aware both of the details of Papian's work and of the status of the electrostatic storage tube program. In response to a request from Forrester, Everett prepared a cost estimate early in January 1950 on the storage tubes, and Hugh Boyd followed this with another in mid-February.[10]

In the summer of 1949 electrostatic storage tube research and development had not yet reached the stage at which assemblies were being built to be incorporated into Whirlwind I. There was no question that an array of tubes could be built and installed into the computer as its automatic, internal "memory," but reliability problems and opportunities for improvement continued to present themselves.

Meanwhile, the other elements of the giant computer, rack on rack and row after row, were being steadily built up, tested, interconnected, tested, further interconnected, and tested again, and it would not be long until Whirlwind I would be in existence as a computer without any storage facilities more ample than the treacle-slow, hand-operated toggle switches, used to check the operation of portions of the machine and the steps in preliminary operations, the success of which would render the machine ready for larger and faster internal storage.

Since Forrester had no intention of allowing Whirlwind to become a computer with a "white elephant" reputation, he took care to assess and reassess the storage situation. But his own and Papian's investigations showed that the promise of the cores could not be realized in time to meet the needs of an otherwise operational Whirlwind. Even before this information was well in hand, he had told ONR in his fall 1949 "Summary Report" that "the next quarter will be used to construct the first set of tubes for WWI." His engineering prudence caused him to qualify this bold assertion a few pages later, however: "The electrostatic storage system will not be connected to the rest of the computer until it has been demonstrated that trouble-free operation can be expected . . . Reliability runs of the complete storage row are not expected until February 1950."[11]

Boyd's February cost analysis of proposed "standard, 100-series" electrostatic tubes, each storing 256 bits of information, in a two-dimensional, 16×16 array, indicated a high cost of approximately $1,500 per tube and a low rate of production of "one and one-half satisfactory tubes per week."[12] The cost was indeed high, but it was the best that could be done, and under the circumstances must be accepted, even though the cost (including all storage tubes) per tube per week to the laboratory approached $2,250.

Necessity alone is never the mother of invention, yet the relatively marginal viability of the electrostatic tube continued to remind Forrester that he needed something better than he had. He sought to put the best face on the situation in reports he sent to MIT Provost Stratton's office in March 1950, in September, and in the following January. In none of these formal letters did he inject a word about the magnetic-core research then being carried forward. He was not making a secret of this research; on the contrary, he was keeping Valley and others on the MIT staff informed in an informal manner as 1950 wore on. He simply was unwilling to speak of his core-storage concept in the same breath with descriptions of the nearly operable, newly operable Whirlwind computer, the first day of "successful" or "real" operations of which was a matter of arbitrary determination depending. upon the standards of performance that might be selected.

Three days before the fateful meeting of March 6, 1950, with ONR representatives—the meeting at which Valley stepped in formally to offer new federal funds—Forrester wrote Stratton's office that "we expect to have the first bank of storage tubes operating before the first of July."[13] He offered this estimate in the context of remarking that "we are probably being much too modest in our claims for the machine." Certain minimum terminal equipment, together with the first bank of tubes, would give by the end of summer "a computer even more complete and flexible (with respect to the entire range of possible computer applications) than any other computer either now in existence or with prospect of materializing within the next two or three years."

He was indeed putting the best face on the situation, perhaps too enthusiastically, for he went on to say of the computer:

It will be better for some applications than others. It will be the only computer which can be applied to many important problems (because of its speed). In a few categories of applications it may not be (in its initial form) as useful as some other machines. The machine at that time should no longer be the limitation on advancement of digital computer utilization; the shortage of enough trained personnel will become the bottleneck.[14]

These were brave (and prophetic) words, drafted in full awareness of the impending meeting on ONR funding, but they were no solution to the internal-storage problem. Forrester himself admitted that one bank of 256-digit storage tubes would provide only one-eighth of the ultimate storage capacity he then had in mind. Unwilling to leave his terms "minimum" and "ultimate" undefined, he pointed up his meaning in typical personal style. Were a stranger to ask, "Can you do my computing job?" wrote Forrester, the answer appropriate to a minimum computer's capacities must be, "Probably, but we must analyze it to find out." But if one possessed the ultimate system Forrester had in mind, then the answer to the question could safely be: "Yes, what is it?"[15] Forrester was after the ultimate.

But the storage tubes were not part of the computer yet, nor were they operating in July, as he had hoped, nor in September. "The final testing and alignment of the first storage bank is moving along steadily," he wrote Stratton in September 1950, injecting first a diplomatic note of tempered optimism, "but more slowly than I had expected," he added matter of factly. He was finding it a touch-and-go business, and a careful reading between the lines indicates again how heavy were the pressures that weekly were becoming heavier as the Air Force phase of proposed application began to take more explicit form. Careful testing of storage tubes and associated circuits in each digit column was producing "numerous small difficulties"; this was to be expected with new equipment, Forrester argued. But "our biggest problem," he confessed, "is that of trying to do in two months what we have had six months to do on other comparable parts of the computer."[16]

Forrester was still able to point out, as he did in his letter to Stratton, copies of which also went to Valley and to C. V. L. Smith of ONR, "Thus far at least, the computer status is not holding up progress of the Air Force intercept program, although a working storage-tube bank will soon be necessary." It was by no means clear that acceptable storage tubes would be ready in time. Meanwhile, he pointed out, the test storage had proved capable of meeting the demands placed on it in "testing out the terminal equipment and telephone line transmission of radar data from Bedford . . .

We have made two trials of transmitting radar data into and through the computer with promising results."[17]

While work on the first bank of storage tubes continued in the Barta Building, Papian reported that same September on his work of the preceding nine months. "The problem is bracketed on the one hand," he wrote, "by a metallic core . . . which has excellent signal ratios and a 20 micro-seconds response time, and on the other hand by a ferritic core . . . which has only fair signal ratios and a 1/2 micro-second response time."[18]

Prospects were sufficiently attractive so that Papian proceeded to a 2 × 2 planar array of cores. In October he obtained "successful operation . . . with 30 micro-second switching time," demonstrating experimentally one of the conceptions Forrester had set forth in a laboratory report he duplicated in May and submitted as an article in June to the *Journal of Applied Physics*.[19] But much core research and testing lay ahead, nor were the results safely predictable.

While this work was progressing, MIT prepared a proposal in October 1950 to present to ONR regarding research problems considered worth pursuing, not by Project Whirlwind alone but by another laboratory. The title of the proposal was "Program of Applied Research at the Laboratory for Insulation Research," and the first project proposed was one urging ONR to support "an investigation of the ways and means by which the hysteresis loops of ferroelectrics and of ferromagnetic semiconductors can be shaped to order." The pertinence of the work to progress in computer research and development was stressed: "The present-day ferrite materials show that this goal can be achieved by dielectrics, if rectangular hysteresis loops can be produced. Project Whirlwind is therefore extremely interested in the outcome."[20]

The project engineers had reason to be. For while the magnetic cores were becoming increasingly attractive prospects for further research, the electrostatic tubes were posing new problems. By the middle of 1950 the smaller tubes, equipped with guns providing a shorter "throw," clearly were not living up to expectations or specifications: ". . . a reliable operating tube with 32 × 32 density has not been achieved." Thirteen of thirty-three tubes produced in one three-month period were research tubes.[21] When the first bank of standard tubes was connected into the computer in July and short programs were run, successful operations could be obtained for several minutes at a time, or even for an hour, but the tubes were not reliable. "The behavior of the storage," said the third quarterly report for 1950, "depended on the programs used and their frequencies, and it varied when different areas of the storage surfaces were used. There was evidently much that we did not understand about the operation of the storage as an integrated part of the computer."[22]

◁

A 4-core, 2-dimensional magnetic memory test set-up.

A 16 by 16 array of ceramic memory cores.

▷

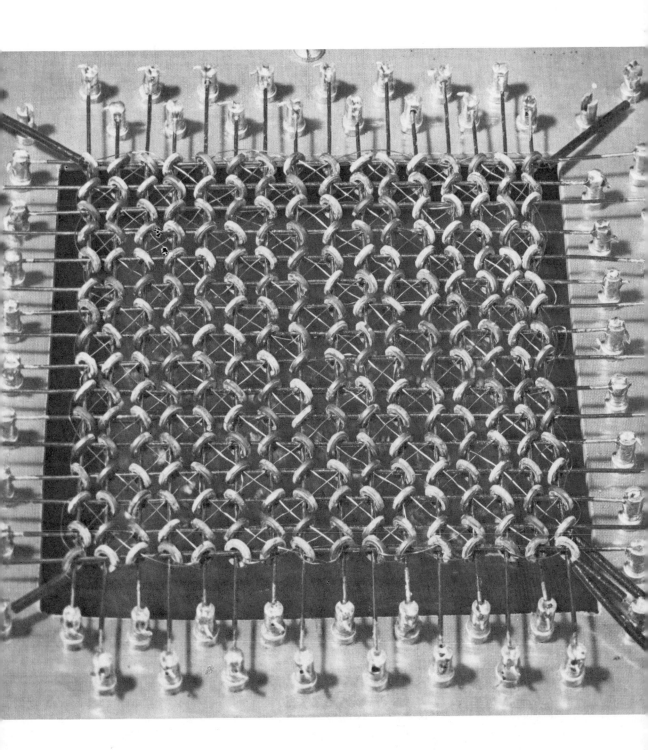

It was in this same fall progress report that the possibilities of magnetic-core storage were first discussed in some detail for the record to the Navy. The report presented the results of Papian's work and indicated the direction of further investigations. It proposed two lines of inquiry, one devoted to "improving materials to reduce eddy-currents and increase hysteresis-loop rectangularity" and the other aimed at "uncovering and solving the problems associated with operating large numbers of these cores in a high-speed memory system."[23]

The article on core-storage Forrester had sent to the *Journal of Applied Physics* appeared in the issue of January 1951. Also during that month Forrester made another formal report to Stratton's office. He reported that since the first bank of storage tubes had been connected (in July), the computer had been "operating satisfactorily much of the time." In consequence, they had been able to make "steady progress" on the Air Force task and at the same time get "organized for engineering application." The storage-tube problem was not one to be solved in a hurry, however, because the complex structure and operations of the tubes posed so many subproblems. Forrester thus felt compelled to admit that "performance of the storage tube bank is not yet good enough to permit predicting future scheduled performance of the machine with complete confidence." Again he made no reference to the possibilities of magnetic-core storage.[24]

He turned instead to the matter of scientific applications of the machine, a goal which Mina Rees had undeviatingly held in view while ONR was bringing Whirlwind expenses into line with those of similar funding operations that ONR sponsored. Comments that Dr. Rees had made to Professor Morse caused Forrester to describe the resources of the four-man mathematics and applications group on the project staff, headed by Charles Adams. While most of the work of Adams's group had been devoted to developing "basic machine techniques and procedures," "a few specific problems" were called to the attention of Stratton's office in order to show that the computer was indeed moving steadily toward being a useful tool.

Integrating the output equipment into the machine and solving the electrostatic storage problems, including increasing the storage capacity beyond the present, unreliable, single bank, remained as tasks that would not be concluded as Forrester had hoped by the end of the 1951 fiscal year. Money problems were by no means over, just because ADSEC had come to the rescue a year ago.

In the preliminary funding discussions during that January twelve months earlier, when Valley and his colleagues had for the first time visited Project Whirlwind, John Marchetti of the Air Force Cambridge Research Laboratories had tentatively suggested an annual expenditure rate of $200,000 from Air Force funds to underwrite Whirlwind's participation in the committee's program.[25] By March 1950 this amount had more than doubled, implying the urgency of the program and the importance the committee had come to attach to the role of Whirlwind I. In addition to the figure of $500,000, which Valley mentioned at the March discussion with ONR, the Air Force the following month redirected the balance in the air traffic control study contract to "the experimental application of digital computers to air defense in accordance with the needs of ADSEC."[26]

This action apparently caused some confusion concerning the amount of money the Air Force would make available. The MIT provost understood the amount would be some $600,000, including $120,000 left in the air traffic control account, whereas John Marchetti believed the $600,000 to be in addition to the air traffic control balance. Marchetti's projected budgets for the following two fiscal years also included an annual allocation of $600,000, again effectively demonstrating the committee's reliance upon Whirlwind I.[27] The actual amount transferred by the Air Force in November was $480,000; this, plus the $20,000 given by ONR and the $120,000 balance from the air traffic control account, made initially available for the ADSEC phase of Project Whirlwind a sum of about $620,000.

The urgency that the Air Force attached to the work of the Valley Committee was illustrated not only by the redirection of the air traffic control study but also by the manpower and financial requirements imposed upon the Cambridge Research Laboratories to support the committee's efforts. Despite the reluctance of his laboratory chiefs John Marchetti, without doubt under pressure from higher echelons, established within the laboratories an "interim Air Defense Group," possessing a "priority in excess of any other job in the house." In his directive Marchetti noted that "the task must be done, and no further delay can be tolerated."[28] In addition to drawing upon the best scientific and engineering talent in the laboratories, the Air Force, in finding funds for the Valley Committee, also tapped the laboratories' appropriation, again to the dismay, if not irritation, of many of its personnel.[29]

In April of 1950, in accordance with its instructions from the Air Force, Project Whirlwind discontinued its work on the air traffic control problem and turned its attention to "the application of high speed computers to tracking while scanning (TWS) in accordance with the needs of the Valley Committee."[30] This TWS phase of Project Whirlwind's activities was continued under the contract for the air traffic control study until its termination on June 30, 1951. Project Whirlwind's participation was then financed through a new contract, AF 19(122)-458, administered by MIT as account number DIC-6889. The new contract reflected, of course, official confirmation of the agreements reached by MIT and the Air Force the previous January, when the institute agreed to implement the ADSEC recommendation, conduct further investigations into the air defense problem under the code name Project Charles, and establish Project Lincoln. All three programs were initially coordinated and supervised by the first director of Project Lincoln, Dr. F. Wheeler Loomis, on leave to MIT from the University of Illinois.[31] As had been the case when ASCA was funded, funding and the level of effort it would support were being subordinated to research and development needs. The pendulum was swinging back from the point it had reached when ONR had cried, "No more!"

Since Whirlwind was still under construction during 1950, the initial work carried out for ADSEC "consisted of (1) studying the TWS problem in order to program (or 'instruct') the computer and (2) devising a means of inserting radar data into the machine." The group anticipated using Missile Early Warning radar located at Hanscom Air Base in Bedford. This radar previously had been used by the Cambridge Research Center to test a Digital Radar Relay, a system it had developed to provide "transmission of range and azimuth data over an ordinary telephone line."[32] The MEW radar and Whirlwind were hooked up together, and experiments were conducted

Whirlwind's peripheral equipment included a 16-inch display oscilloscope.

that produced flight data. But the data were of poor quality because of erratic behavior on the part of the MEW radar. So between February 12 and March 12, 1951, the system was shut down for overhaul and repair.[33]

Once back in operation the system received further minor technical corrections until it successfully "tracked a single aircraft and computed the proper magnetic heading instructions to guide the aircraft to an arbitrarily chosen geographical point." Subsequent similar successes led to an attempt to perform "a computer-controlled collision-course interception." On April 20, 1951, three such interceptions were successfully completed. The pilot of the intercepting aircraft reported that from a distance of about 40 miles he was brought to within 1,000 yards of his target on each occasion.[34]

Whirlwind and ADSEC personnel hailed the interceptions as a success, for they demonstrated the feasibility of the concept. They vindicated, in a preliminary way, the predictions Crawford, Forrester, and Everett had held to for years, that such practical, real-time operations lay within the power of electronic information systems. And they provided the basis for the next air

Magnetic tape units were installed in 1953.

defense step: an expanded, experimental, multiple-radar warning system to be established later in the Cape Cod area. The Bedford MEW tests also offered "valuable experimental experience in preparation for operating" Whirlwind in the expanded system.[35]

Among those who commended the successes achieved by ADSEC and Project Whirlwind was Air Force Chief of Staff Vandenberg. In a letter to George Valley, he observed that the "successfully accomplished digital computation of interception courses with the Whirlwind Computer" gave "real hope of being able to eliminate some of the delays and inaccuracies inherent in conventional manual Air Defense control systems."[36]

The success of the Bedford intercept tests demonstrated only one aspect of Whirlwind as a fully operating computer. There are as many ways of determining when a computer is "in operating condition" as human ingenuity can devise, because the digital computer is an integrated system of electronic circuits that evolves through many stages of testing and preliminary electronic operation of, first, its elements, then groups of its elements, then eventually all of the elements together. Further, there is the repetition of this pattern, once the entire machine is considered operable, through many levels of logical complexity as determined by the programs and information-processing paces through which the machine is put. However, long before the electronic capacities of the components of the machine have fin-

An operator at a Flexowriter verifies a coded tape.

ished being checked out, the logical calculational capacities have begun to be explored, inasmuch as these logical capacities take expression first in the electronic operations of the machine.

If one is most concerned about whether a computer will perform the basic arithmetical operations, then these may become one's principal criteria of its operability. If a given storage capacity must be demonstrated first, then that is the consideration which may determine whether a particular computer is "really" in operating condition. If a computer is expected to carry out a certain type of program, then that may become the standard of its "true operating condition." Nor are these the only examples.

Forrester, Everett, and their engineering staff recognized full well that the usefulness of this computer which they had been touting as a "general-purpose" machine depended on the size of its internal, automatic storage. The manually controlled test storage could be set to put the other control and calculational elements of the machine through enough paces to demonstrate their capacities, their speed, and their reliability, and in this respect determine whether they would "really" operate or not. But an operating standard which could only be demonstrated with the passage of time was that of how dependably the machine would perform its multiple operations and how often it would have to shut down, or even pause, for repairs.

Long before the intercept tests were run, the project engineers and many of the technicians had sufficient evidence, and from that evidence satisfactory knowledge that the computer would calculate as they had expected. They did not know how it would operate with full storage capacity, because such capacity had not yet been achieved. Meanwhile, the success of the first air-intercept tests was another milestone, and a dramatic one, demonstrating the potentiality of Whirlwind as a truly useful machine.

In this perspective, the chronic troubles the project had been having with the electrostatic storage tubes were not crippling, for those troubles had not prevented the tubes from contributing to the success of the intercept tests of the spring of 1951. Since June 1950 the first bank of 16 tubes, comprising a storage capacity of 256 registers, had been connected to the rest of the computer.[37] Preliminary results were at once gratifying and irritating. The tubes worked, but not all of their storage capacity was dependable. Parts of the storage surfaces would operate without error for over an hour, while other parts would not hold up beyond five minutes. It was the overall delicacy and instability of the tube-bank's performance that caused Forrester, Everett, and their staff to remain profoundly dissatisfied. The reliability prospects were quite intolerable when measured by the standards originally laid down. Improved quality control in the design and manufacture of the tubes was imperative.

However promising magnetic-core storage appeared to be, the research and development problems involved in magnetic-core applications were altogether too formidable and time-consuming to meet the current needs of Whirlwind, for it was now a computer going through shakedown operations. So there was nothing for it but to continue testing and adjusting present tube and circuit designs while continuing also to construct and test special research modifications on tubes not wired into the rest of the computer. Obviously, the key lay in controlling the characteristics of the individual tubes that were to serve as the building blocks of the total internal storage element.

During 1950 and 1951, then, Project Whirlwind was engaged in exploring and improving the operating capacities of the entire computer with one hand, so to speak, while carrying on development work on the elements of its components with the other hand. The principal elements needing improvement were the internal storage and the input-output equipment. Aware that the possible modes of input and output were many and varied, and estimating at the start that the design and development problems were far less formidable with regard to this terminal equipment than with regard to overall machine control, arithmetic computation, and internal storage, Forrester had been willing to let the Special Devices Center contract for part of the terminal equipment separately. After he had participated in establishing the requirements needed for compatibility with the rest of the computer, he had been satisfied to have the Eastman Kodak Company take on the job of designing and developing the reading and recording unit. Eastman would work with Project Whirlwind at the engineering level but would be responsible contractually, fiscally, and administratively to the Special Devices Center. The input-output control element would be developed at MIT, in order to ensure that numbers would be transferred satisfactorily between the input-output register of Whirlwind and whatever external memory and recording devices were used—in this instance, the Eastman reader-recorder.

The Eastman Company had delivered the first reader-recorder unit on September 13, 1949, after testing it during the preceding three months.[38] Reliability tests were next in order, to find out how well and consistently the unit would "record binary numbers on photographic film by . . . light from . . . a cathode ray tube," and how well and reliably it would "read such recorded data by scanning of the processed film with a cathode ray tube."[39]

By the beginning of summer 1950 the reader-recorder unit was proving unreliable when connected to the computer, indicating the need for more extensive testing than had been planned. Characteristically, the "Summary Report" issued that spring began discussing other forms of input-output equipment: "The input-output requirements have been studied," said the report, "and a proposal has been made for the minimum amount of terminal equipment needed to make the computer useful in handling general problems." Input equipment called for included a typewriter, a coded-paper-tape punching device, and film units. Output equipment would include a typewriter, a paper-tape punch, film units, and "a versatile oscilloscope display." Acquisition and integration of such units would occupy the coming year.[40]

By the time the successful air intercepts occurred in the spring of 1951, the Eastman units had been quietly discarded, a Flexowriter typewriter and punched-tape units were in service, and plans were laid for "a flexible system that will accommodate various kinds of terminal equipment," including paper tape, magnetic tape, oscilloscopes, a scope camera, and a control to introduce preprogrammed marginal checking whenever desired.[41]

More important than the incorporation of improved input-output equipment was the progress achieved by the beginning of 1951 in the design of electrostatic storage tubes. As a result of this advance Forrester felt free to proclaim to ONR in his official report of the spring of 1951 that Whirlwind had become "a reliable operating system." By the end of March 1951 applications were being programmed on the machine a scheduled thirty-five hours a week. "Of this time, 90 percent is useful." The computer more than once had achieved as many as seven consecutive hours of error-free operation.[42]

Alterations in the "charge on the glass windows" of the electrostatic tubes were identified as a major source of trouble and led to a redesign, the 300-series tube, in which coating "the entire inside of the envelope . . . with aquadag" removed the earlier fluctuations of the high-velocity gun's beam. Once all sixteen tubes had been replaced, Forrester was willing to call the computer "a reliable working system."[43] Five years had passed since Forrester made the decision to abandon the analog-computer approach to the aircraft stability and control analyzer problem and had committed himself to the alluring but virtually untried electronic digital computer.

Another achievement was in evidence by the spring of 1951. The hundreds of regular vacuum tubes employed in the pulsed circuits had become so reliable after the interface problems had been solved that wholesale replacement of tubes within less than 20,000 hours was considered to be not only unnecessary but "unwise."[44] A new high in reliability and longevity had been achieved in the course of Whirlwind's development, potentially increasing the life span of many standard-design vacuum tubes from a few hundreds of hours to several thousands of hours.

But Forrester remained far from satisfied with the performance of the electrostatic internal-storage tubes.

13

The End of the Beginning

During 1951 the days when Project Whirlwind could single-mindedly do its own thing (design and develop a really new kind of machine) came to an end. Increasingly the project began to be swallowed up in the larger enterprise conceived by ADSEC, expanded by Project Charles, and implemented by MIT's Lincoln Laboratory, of which Whirlwind became a subdivision. In short, Project Whirlwind began subtly to lose the independence that had been its unique and irritating hallmark.

During the early and middle fifties the Whirlwind computer became a fully operating machine, and the research and development challenge that for more than half a decade had been the project's reason for being came to an end. But the engineers found their work was just beginning. The pressing need to construct a continent-wide warning system against possible air attack centered their attention on the problem of designing the next-generation computer for specific application. This prospect became increasingly unattractive to Forrester and Everett as it became more routine, and each man, in his own way, sought new frontiers.

Concurrently with the establishment and organization of Project Lincoln in 1951, MIT, as discussed above, was in the process of reorganizing its computer program. Project Whirlwind, detached from the Servomechanisms Laboratory, was assigned to the newly created Digital Computer Laboratory, which was placed under Forrester's direction. The reorganization not only served to placate ONR, but it facilitated administrative relations between Project Whirlwind and Project Lincoln. When the reorganization took place, Forrester discussed with Wheeler Loomis, Lincoln's director, the nature of the relationship between the groups. Loomis mentioned two administrative possibilities: "one a sort of sub-contract arrangement . . . the other a closer administrative tie." Forrester, as could have been anticipated, noted a preference for an independent status and suggested that the Digital Computer Laboratory's part of Lincoln's program remain at Cambridge until the computer his group was to design especially for air defense had been assembled or put "into initial operation." This, he estimated, would not be until 1954.[1]

When Project Lincoln was first organized by MIT, responsibility for digital computer research and development had not been assigned to it. Second thoughts, however, added this task to Lincoln's program, and six months later those operations and staff members of the Digital Computer Laboratory concerned with Whirlwind I and its application to air defense were incorporated as "Division VI" into Lincoln Laboratory.[2] Although integrated into Lincoln's organization, the division remained in Cambridge. Consequently, Jay Forrester came to wear two hats: one as director of MIT's Digital Computer Laboratory, the other as head of Lincoln Laboratory's Division VI. In the latter capacity, he was responsible for Whirlwind's participation in the Cape Cod experimental warning system and for the design and construction of a digital computer possessing the characteristics "desired for a future operational air defense system."[3]

Forrester and his colleagues within Division VI faced four major tasks from the outset: (1) the organization of the division and the formulation of guidelines for its relations with the rest of Lincoln Laboratory; (2) the design, construction, operation, and expansion of the Cape Cod system in cooperation with Division II; (3) the design and construction, with concomitant research and development, of a prototype air defense computer and its ancillary equipment; and (4) the selection of an industrial source for production of the computer. All four tasks were pursued concurrently during the closing months of 1951 and throughout 1952–1953.

Administratively, Division VI was divided into six groups, each charged with a specific responsibility within the overall program. Group 60, under the direction of Harris Fahnestock, was responsible for administrative services. Group 61, under C. Robert Wieser, was responsible for the Cape Cod system. Group 62, under Norman Taylor, bore responsibility for the design and construction of the air defense computer. Group 65, under David R. Brown, was responsible for magnetic materials. Group 64, under Stephen H. Dodd, was responsible for the maintenance and improvement of Whirlwind I. And Group 63, under Pat Youtz, conducted the electrostatic storage tube development program.[4]

Later, the Sage System Production Coordination Office and the AN/FSQ-7 Systems Office were organized within the division. The Production Coordination Office maintained "liaison with industrial and military organizations outside Lincoln" and acted "as the coordination agency for Division VI portions of SAGE system planning and implementation, thus providing suitable direction and control of the program with respect to Lincoln's over-all responsibility for the system." The Systems Office maintained coordination with the International Business Machines Corporation, which subsequently became the manufacturer of the production model of the air defense computer, the AN/FSQ-7.[5]

To a considerable extent Forrester and his engineers during the early fifties enjoyed the same independence and freedom of action within Lincoln Laboratory that they had enjoyed when attached to the Servomechanisms Laboratory. Although nominally attached to the latter, Project Whirlwind had been virtually self-sufficient and independent. This was especially true after the project had so expanded in size that it became necessary for it to move to separate quarters in the Barta Building. Here the project established its own shops and maintained its own service crews, an autonomy acceptable to Nat Sage's Division of Industrial Cooperation, which administered the contract. Thus, the freedom of action that Sage permitted in technical matters he had also permitted in administrative matters. The cumulative effect confirmed Forrester's desire and belief that Project Whirlwind was actually, if not contractually, a free agent.[6]

During 1951 and 1952, prior to the physical integration of Project Whirlwind into Lincoln Laboratory, Forrester and Everett worked with the parent organization as Forrester had previously worked with ONR. No members of the Whirlwind staff, for example, attended Lincoln's meetings. So from the start Division VI established a pattern of autonomous behavior within Lincoln Laboratory. It was a pattern that Forrester and Everett were careful to maintain as the attention of the project shifted from finishing and perfecting Whirlwind to designing and developing the FSQ-7 computer, and as common technical problems of SAGE brought Division VI into closer association with the other divisions of Lincoln Laboratory. Even after Forrester's departure in 1956, Everett as the new director of Division VI continued its semiautonomous and highly individualistic role, until he led a large contingent of the division's personnel from the laboratory in 1959 to form the MITRE Corporation.

When the division personnel finally moved during the summer of 1953 to the Lincoln Laboratory quarters in Lexington, the giant Whirlwind computer was left behind in the Barta Building on the MIT campus.[7] The division took its service organizations with it, however: the print shop, machine shop, purchasing office, and so on. These services duplicated those already provided by Lincoln, but Forrester and his associates refused to disassemble the smooth-functioning organization they had created at MIT. There were those within Lincoln who were irritated by this display of independence and saw it simply as a determination to continue going "first class" regardless of the cost. But there were also those who took advantage of the efficiency that the additional facilities and services offered. Among the latter was George

Valley, head of Division II, who when in need of immediate assistance would resort to the division's supporting facilities.

At the same time Division VI remained highly individualistic, continuing to do business its own way and working effectively with the radar engineers in Division II. The latter, under the direction of Valley, were responsible for aircraft control and warning and possessed that special competence and experience which Whirlwind's personnel lacked to set up the preliminary, experimental, Cape Cod system employing several radar stations to feed data into Whirlwind.

This particular kind of practical application of the general-purpose computer, of which Whirlwind was the first example, required dimensions and directions of technical electronic knowledge and experience that Project Whirlwind personnel had never acquired and very likely could not have mastered in the brief time that development schedules allowed. The engineers took this situation for granted, and there was from the start the view that such pooling of resources and talents as Division II and Division VI possessed was the natural course to pursue. It was the efficient way to proceed, and became the way they successfully proceeded during 1952-1953.

In this respect then, Whirlwind was not ruggedly independent. Rather, its independence manifested itself in the group's self-resourcefulness and daily conduct of its affairs. Although later, by the move from the MIT campus to Lexington, it lost the injection of rich new blood that had been contributed by the graduate students, the project's firmly established way of doing things persisted for some time and helped maintain its special character and vitality against the pressures imposed by the more conventional organization of Lincoln.[8]

Two of the four major tasks facing the administrators of Division VI were of vital importance to the overall program of Lincoln Laboratory, for unless they were successfully completed, the program could become a total failure. These were the construction, operation, and evaluation, in cooperation with Division II, of the Cape Cod experimental system and the design and construction of a high-speed digital computer that would possess the characteristics "required for an operational air defense system."[9]

One of the follow-on test projects that the planners working on Project Charles had recommended was the more elaborate Cape Cod multiple-radar intercept system. Whirlwind would be the machine element at the information-processing, command and control center of this system. This solution of the air defense problem was essentially similar to that proposed by the Valley Committee. Project Charles's investigators were familiar, of course, with the successful experiments of Project Whirlwind and ADSEC. They had been unable to find any "other solution to air defense data processing . . . equal in long term value to the digital transmission and automatic analysis of data." Hence they had recommended the construction of a model system in the Cape Cod region of Massachusetts. This system would consist of a series of radar stations tied to Whirlwind at MIT. The data obtained from this experimental network, it was anticipated, would provide guidelines for the design, development, and construction of a more sophisticated digital computer. This next generation computer was to incorporate the unique functional characteristics required by the information and control center of the proposed centralized air defense system.[10]

The Cape Cod system became the particular joint responsibility of Divisions II and VI of the Lincoln Laboratory pursuant to the laboratory's overall responsibility for coordinating and implementing the recommendations of ADSEC and Project Charles as well as for performing within its own facilities research, development, and tests in the general area of air defense.[11] The primary task confronting Lincoln Laboratory at this time was the "development of a system using a high-speed digital computer to receive, process, and transmit air-surveillance, identification, and weapon-guidance information."[12]

As an experimental system, Cape Cod then served several purposes: it developed "system concepts for a high-track-capacity system"; it permitted new components to be tested in an operating prototype of the air defense system envisaged by ADSEC and Project Charles; it furnished data and other information necessary to the preparation of "specifications for digital computers designed specifically for air defense"; and it permitted verification of the "soundness of the whole concept by experiments using live radar data and controlling live aircraft."[13]

Division VI's responsibilities for the Cape Cod system included "air defense center planning, automatic information processing (including data screening and automatic tracking), the computation of control orders for weapons, and the provision of the digital equipment necessary in the air defense center." These responsibilities fell mainly upon groups 61, 64, and 65.[14] When work upon the system was commenced by the groups concerned, it was anticipated that the program would consist of three parts: "(1) Construction and operation of a three-radar network; (2) construction of a fourteen-radar network; and (3) planning for a future operational system." The first part, which was scheduled for completion during fiscal year 1952, called for expansion of the single-radar system with which the Valley Committee had conducted its successful intercept experiments in the spring of 1951.

Throughout fiscal year 1952 the primary objective was "aimed at learning how to track an aircraft through a network of radars having overlapping coverage," in order to gain the knowledge and experience necessary to implement the second part, expansion into a fourteen-radar network. The hope was that by July of 1952 the larger network would be under construction and that in the course of the year, Whirlwind would be sufficiently improved technically, by the installation of magnetic storage drums, to expand the computer's capacity to handle the requirements of the full Cape Cod radar net. If this schedule were met, then it was anticipated that prior to June 1953 Division VI would be able "to commence operation with the fourteen-radar network with automatic data-handling capacity for data screening, automatic track-while-scan, and the control of a large number of aircraft."[15] Realization of these plans was of extraordinary importance to the total air defense project, for in addition to laying the groundwork for an expanded experimental system, the initial efforts would permit the military to evaluate the concept even as it was in process of implementation.[16]

Military evaluation of the project was more important than it appeared to be on the surface, for while Project Lincoln had been in the process of organization by MIT and the national military establishment, another air defense program had been under way at the Willow Run Research Center of the University of Michigan. This was a program similar in goal but different as to the proposed method of attainment. The competition between the two programs could be "sticky," not solely because of the impact upon the educational institutions involved, but also because the situation reflected the competition between the Rome Air Development Center at Rome, New York, and the Air Force Cambridge Research Center at Cambridge, Massachusetts. Both were Air Force agencies, but both were striving to become preeminent in air defense research and development and in the concomitant area of military electronics. Furthermore, the competition was not divorced from politics. Political representatives of the two regions concerned sought to keep the program, since it held great potential for economic growth and stability. Industry also did not remain uninvolved, although the concern there was less narrowly regional. IBM eventually became involved in Lincoln's program; General Electric expressed interest in the program conducted at Willow Run.[17]

The problems raised by the competing programs were finally resolved in May 1953 when the Air Force terminated the University of Michigan's program and concentrated its whole effort upon the centralized concept under development by Lincoln Laboratory and the Cambridge Research Center.[18] There were the unavoidable mutterings that the decision had been politically motivated, and it would be naive to assume that political and economic pressures played no role. Nevertheless, the feasibility of the concept Lincoln was implementing had been demonstrated by the experiments first conducted for ADSEC and then expanded under Divisions II and VI of Lincoln Laboratory in the Cape Cod system. In comparison, the Michigan system had "not been demonstrated as successful."[19]

By March 1953 the Cape Cod system, though incomplete, was supplying "valuable experimental data from existing equipment." The nucleus of the system was the network that had been put together for the ADSEC experiments, but two smaller radars located north and south of Boston, at Rockport and Scituate, Massachusetts, using slowed-down-video data transmission links, had also been used in some tracking tests. The data generated by the radars were fed into Whirlwind. The computer processed the information and provided "vectoring instructions for mid-course guidance of manned interceptors and . . . special displays for people who monitor and direct the operation of the system."

The information and experience gained from such tests, using "live aircraft, live radar, and an operating computer" proved immensely "valuable in planning an advanced air defense system."[20] By December 1953 the system was operating with a large radar set (FPS-3) located at Truro on Cape Cod and two gap-filler radars. The data provided were processed automatically by Whirlwind, which was able to "carry the tracks of as many as 48 aircraft." Guidance instructions based on Whirlwind data were transmitted to intercepting aircraft.[21] Although the "electronic systems and the programs" were functioning well, good radar data were still lacking.[22]

The role Whirlwind was able to play in these December exercises hinged crucially upon the progress made in magnetic-core development work since Bill Papian had built his first 2 × 2 planar array of cores in the fall of 1950. During 1951 Papian continued his efforts to identify core material that would hold its polarization in spite of unwanted electronic system "noise" unavoidably generated by the pulses passing through the circuitry. The core should also be made of material that would permit it to switch rapidly from one electromagnetic state to the other when required, that is, from plus to minus (from "yes" to "no"). A 16 × 16 array of cores in one plane was constructed in order to test and observe several effects of electrical "noise," such as those of the switching of nearby cores, that might unintentionally trigger another core or the multiple effects of running program patterns through the array. By the end of 1951 "a fair demonstration of the practicability" of the arrangement had been achieved: "Error-free operation for periods as long as several hours is highly encouraging in view of the very large variation of characteristics among the 256 cores and the incomplete state of development of the logical test equipment surrounding the array."[23] The cores continued to appear promising indeed, yet they were still far from achieving the operating standards required.

The addition of a second bank of electrostatic storage tubes to Whirlwind at this time increased its storage capacity by 1,024 registers without adding to storage access time.[24] But experience with the new tubes during 1952 revealed that, contradictory to earlier judgments, the internal-storage problem was not yet out of the woods. The new bank of tubes possessed a larger storage density of 32 × 32 registers, compared to 16 × 16 in the first bank.

A close-up of a 64 by 64 array of ferrite cores.

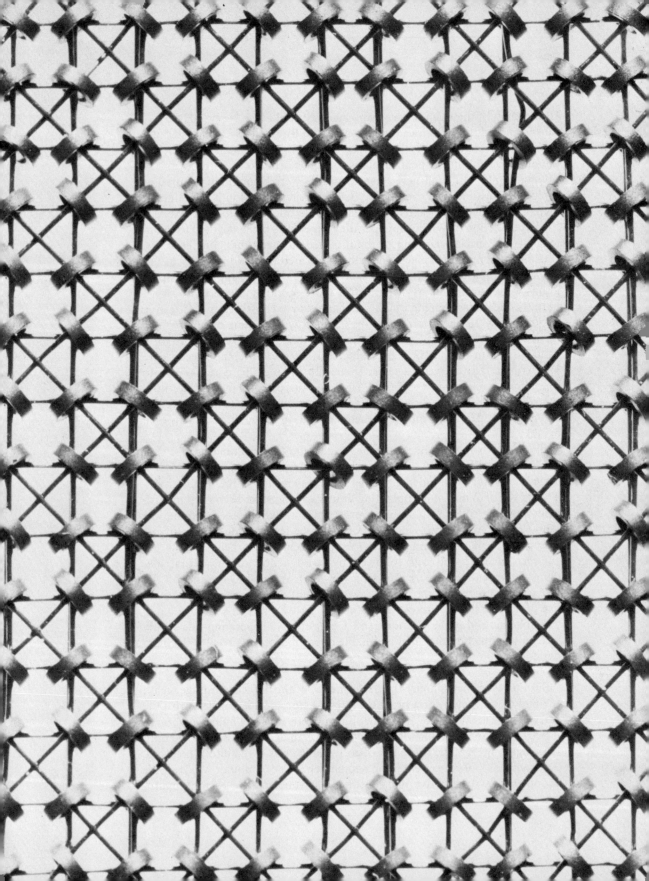

Unfortunately, these tubes were by no means trouble-free. New "400-series" tubes replaced the 300-series tubes to no avail. By April 1952 Forrester and Everett decided reluctantly to hold up adding any more banks of tubes of the new design, and suspended plans to replace the 16 × 16 tubes in the original bank. Although new 500-series tubes were being manufactured as rapidly as possible, and even if they proved reliable, it would take time to increase production sufficiently to maintain an adequate stock of reserves. "A large fraction of Whirlwind operating time" was being devoted to maintenance and special checking of the installed storage tubes. Furthermore, the limited supply of replacement tubes indicated it would be risky to put Whirlwind on a three-shifts-a-day schedule, even though applications programs were stacking up as demands for more machine time grew.[25]

In the meantime, Papian and his assistants were constructing and testing another 16 × 16 planar array of cores, composed this time of nonmetallic ferritic material instead of rings of thin metal ribbon wound on itself to form a doughnut. In May 1952 it became clear that the switching speeds were approximately twenty times faster than with the metallic cores—down to one microsecond or less. So promising was the performance of the non-metallic ferrites that by July Forrester, Everett, and their engineers decided to build 32 × 32 arrays and stack them 16 high, in a true three-dimensional arrangement.

Since Whirlwind was by then in heavy demand for preliminary Cape Cod and other applications, it would not be possible to use it to test the 16,384-bit core memory, comprising 1,024 registers, which was then being built. The design of Whirlwind's operating units had long since become standardized, however, so the solution most practical to the engineers was to build a semicopy of Whirlwind—another computer to test the magnetic storage. The concept of the Memory Test Computer came into being during the summer of 1952 and was followed by construction of the actual machine—more modest in size and capacities than Whirlwind—in the fall. By November, Forrester and Everett were committing themselves fully to the use of nonmetallic ferrites for the Memory Test Computer's storage bank. The following May the Memory Test Computer was operating sufficiently well to demonstrate the "highly reliable operation of a 32 × 32 × 16 magnetic ferrite storage."

To Forrester that summer the performance of the new core storage meant the end of his search for a practical internal storage element. Electrostatic storage tube manufacture and development were abruptly halted as soon as it became clear that Whirlwind would receive an existing core-storage unit. On August 8, 1953, the first bank of core storage was wired into Whirlwind. A second bank of cores went in on September 5. The computer's access time dropped from twenty-five microseconds for tube storage to nine micro-

Forrester with a 64 by 64 core memory plane.

seconds for the magnetic cores.[26] But best of all, the chronic, incurable maintenance troubles and the high costs of tube manufacture were at an end. A brief valedictory in behalf of electrostatic storage was nevertheless in order; the "Summary Report" for the third quarter of 1953 pointed out that Whirlwind "could not have reached its present state of development without ES. No other form of high-speed storage was available when Whirlwind I was put in operation."[27]

Four years had passed since Forrester had set Papian to work on the magnetic core development project, sorting, testing and analyzing the electromagnetic properties of the tiny rings. During those four years Whirlwind had found a mission and was about to spawn a successor that would take advantage of advances in the electronics state of the art since Whirlwind had been conceived. Long before the end of 1953 Forrester's engineers had begun to consider the design parameters that the new defense computer should have. The Cape Cod tests added valuable data and experience. All of these would be of assistance in designing and constructing the computer to be used in the projected continent-wide air defense system.

Existing computers, including Whirlwind, were "suitable for studying the digital control of air defense," but they did not possess the unique character-

▷
The Memory Test
Computer, built to
test the magnetic-
core memory bank on
the left.

Close-up of a magnetic
memory bank. Two
memory banks were
installed in Whirlwind
in 1953, increasing its
storage to 2,048 words
of 16 bits each.
◁

istics necessary to an air defense system. Moreover, the design and construc-tion of an air defense computer was urgent; national security required the "availability of an improved Air Defense System" as promptly as possible.[28] As early as 1951 the question was not "whether to build a machine or not, but rather to build the best machine possible, considering speed, cost, capac-ity, and complexity."[29] In consequence, concurrently with the construction and operation of the Cape Cod system, groups 62 and 63 of Division VI embarked immediately upon a research and development program pointed to the construction of an air defense computer.[30] This computer was first thought of as "Whirlwind II," then it became the "XD-1" and finally the "FSQ-7."

When in 1951 it took on the research and development program that eventually produced the FSQ-7, Division VI operated upon three premises. First, Project Charles's recommendation for an "improved air defense sys-tem using a digital computer information center" had to be implemented and realized "as soon as practical." Second, no contemporary digital com-puter could be more than a "laboratory model" for the proposed system. An advanced design was needed that would "improve reliability, reduce maintenance, be tailored to the air defense application, and incorporate the necessary facilities for the required terminal equipment." Third, the Digital Computer Laboratory would furnish the "key personnel and background experience for the estimated design program."[31]

In a series of meetings held that fall to plan and schedule the research and development program for the air defense computer, those members of Divi-sion VI participating decided that the computer should be fast, flexible, and reliable. It should be as fast as, if not faster than, Whirlwind I. It should possess a register length of twenty-four bits. The group considered the use of marginal checking, magnetic cores, and transistors in order to achieve max-imum reliability, even though the technology in these areas was not yet fully developed. Reliability was so important, the conferees believed, that they even considered the installation of additional machines in the command and control center, to be available as an instant reserve. A general-purpose com-puter was essential, since flexibility was another major requirement. The time estimated to complete the program was three years.[32]

By January of 1952 the design staff for Whirlwind II was in process of organization. Its schedule called for the first half of fiscal year 1953 to be spent in determining and establishing the air-defense computer's character-istics and selecting its components; the second half of the year was to be devoted to its design. The engineers selected four major areas of effort: "(1) a study of new components and circuits, (2) the determination of optimum machine logic to utilize these new techniques, (3) the development of new magnetic materials for reliable high-speed storage and for switching purposes, (4) close liaison with the Cape Cod System to formulate the computer characteristics peculiar to air defense data processing."[33]

A problem of primary importance, which beset the leaders of the Digital Computer Laboratory and of Division VI and which possessed special significance for groups 61, 62, and 63 responsible for the Cape Cod system and Whirlwind II, was the shortage of personnel trained and experienced in computer technology. The problem was acute enough in itself, but it was further complicated by the rapid physical and organizational expansion of the Digital Computer Laboratory as it sought to meet its responsibilities, not only to the Air Force but to the Navy and MIT as well, for as Whirlwind had become operational, programs other than those in air defense were also assigned to it.

To cope with these complications as they bore upon Division VI, Everett and Fahnestock recommended the institution of regularly scheduled formal meetings of group leaders and laboratory chiefs to keep all aware of the activities going on within other groups, permit critical analysis of the program, and assist in the assignment of personnel and job priorities. The engineer's biweekly reports and the Friday afternoon teas from the early days of Project Whirlwind were no longer adequate for the dissemination of information. The responsibilities of the Digital Computer Laboratory were just too complex, too great.[34]

The first meeting, held on March 26, 1952, considered the seriousness of the shortage of experienced personnel and the impact of the shortage upon the Whirlwind II and Cape Cod programs. Norman Taylor, responsible for Whirlwind II, predicted that the schedule established for the design and construction of the production model of the air defense computer would prove "unrealistic," for of the twenty-three members of his group, only four, excluding David R. Brown and Taylor himself, had any previous experience with Whirlwind. Requesting the transfer to his group of one or two more men possessing Whirlwind training, Taylor estimated that even if all effort were taken off Whirlwind, completion of Whirlwind II would not be accomplished until January 1, 1956, two years later than scheduled. If Whirlwind personnel were not used, then completion of a production model would be extended two years beyond that point.

In response to Taylor's predictions and pleas, Steve Dodd, head of Group 64, argued that a similar lack of experienced personnel would interfere with and delay the planned program for the improvement and enlargement of Whirlwind. Whirlwind had been considered a "training ground for Whirlwind II," but already the requirements for the former's program had increased "faster than the training"; consequently, no surplus of personnel existed for transfer. Furthermore, he warned, dilution of "the effort on Whirlwind and Cape Cod might easily push Whirlwind out to the original time estimates for Whirlwind II." Forrester concluded the discussion by recommending that the problem be taken under consideration and investigated further by Dodd and Wieser.[35]

The conclusions reached by Dodd and Wieser were presented at the group leaders' meeting of June 9. Dodd, acting as spokesman, told his colleagues that "no experienced staff could be transferred without seriously cutting into the Cape Cod program."[36] This could have been particularly damaging to the overall program, especially if Wieser's earlier warning—that the Cape Cod system would be "running too late to be of any use in affecting decisions in the design" of Whirlwind II—proved accurate.[37] Forrester's decision, given at the end of the meeting, was that a transfer of experienced personnel from Group 64 to Group 62 would not be in "the best interests of the laboratory." Consequently, Taylor was required to train his own men and to make his assignments accordingly.[38] Although this time around the specific problems were different, the research and development challenge was reminiscent of the early days of Whirlwind: Forrester was allocating scarce resources. The technical knowledge and experience, however, were vastly deeper.

The fourth major task that faced the directors of Division VI was a new one: selection of a manufacturing source for the air defense computer. From the middle of 1951 on, analyses were undertaken and applications from qualified manufacturers were solicited, informally at first. Ultimately, the Air Force placed the International Business Machines Corporation under contract. From the outset of contractual negotiations, IBM had preferred a "prime contract." This view was shared by MIT because the institute's administration was loath to expand its budget through "additional funds for large subcontracts."[39] On the other hand, the Cambridge Research Center, representing the Air Force in the day-to-day negotiations, believed that a prime contract was impossible at the start because revised Air Force regulations made difficult if not impossible the justification of IBM as a "sole source." Consequently, John Marchetti, speaking for the center, recommended a temporary subcontract with Lincoln Laboratory.[40]

Although MIT and IBM pressed the matter on principle, using it as a means of inducing the Air Force to ease its contractual procedures,[41] both ultimately accepted a subcontractual relationship that, it was anticipated, would within a matter of months be replaced by a prime contract between the Air Force and IBM. Marchetti, however, made very clear the Air Force's intent to have MIT bear primary responsibility for the program, for it was to "continue to monitor the prime contract," even after the Air Force had taken over with "production money."[42]

These were not the kinds of considerations that SDD and Gordon Brown's Servomechanisms Laboratory had had to contend with during World War II and immediately after, when Project Whirlwind was born. But they were inescapable facts of life in the highly organized days of Lincoln and SAGE. Forrester had to deal with them whether he wanted to or not. In many ways it had become a different ballgame, a "business as usual" environment.

On October 27, 1952, MIT issued a letter of intent under the terms of which IBM commenced a cooperative project with Lincoln Laboratory. The contract was ultimately to involve the Western Electric Company, the Bell Telephone Laboratories, the Burroughs Corporation, and the Systems Development Corporation, and it culminated in the development and construction of the SAGE continental air defense system. The story of the preliminary success of the Cape Cod system and the subsequent building of SAGE, however, is not a part of the Whirlwind story. It is Whirlwind's sequel and is a story the research and development aspects of which involved Lincoln Laboratory, IBM, and the Air Force in development and production problems such as Project Whirlwind had never had to face. Project Whirlwind had run its creative, independent course as an on-campus research and development organization and was being shunted by ever stronger external forces, such as ONR in different ways had once sought to generate, along a course that would bring it into closer alignment with the larger organization of Project Lincoln and into an increasingly subordinate, assisting role, supporting and implementing the specific technological needs of the growing military defense establishment.

It was one thing for a young graduate-student engineer to attack an aircraft simulator problem in the closing years of a great war, another thing to open a door onto undreamt-of vistas of pioneering computer research and development waiting to be traversed, and still another to become a training and development organization ten years later, trapped in the detailed implementation work of devising third- and fourth-generation computers for increasingly routine, even though more complex, military assignments. When Forrester perceived what appeared to lie ahead of the organization he had built up, he found he was not particularly challenged by the prospect. Firmly convinced he could not restore the past and possessing extensive organizational experience acquired over a decade, he left the rapidly growing "computer business" in 1956 to immerse himself in the serious academic study of principles and techniques of industrial and engineering organization. He joined the MIT faculty in a professorial capacity that took him out of the administrative chain of command.

Subsequently, Everett left Project Lincoln also. Convinced the past could not be restored but still keenly attracted to other untrodden vistas in the realm of computer research and development, he became instrumental in forming a new organization to probe the engineering unknown, the MITRE Corporation of Bedford, Massachusetts. But these are other stories, still unfolding, better told elsewhere, and not a part of this account.

14

A Retrospective

For all the adventures that befell Project Whirlwind and for all the changes that occurred in the aims and procedures of the project, from the days of the airplane analyzer to the days of continental air defense it enjoyed a remarkable constancy of identity as a team of investigators dedicated to the pursuit of research and development. In the continuity of its style of carrying on its inquiries and in the depths of its commitment to producing practical machinery where none had existed before, it maintained a unity of character and a philosophy of investigation that marked it as unique among research and development projects.

Superficially the story of Whirlwind divides quite naturally into two parts which although interrelated stand distinct. This distinction is the more evident from the fact that the divisions are chronological, covering the periods 1944 to 1950 and 1949 to 1956. Moreover, each period correlates with a distinct, minor era in the nation's transition from World War II through the retrenchment of peace to the Cold War and the Korean War, and each period can be further defined by the dependence of the project upon either Navy or Air Force financing and managerial assistance, interference, and supervision.

The years between 1944 and 1950 were for Project Whirlwind a period of gestation, for it was during these years that emphasis shifted from the restricted-purpose simulator to the general-purpose computer, and it was during these years that the computer was brought to birth as an operating machine. Also, these years broadly delimit the period in which the Navy played the primary role in the program, and—perhaps of greatest importance for the climate in which research and development operated—they approximate the interlude between the end of World War II and the beginning of the period of American military adventures and misadventures that started with the Korean War. This interlude between wars was dominated in the United States by a policy of military retrenchment that significantly affected the magnitude and momentum of Project Whirlwind.

The years between 1949 and 1956 reflected the anxieties of a world increasingly hostile in its divisions and were marked by a reemergence of concern over the nation's air defenses and by programs mounted to study and correct their inadequacies. One of these programs led to the successful demonstration by Whirlwind of the feasibility of an air defense command-and-control center equipped with the digital computer as the principal information-coordinating element. As a result the Air Force displaced the Navy as the major source of funds and purpose for the project. The Whirlwind team became assimilated into the Air Force program and into the development of the semiautomatic ground environment (SAGE) air defense system, which prior to the missile age was intended to provide maximum security against attack from the air.

This same concept—a centralized computer of large capacity fed by geographically scattered radar sensors—was subsequently modified and applied to continental defense against missile attack. Thus the concept of "command and control" which Whirlwind had demonstrated as feasible, and in the development of which Whirlwind had played a vital role, was incorporated as an enduring element in the national defense structure. Further, the concept of command and control was to expand well beyond military use through application to other governmental needs and to the needs of industry and society in general, as the computer moved in the direction of becoming a true public utility, which, so proponents argued, would rank with the telephone and the water faucet.

In addition to advancing the state of the art in air defense, Project Whirlwind also advanced the state of the art in computer technology. There are among its technical contributions several accomplishments that should be singled out.

Forrester, looking back from the perspective of more than a decade, noted over a dozen devices, processes, and applications that Whirlwind contributed or brought to a practical working level.[1] Though the details of their operation belong more properly in a technical engineering history of the development of the SAGE air defense system—a technical story that would begin with Whirlwind (not with the aircraft analyzer) and include the next-generation AN/FSQ-7 production computer that demonstrated the worth of the Whirlwind technical concepts—the technical accomplishments Forrester enumerated provide a measure of the practical success of Project Whirlwind as an innovating engineering enterprise.

The most famous contribution was the random-access, magnetic-core storage feature, which was to be widely employed in succeeding generations of faster and more compact digital computers. Marginal checking, to detect deteriorating components, was another novel and highly practical feature. The Whirlwind computer was also first and far ahead in its visual display facilities. One form of information output was a cathode ray tube display "capable of plotting computed results on airspace maps."[2] Associated with it was the "light gun," or light pen, with which an operator could "write" on the face of the CRT display and provide new information which the computer could store and use. As a consequence of these two features, direct and simultaneous man-machine interaction became feasible, adding to the versatility and usefulness of the digital computer.

The perfection of simulation techniques by which hypothetical aircraft flights could be programmed into the computer for study and training purposes enhanced the practical prospects for exploiting digital simulation in a wide variety of fields. The crystal matrix switch designed by David Brown, the magnetic matrix switch developed by Kenneth Olsen, and the cryotron invented by Dudley Buck were all Project Whirlwind products that had continuing use and development later as digital computer electronics design progressed.

The Whirlwind machine was extensively programmed to carry out the novel procedure of self-checking, including the tasks of identifying defective components and typing out appropriate instructions to the operator. Early random tube failures posed another hurdle that the Whirlwind project negotiated successfully, for scrutiny and modification of tube-fabrication techniques led to dramatic increases in length of tube life through procedures applicable to the manufacture of hundreds of standard radio tube types.

The need to send radar-gathered data long distances to a computer control center caused successful techniques to be developed by the Lincoln Laboratory for sending digital data over telephone lines and opened the way for later commercial applications. The incorporation of a computer in a control network led to the development of a practical "feedback loop," in which the computer changed its control instructions as it received new information and thus maintained pertinent control, as when directing interceptor aircraft toward their targets in the early Whirlwind air defense tests. Here lay the prophetic significance of Reports L-1 and L-2 of 1947, and here was another practical application of the computer—the feedback control loop—that would have military and commercial use in the years to come.

A related pioneering development is to be seen in the doctoral dissertation of a Project Whirlwind engineer, William Linville, on "sampled data control theory." Linville investigated the effects of sampling operations upon the stability of feedback control loops in those situations in which different users would be sharing the services of a large computer to solve their separate problems.

Last, and of profound influence upon subsequent computer design, was the working out for Whirlwind of the intricate systemic details of "synchronous parallel logic"—that is, the transmitting of electronic pulses, or digits, simultaneously within the computer rather than sequentially, while maintaining logical coherence and control. This feature accelerated enormously (compared to other computers of that day) the speeds with which the computer could process its information. As Forrester has noted, "The parallel synchronous logic worked out for the Whirlwind computer and first appearing in the block diagram reports done by Robert Everett and Francis Swain set the trend for many later computer developments."[3]

Such, in brief, is Whirlwind's national historical and technical significance. In addition, Whirlwind is significant as an example of innovative engineering that happened to produce at the right place and time the right instrument. It met a national defense need for which there existed no other solution so apt or so elegant.

There was something of a storybook quality about the perils and successes of Whirlwind the project and Whirlwind the computer. Brilliant young men had shown seasoned, middle-aged veterans how such a thing should be done, and they had done so largely on their own terms. Young Perry Crawford had had the vision first. He began to translate his vision into action by joining the enterprising young engineers and program managers at Luis de Florez's unorthodox Special Devices Division, which encouraged and funded a variety of specific computer programs. Serendipitously, Crawford had "infected" young Jay Forrester, and Forrester's ASCA project was transformed into one of those programs.

Crawford had taken the strategist's approach, so to speak, while Forrester took the tactician's approach, more limited in scope, only to find himself moving into the realms of strategy and taking a third young engineer, Bob Everett, with him. The two young men quickly realized that they would not be developing simply a sophisticated flight trainer. Instead, they had stumbled upon a design concept so fundamental that its generality of application was almost staggering to contemplate. But Forrester was not staggered. The stunning generality of the abstract concept challenged him to incarnate it as a physical machine and solve a practical problem of his own. Archibald's postwar computer conference and Mauchly and Eckert's ENIAC, then under construction, pointed the way.

Both Forrester and Everett had formed their philosophy of research and development management in the unusual, creative intellectual and administrative environment of Gordon Brown's Servomechanisms Laboratory. Characteristically, they took their own path. It was a path that no one involved with computers had trod before them, and as they made their way, they encountered formidable policy resistances to their way of managing research and development. These resistances were so deep-rooted, powerful, and inimical that in the end, even though the achievements of Project Whirlwind triumphantly demonstrated the rightness of the path that Forrester and Everett had taken, research and development managers who came after concluded that either the project had succeeded in spite of, rather than because of, the way it managed its affairs, or it had been too unusual to try to duplicate.

The path Forrester and Everett had followed became lost to view amid a tangle of misapprehensions, indifference, and conservative tradition. Whirlwind the computer flourished long enough to accelerate dramatically the progress of computer design, but Whirlwind the project proved to be only as fresh, exciting, transient, and fragile as fabled Camelot. Then it was swallowed up in Lincoln Lab, and part of it was transformed into MITRE, and even the wondrous computer itself became obsolete.

True, Kenneth Olsen was able to apply his experience from Project Whirlwind to start the Digital Equipment Corporation, and he included Forrester on his board of directors. But it is doubtful if Olsen and his associates, when they formed their corporation, enjoyed the freedom from fiscal and operational restraints that had marked the initiation of ASCA and set the pattern for Project Whirlwind. Whirlwind's roots lay deep in the academic laboratory with its tradition of tolerance and freedom in the search for knowledge, pure or applied, a tradition which has more often backed the man rather than the project. The crisis of war may have narrowed the focus of research and development, but the tolerance of the academic climate was expanded by the generous flow of funds from a government willing under the urgency of war to underwrite the costs of any research and development activity that would further the war effort and hasten the day of victory. Educated, trained, and their experience gained in such a climate, the young engineers responsible for Project Whirlwind were loath to accept the imposition of peacetime restraints that took the form primarily of resistance to the continuation of a level of expenditure which, though acceptable in war, was excessive in peace.

The first serious policy resistance to the course Project Whirlwind had taken appears to have sprung from the circumstance that mathematicians involved with the computer already had set out down a different path. Since this new machine would be preeminently a mathematical machine, the presumption had taken root that no one understood the potentialities, the hazards, and the limits of the computer so well as they. So firmly had this idea taken hold by 1947 that the Navy appeared to be following only sensible managerial guidelines when it placed the computer projects it was sponsoring under the funding and programming guidance of the Mathematics Branch in ONR.

But Forrester and Everett had taken a different direction. Realizing that the computer would be electrical before it could be mathematical, that for the designer the so-called mathematical operations of the machine would derive only from the ordering and the operating of the electrical components, they knew that the engineering would be all. The mathematicians agreed, to a point, but failed to appreciate two conclusions that Forrester and Everett had placed front and center in their managerial considerations: superbly reliable components would be essential; and designing, developing, and integrating the many, many parts of a computer into a working system would require a massive, many-pronged, and expensive attack upon the engineering problems involved. Especially difficult to solve would be the problem of internal storage. Some of the mathematicians disagreed, others were neutral, but none came forward to agree or endorse.

These were not the only differences in philosophy of program management that mattered. While ONR preferred to support *projects*, Luis de Florez, Gordon Brown, Nat Sage, and MIT President Karl Compton preferred to back *the man*. Their attitude allowed Project Whirlwind greater freedom of operational choice than many responsible executives contemplate granting enthusiastic subordinates and had a subtle, unanticipated effect upon their perception of available alternatives. Had MIT and the Special Devices Division insisted upon backing the project instead of the man, then the original ASCA concept would have dominated judgments regarding allocation of research and design effort and would have ruled out the shift to a computer of general-purpose, command-and-control characteristics. A focus of effort judged fitting and coherent by project-defined aims would, in Whirlwind's case, have made impossible Forrester's and Sage's proposal to change direction and metamorphose ASCA into Whirlwind.

The policy of backing the man in Project Whirlwind had immediate precedents. The special innovative climate that Captain de Florez had fostered in his Special Devices Division was itself the consequence of wartime naval judgment to back the unorthodox engineering approaches that were the hallmarks of de Florez's highly successful career. Once the war was won, that style of management which permitted the Navy to gamble on de Florez, which enabled MIT to back Brown and his unusual Servomechanisms Laboratory, and which allowed Brown, Sage, and SDD to back Forrester became less attractive amid the less demanding routines of peacetime. In the name of sound management, their entrepreneurial approaches were judged too risky. They were also considered too costly, and Forrester's later funding demands appeared to support this common wisdom.

The conventional wisdom of backing the project triumphed in ONR, so from the naval administrator's point of view Project Whirlwind was "lucky." But from the MIT administrators' point of view, luck did not adequately characterize the situation. Rather, it was Forrester's technical foresight demonstrated in the letter he had written to Lieutenant Commander Knutson in January 1946, in the L-1 and L-2 reports of October 1947 that

Valley found so convincing in 1950, and in the assessments Forrester and his engineers prepared for President Compton in October 1948. Project Whirlwind in this way offered a solution of its own to the difficulty of backing the man, for the MIT administrators were not relying upon blind faith; they were kept informed. Curiously, this solution appears generally to have been ignored. Instead, the same information that MIT interpreted as reassuring was given different meaning by ONR. The latter not only was backing the project but also was following the mathematicians' inadequate accessment of the engineering approach such a project should require. Certainly, ONR was to a great extent backing the man in its support for von Neumann and his program at the Institute for Advanced Study, but von Neumann was a mathematician of international stature, conducting a program at less cost and with primarily a mathematical purpose. By comparison, the Project Whirlwind group were young unknowns whose strength lay not in demonstrated accomplishments but in their sponsoring organization, the Massachusetts Institute of Technology.

It is too easy to turn ONR into either the whipping boy or the villain of this story, when in fact ONR was neither. The funding constraints imposed on ONR from above would still have been there, and it makes little sense to argue that ONR should have backed the man regardless of the dollar cost. Had ONR indeed been inclined to back the man instead of the project, it is still unlikely that the Navy could have endorsed Forrester's and Sage's extraordinary demands for funds, demands that became more extraordinary as the Truman administration imposed increasingly austere restrictions upon military budgets during the interim between World War II and the Korean War. Where genuine controversy arises, neither party is without blame, and such was the situation here. The funding controversy could only obscure the relative merits of backing the man versus backing the project.

Project Whirlwind flourished under the approach that backs the man because it showed how research and development costs could be controlled, justified, and recovered. Recovery of costs is a hallowed economic doctrine that means just what it says: costs invested in an enterprise must be recovered in some form if that enterprise is to continue or be judged worthwhile. The circumstance that escaped the notice of traditional-minded observers at the time was that the research and development process was (and is) redefining this venerable economic doctrine, and Forrester and Everett were doing just that (probably without realizing it) in Project Whirlwind. Indeed, their efforts to modify traditional judgments of how costs may be recovered made their entire enterprise suspect to conservative managers, who found that their view of what was going on in Whirlwind was obscured by the unorthodox methods of marshaling resources and carrying on research and development that the project resolutely maintained.

Forrester and Everett appear to have redefined "recovery of costs" in at least three ways. First, they interpreted it to mean the balance that should be maintained between creativity and costs, or to put it another way, between level of effort and expenditures. Forrester made it quite clear to Compton, for example, that costs should be subordinated to and determined by the level of creative effort and not the other way around, if research and development costs were to be recovered.

Project Whirlwind redefined recovery of costs in a second way. This was the powerfully instrumental short-range approach that Forrester had mastered in the early 1940s in the Servomechanisms Laboratory and that he applied to Project Whirlwind. It focused elaborate, expensive design attention on every component part that would go into the computer. It regarded the computer as a system, the operating requirements of which could be represented in an engineer's mathematical model, and it "plugged into" this abstract model the numbers obtained from extensively testing each component as it was developed. This information-intensive approach was not cheap, but by matching test results against the theoretical model and avoiding time-consuming, costly "cut and try" experimenting, it produced effective hardware sooner.

Forrester and Everett redefined traditional recovery of costs on still a third level of research and development analysis, that of the ratio to be maintained between the cost of supporting services and technical costs. The ratio of supporting-services costs to technical costs was high in Project Whirlwind; it exposed the project to accusations of "gold plating" practices by those who were unwittingly committed to a "philosophy of scarcity" that regarded frugal conduct of research and development as an absolute virtue.

But from Forrester's and Everett's point of view, a more resourceful course of action lay open, one that balanced these two necessary kinds of costs by going beyond common-sense convention. "There is a need to subordinate these problems of balance," Everett remarked, "to a philosophy of creative force and inherent growth which tells you how to proportion your services to your technical effort."[4] The Whirlwind project eloquently demonstrated this, as far as Forrester and Everett were concerned in after years. Yet the lesson remained unappreciated in the thronging halls of research and development; and this, too, the two men felt keenly. After a first visit to the Whirlwind installation, young Thomas Watson of the International Business Machines Corporation had asked Forrester, "How do you achieve so much with so little?" It was as clear in the early fifties when Watson visited the Barta Building as it was a decade and a half later that research and development managers had failed to grasp the essential intangibles of the Whirlwind philosophy of conducting research and development. That philosophy involved far more than conventional evaluation of a proper ratio of services costs to technical costs, as this case history has shown.

Because Project Whirlwind succeeded does not mean that it was inevitably destined to succeed. It was, like all challenges, a creature of human endeavor. It did achieve its goal, however, and it did accelerate computer progress both by the concepts it demonstrated and by the talented engineers it developed. As a consequence, one may hail it as a model of research and development. But had its funds been cut off, it would likely have joined that ever growing number of military research and development enterprises that come to an end on the scrap heap. Whatever the resourcefulness of its leadership, Whirlwind was in part master of its fate and in part a creature of larger circumstance. The words of another observer of American science and technology, uttered in another context, are relevant to Whirlwind. "We must realize," remarked W. Carey of the Bureau of the Budget in 1957, "that when science and education become instruments of public policy"—and, we should add, of public funding—

pledging their fortunes to it, an unstable equilibrium is established. Public policy is, almost by definition, the most transient of phenomena, subject from beginning to end to the vagaries of political dynamism. The budget of a government, under the democratic process, is an expression of the objectives, aspirations, and social values of a people in a given web of circumstances. To claim stability for such a product is to claim too much. In such a setting, science and education become soldiers of fortune.[5]

The story of Project Whirlwind, as well as the story of what became of this research and development enterprise in the years after 1956, is that of a soldier of fortune—but of a soldier that could not join the ranks where the other computer projects marched and that would not march to the usual drum. Was Project Whirlwind perhaps a sport then, ahead of its time? It was a rare example of the kind of research and development operation that *could* be mounted a mere century and a half after the research and development process had emerged upon the scene of human affairs.

It may be that Project Whirlwind's resemblance to Camelot is simply a consequence of the fact that the research and development process has been with us too short a while to be well digested into human understanding and prosecuted with wisdom and efficiency. The behavior of many experts suggests they are scarcely yet aware of how different a human activity it is. Because research and development is an economic activity, a technological activity, and a scientific, engineering activity, it straddles at least three currents of human affairs: the conserving economic, the practical technological, and the philosophical scientific, each of them heavily traditional and committed to its own way of doing things. The emergence of scientific technology, alias research and development, by syncretistically combining elements and values from these three traditions to form a new scientific-industrial revolution during the eighteenth, nineteenth, and twentieth centuries revolutionized not simply man's technology but his whole way of dealing with the world and estimating his prospects in it. Whirlwind was an integral, tiny episode in this grand scenario. At the same time and in its small way it contributed to the new Information Revolution, pushing the computer state of the art to fantastic limits with a rapidity that could only leave sensitive observers gasping.

Whirlwind is a reminder that the new ways of doing things that research and development creatively encourages are not efficiently or wisely manageable according to the dictates of the old traditions alone. This fact escaped the attention of most administrators at the time and is one of the reasons that Whirlwind's precedent was not widely followed. Instead, a central article of faith out of the past continued to dominate the activity that Whirlwind pursued. This article holds, loosely spoken, that economic determination of recovery of costs should preselect the research and development options available at any time. Forrester, however, put his research and development options first. Had he and his MIT superiors accepted the traditional article of faith, they would have found it safer to back the project rather than the man, safer to stay within the conceptual confines imposed by ASCA (rather than consign the cockpit to the junkpile to cut costs), and safer to keep costs generally recoverable by setting a more modest and conventional level of effort within the laboratory (as the Ad Hoc Panel noted all other computer projects were doing when it priced their dollar costs).

The vital element of the larger historical equation that ONR and the Ad Hoc Panel, for example, appeared to ignore and that Forrester and Everett did not is the new independent variable of the ability of the research and development process to find superior solutions and in doing so to create wealth on a scale and at a rate that quite destroys the efficacy of venerated economic doctrine to control events. Project Whirlwind was well run. It had succeeded in part not because it refused to pay attention to recovery of costs, but because Forrester and Everett chose to subordinate traditional economic doctrine to their research and development doctrine of running the project "on our terms, or let it be shut off." They simply maintained the type of effort and the level of effort that they perceived, from their technical analyses, to be necessary, and in five years at a cost in round numbers of a million dollars a year, they had forced the state of the art of computer technology far beyond that of any contemporary effort. As the members of Project Whirlwind realized then and in later years, they had done it sooner than anyone else and they had done it better. For a while, *their* Camelot had been real.

Epilogue

Whirlwind the project was gradually absorbed within the Lincoln Laboratory during the early 1950s. Whirlwind the computer continued to operate in the Barta Building as part of MIT's computer facilities until 1959, three years after Forrester's departure and the year Everett joined the newly formed MITRE Corporation. A memo of May 26, 1959, announced the closing down of the computer after almost ten years and 62,000 filament-hours of operation: "Whirlwind I will be shut down for the final time on Friday evening, May 27, 1959, at approximately 10:00 p.m. The entire evening will be available for running demonstration programs and other activities as are appropriate to the occasion. Although no formal ceremonies are planned, it is hoped that as many as possible of Whirlwind's long-time friends will be present during these last hours. Please feel free to circulate this notice to others who may be interested in attending." Thus this first-generation, high-speed digital computer—which by December 1954 had grown to include over 12,500 vacuum tubes and 23,800 crystal diodes—appeared to have become the victim of technological obsolescence.

The closing down in the Barta Building did not, however, mark the end of Whirlwind the computer. In 1963, under lease from the Navy to an alumnus of the project, William Wolf, Whirlwind recommenced operations. For another decade, it was to serve the Wolf R&D Corporation in new quarters in West Concord, Massachusetts. Not until the sale of the corporation in the early 1970s was Whirlwind permanently shut down. Later, it was dismantled and selected components were deposited with the Smithsonian Institution in Washington, D.C., and the Digital Computer Museum in Marlboro, Massachusetts. Thus, finally recognized for its contributions to computer technology and national defense, Whirlwind the computer came to the end of its days.

APPENDIX A

Whirlwind and High-Speed Computing

by Jay W. Forrester

Project Whirlwind is a high-speed computer activity sponsored at the Massachusetts Institute of Technology by the Office of Naval Research. There are several aspects of the work to be discussed in this paper. First will be considered present work of the project in the field of digital computers. A few operating characteristics of the Whirlwind I computer now under construction will be given as well as a report on the present status of the project. Some attention will be given to test equipment which is being developed by the laboratory since these devices may be valuable to other laboratories doing work on computers. Finally, we will look briefly at some future plans of Project Whirlwind and will examine the outlook for the future in large-scale computers.

The Project Whirlwind group considers its principal long-range objective to be research in digital computer applications, although such research does normally imply a substantial effort in the development and construction of required equipment. In the past and up to the present time the entire facilities of the project have been devoted to the design and construction of the Whirlwind I computer. A staff of 70 with total personnel of 200 are now engaged in this work.

Digital computers show promise of almost revolutionary contributions to many branches of science and engineering, as well as to the social sciences and large-scale accounting. Although the equipment and methods being developed by the project can be applied to most of these fields, it is necessary that the group restrict its interests to one region. This chosen region for the

This paper was delivered July 29, 1948, at the Modern Calculating Machinery and Numerical Methods Symposium at the University of California, Los Angeles. It was also issued as Report R-142, Servomechanisms Laboratory, Massachusetts Institute of Technology.

Project Whirlwind group is the application of digital computers to control problems. Control in this sense includes the use of computers for simulation. In control applications the computer is an operating part of a larger system. By way of illustration we might mention the control of industrial processes, military gunnery and fire control, and the centralized control of air traffic. Enough study of these problems has been completed to indicate that the more interesting control applications become feasible only with the highest speed machines which appear possible in the next few years. As a result, the Project Whirlwind work lies in the region of machine speeds of 20,000 arithmetic operations (complete multi-digit multiplications, etc.) per second. Although this speed is 10 to 100 times that of many other digital computers now being considered, the complexity of the equipment is only a few times greater. A much higher computing efficiency, measured in multiplications per second per vacuum tube, is thereby achieved. Although required in control, it is probable that these speeds can also properly be applied to routine engineering computation.

To make this use of the enhanced computing efficiencies of the ultra-high-speed machines in computation work will require extensive studies in the administration of high-speed traffic flow and will necessitate some auxiliary equipment. High-speed traffic flow will be discussed in a later section.

At the present time the principal technical subdivisions of the laboratory are those working in electronic circuit research and design, the electrostatic storage tube group, the mathematics staff, and the block diagrams and systems planning group. These men have laid down the general outline of the computer now under construction, and have reduced most of the machine to detailed block diagrams, circuits, and production drawings.

Let us now turn our attention to this Whirlwind I computer. The machine was originally planned merely to demonstrate circuit and construction techniques. It has, however, been extended to a full-scale operating machine which is entirely suitable for studying computer applications. It has a short register length of 16 binary digits, which is the minimum size necessary for a satisfactory control order. It uses the so-called single-address code for greater flexibility and programming ease. The 16-digit register length is entirely suitable for many control problems, though machines of the future for this purpose might better have 20 or 24 digits. For calculations requiring a greater number of significant figures, there are special built-in facilities to permit the use of multiple-length numbers with the same ease as obtained for the single register length.

Because there exists nowhere in the world a large-scale digital computer entirely successful from the standpoint of reliability and maintenance, every effort has been made to facilitate servicing and trouble location. No attempt has been made to achieve a compact design. Electronic circuits are housed in cabinets on flat panels in two-dimensional, rather than three-dimensional,

Figure 2. B register, rear view.

arrangement. It is possible to apply test scopes and measuring equipment to any resistor, condenser, or circuit connection in the entire machine while the computer is in normal operation. Extensive facilities, amounting to some 25 percent of the entire machine, are being provided to aid in trouble location. Part of these, the marginal checking equipment, is expected to detect those components in the machine which are still operating satisfactorily but which have deteriorated from acceptable component tolerances. Most potential failures can thereby be located before creating machine failure. Several studies are in process on trouble location problems. It is anticipated that for about 60 percent of the machine, failures can, if desired, be identified automatically with an indication showing the particular vacuum tube circuit at fault.

Looking now at the status of Project Whirlwind, we find the first finished parts of the Whirlwind I computer arriving for installation. Certain parts of the central control are now completed and undergoing tests. The first production line shipments of completed chassis for the arithmetic element will be made from the Sylvania Electric Products factory in about eight weeks. The air-conditioning system for heat dissipation is now being installed. It is to be anticipated that some circuit troubles will be encountered and that minor corrections will be required. Initial testing and research into trouble location methods can be started as soon as the complete arithmetic element

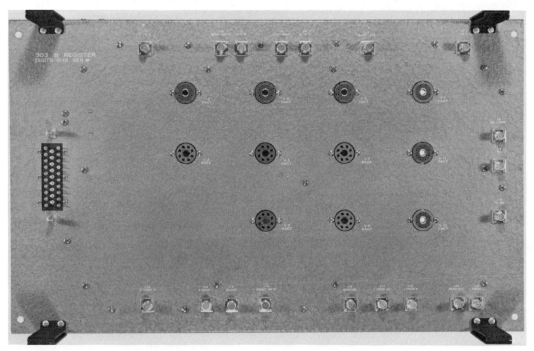

has been received this fall. Subassemblies for the computer will continue to arrive over the next twelve months, and it is expected that the entire machine will operate about December 1949.

The storage tubes to be used in the computer are of the beam deflection type. In such a tube positive and negative charges representing the two binary digits are stored in a rectangular array on a flat plate. Laboratory research tubes of smaller than final size have demonstrated performance which would be satisfactory for initial computer operations. However, before complete tubes can be built for machine applications, it will be necessary to improve laboratory facilities and to improve certain construction techniques. A vacuum system with higher pumping speeds must be built and some additional design of electron guns is needed. It is expected that satisfactory sample tubes will be built yet this year and that pilot quantities will be constructed in the first half of 1949.

Let us now examine illustrations of a few phases of the Whirlwind work. Figure 1 is a picture of the MIT Barta Building [reproduced above, page 86], all three floors of which are used by the computer project. Figure 2 shows the final design of the vacuum tube and connector side of the B-register of the arithmetic element. Numbers in the computer are transmitted as video pulses, one-tenth microsecond wide. All video circuits are handled through

◁

Figure 3. B register,
front view.

Figure 4. B register
prototype, close-up.

▷

coaxial cable. For convenience and to achieve an orderly arrangement, circuits have been arranged to place connectors on the edges of panels. The reverse side of this panel is shown in Figure 3. All circuit components are laid out in two-dimensional arrangement to achieve the utmost ease in servicing. In Figure 4 is a close-up of a small section of one of these panels to show better the physical construction. All components are mounted on turret lugs, and design standards equivalent to those required for production Army and Navy equipment are used except that protection against shock and vibration is not required. One will note in this figure that the germanium crystal diode rectifier is an important circuit element. The rectifier is used for pulse clipping and for d-c restoration of bias levels. Also shown in the figure are pulse transformers which have been developed at the laboratory for use with circuits employing one-tenth microsecond pulses at repetition rates from zero to two megacycles.

In Figure 5 are shown two experimental deflection voltage generators designed for storage tube control. These circuits decode binary numbers into deflection voltages for positioning the cathode-ray beam in electrostatic storage tubes. Two identical units, one for the X-axis and the other for the Y-axis are used. The output of these circuits when sequenced through the 1,024 positions of a 32 by 32 array are shown in the scope display of Figure 6.

The next two illustrations, Figures 7 and 8, are included to call attention

to the laboratory's test equipment program. As is well known, the available measuring equipment in any scientific field may limit the rate at which progress is possible. Just as an entirely new line of test equipment was required for radar research, likewise special equipment is required for work on computer circuits. A substantial fraction of the laboratory effort is now being devoted to development of an interrelated line of standard test equipment. With units of this equipment properly connected it is possible to obtain the variety of pulse patterns necessary for research and test work in computer circuits. As rapidly as these units are designed, descriptions of their operation are being written. In addition, there will be prepared within the next two months a discussion showing examples of how assemblies of these equipments can be arranged to meet the problems that arise in computer research. Information on this test equipment can be obtained from the Servomechanisms Laboratory and in the future it may become possible to obtain the equipment itself from the Sylvania Electric Products Company.

Figure 7 shows the gate and delay unit. This is a double unit. Each section will provide a gate pulse of any desired duration between 0.5 microseconds and 2,500 microseconds, or if preferred, the unit will provide a delayed pulse over the same time range following receipt of an input pulse. Figure 8 shows a variable frequency clock operating over the range of 200 kilocycles to 5 megacycles putting out pulses which are 0.1 microseconds wide and up to 40 volts high. Other units of the standard test equipment will include pulse mixers, coders, gate amplifiers, scope synchronizers, pulse standardizers, push button synchronizers, register panels, video amplifiers, and probes.

Let us turn our attention to possible future plans of Project Whirlwind. Computing machine design has now reached a point where the attentions of some of the staff should be directed toward computer applications. Studies of the way computers should be used are now being started. Although the use of computers as control mechanisms may be of first interest, it is true, however, that control applications will require extensive auxiliary equipment and probably several years for development. On the other hand, one can now begin plans for applying high-speed computers to computations in science and engineering.

The reader may be surprised and may not agree, but I believe that if a high-speed computer capable of 1,000 to 20,000 arithmetic operations per second were sitting here today, it would be nearly two years before the machine were in effective and efficient operation. One would be caught totally unprepared for feeding to this equipment problems at its high acceptance rate. On the other hand, this represents but one-half of a vicious circle in which an adequate national interest in computer training cannot be developed until the equipment is actually available.

Many people believe that one is not obligated to use the new machines efficiently and that their existence can be justified for occasional use on a

Figure 5. Deflection voltage generators for storage tube control.

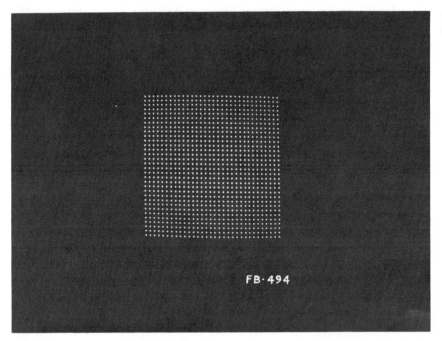

Figure 6. Oscilloscope display.

few problems of great importance. It seems to me, however, that the high cost, upwards of a half-million dollars, and the high maintenance and operating expenses which will certainly be encountered in the next few years will force development of the administrative procedures necessary to make effective use of centrally located computers. The development of high-speed traffic through such equipment is a promising approach.

Much has been said about the new advances in mathematics which will be required to use high-speed computers, and about the problems, notably in partial differential equations, which are at the limit of our present mathematical comprehension. It has been pointed out that even with high-speed machines certain of these problems will require hours, days, or weeks for a solution. On the other hand, very little consideration has been given the use of high-speed machines for those problems which are even now being solved by other means and for those problems which are mathematically well understood but are just beyond the practical limits of solution by present equipment.

We feel that the first effective use of high-speed machines will be for those problems which are straight-forward in formulation and those problems which people are now attempting to solve by presently available computing equipment. To use effectively the high-speed digital computers on such problems, it will be necessary to develop some auxiliary equipment and in

Figure 7. Gate and delay unit.

particular the administrative procedures required to maintain a schedule of high-speed traffic flow. In other words, it should be possible to pass such problems through a machine just as the telegraph company transmits messages. The machine would be available to a large number of groups through wire communication facility, probably teletype initially. The persons responsible for machine operation should need pay no more attention to the nature and outcome of a computation problem than the individual employees of the telegraph company need examine, understand, and criticize the contents of messages which they handle. Such a procedure would be a radical departure from present practice in large-scale computers but one no more radical than the new computers themselves. The person preparing and transmitting the problem would be fully responsible for its outcome, and if the problem were improperly set up for solution, the erroneous results would be returned for his use in correcting the formulation. Checks and the desired level of protection can be specified in the program setup. Computing programs repeatedly used by a particular subscriber can be made a part of the computing machine program library in order that only initial data need be transmitted for the majority of routine problems.

With machines such as Whirlwind I and others now under development, no manual switching or plugboard operations are required and the setup and solution of a problem can be completely and automatically controlled through signals received by teletype connection. This is even true down to a specification of page composition in printed results and graphical presentation for facsimile transmission. Because of the low transmission rate of teletype circuits the problems transmitted from a remote point would be collected together on magnetic tape or photographic film to permit high-speed entry into the computing equipment.

To avoid the delays and administrative difficulties surrounding present large-scale computers, such a service must be as easy for an accepted subscriber to use as present teletype. The success of the administrative organization will be measured by the degree to which such computer service can compete in problems of the size requiring but a few man-hours of hand-calculating machine operation.

As I have already mentioned, the Whirlwind I computer should be in operation by the end of 1949. During 1950 the equipment and administrative procedures for high-speed traffic flow can be worked out, and during 1951 such a problem solution network should actually become possible. On a machine operated by a research group such as the Servomechanisms Laboratory, only part of each day could be devoted to such routine traffic since the machine would be kept available during normal laboratory hours for the study of new applications. Heavy loads as they develop would be shifted elsewhere to machines established with the intention of accepting routine work.

Simultaneously with the development of high-speed traffic flow, studies of control problems will be initiated. Devices must be developed for converting mechanical motions and electrical voltages to digital quantities for machine use. Special equipment for the continuous receipt of information from teletype, from radar systems, and other forms of communication must

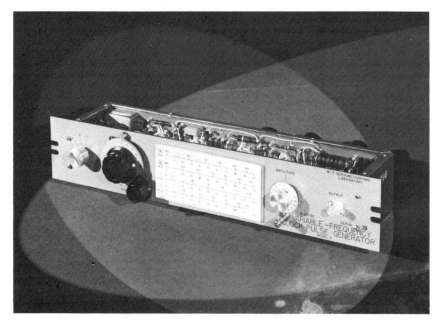

Figure 8. Variable frequency clock-pulse generator.

become available before the uses of computers as control devices can be fully explored.

Let us now examine the outlook for large-scale digital computers. A great deal of unfounded optimism has and still does exist regarding the availability of such machines and the rapidity with which they can be put in service. I believe that, barring an all-out emergency effort such as went into the development of radar, large-scale computers will for several years need the sympathetic care of a laboratory crew. During these several years, personnel must be trained in the proper use of the machine. Trouble location methods must be designed and suitable facilities provided in the machines for rapid and probably automatic location of faulty parts. Until this exploratory period has elapsed the machines will not be suitable as a packaged product for the user interested only in the results and not in the advancement of the computer art. It must be borne in mind that there is not a single machine in existence today which incorporates the most important features of the proposed digital computers. In other words, none of the present machines are designed for high-speed problem set-up through completely automatic means without the use of manual switches or plugboards.

I have indicated our expectation of operating a high-speed computer by the end of 1949, the hope of developing procedures and equipment for high-speed traffic flow by the end of 1950, and for getting this equipment into operation by the end of 1951. I doubt that this schedule will be improved upon and it is possible that even with the combined efforts of all groups in the field such a time schedule cannot be met. One must remember that by comparison a radar set is a very simple and straight-forward device, yet hundreds of millions of dollars went into the development of this equipment. True, we are building on the results of that work, yet I believe that corresponding millions of dollars will be spent in computer development before achieving even a representative sampling of the objectives which this audience visualizes. An all-out national effort such as was devoted to radar or atomic energy would, of course, accelerate the time schedules listed. Such an accelerated program would be much less efficient in a dollar and man-hour sense than the present course of action. I believe that the recent high-speed electronic trend in computers has very little engineering in common with that of the differential analyzer and the many digital computers which have proven successful in the past. We must, therefore, look upon it as a new field in its earliest stages of physical development and that it will require the same growing period as any other branch of engineering.

Furthermore, in the matter of operating personnel I believe there is a strong tendency to underestimate the size of the group which will be necessary to make reasonable use of a large-scale digital computer of the future. We have made rather careful estimates of the size group necessary to operate a computing machine at the center of the high-speed traffic network which I have already discussed. We believe that a minimum of 150 people will be required and even this assumes that most problem setup is done at the remote point and does not fall to the responsibility of the local group.

To summarize, Project Whirlwind is directed primarily at computer applications though it will continue to carry a heavy responsibility in machine development. The problems which will receive greatest attention are those requiring high-speed machines of some 20,000 arithmetic operations per second giving high computing efficiencies. The Whirlwind I computer, assembly of which is now underway, will permit such applications and studies and will be a proving ground for trouble location methods and circuits in order that improved high-speed computers may follow. One of the first applications for high-speed computers which will be developed will probably be the high-speed traffic flow network. This is chosen first because it is one of the simpler systems applications and one which can be achieved in the near future. The lessons learned can be applied in the problems to follow. With the present size staff and expenditure rate, this objective will require some three to four years. While computers appear to be capable ultimately of accomplishing most of the functions with which they are credited, it is almost certain that they will not do so at as early a date as anticipated. Many years, and large sums of development money lie between this audience and the realization of many of their hopes.

APPENDIX B

The Whirlwind I Computer

by Robert R. Everett

The Project Whirlwind is a high-speed computer activity sponsored at the Digital Computer Laboratory, formerly a part of the Servomechanisms Laboratory, of the Massachusetts Institute of Technology, by the Office of Naval Research and the United States Air Force. The project began in 1945 with the assignment of building a high-quality real-time aircraft simulator. Historically, the project always has been primarily interested in the fields of real-time simulation and control; but since about the beginning of 1947, most of its efforts have been devoted to the design and construction of the digital computer known as Whirlwind I (WWI). This computer has been in operation for over a year and an increasing proportion of project effort now is going into application studies.

Applications for digital computers are found in many branches of science, engineering, and business. Although any modern general-purpose digital computer can be applied to all these fields, a machine is generally designed to be most suited to some particular area. The WWI was designed for use in control and simulation work such as air traffic control, industrial process control, and aircraft simulation. This does not mean that the WWI will not be used on applications other than control. About one-half the available computing time for 1952 will be assigned to engineering and scientific calculation, including research in such uses supported by the Office of Naval Research through the Massachusetts Institute of Technology Committee on Machine Methods for Computation.

These control and simulation problems result in a specialized emphasis on computer design.

©1952 AIEE (now IEEE). Reprinted, with permission, from Joint Computer Conference AIEE/IRE, December 10–12, 1951, Philadelphia, Pennsylvania.

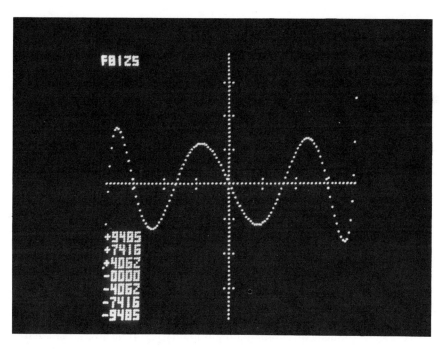

Figure 1. Sample computer output.

Short Register Length

Control problems are usually very simple mathematically. Furthermore, the computer is almost always part of a feedback rather than an open-ended system. Consequently, roundoff errors are seldom troublesome and the register length can be shortened to something comparable to the sensitivity of the physical quantities involved, perhaps five decimal places or less.

WWI has a register length of 16 binary digits including sign or about four and one-half decimals. The register length was chosen as the minimum that would provide a usable single-address order, in this case 5 binary digits for instruction and 11 binary digits for address. In a future machine we probably would increase this register length to 20 or 24 binary digits to get additional order flexibility; the increased numerical precision is less important.

For scientific and engineering calculation, greater than 16-digit precision is often required. There is available a set of multiple-length and floating point subroutines which make the use of greater precision very easy. It is true that these subroutines are slow, bringing effective machine speed down to about that obtained by acoustic memory machines. It is much more efficient to waste computing time occasionally this way than to waste continuously a large part of the storage and computing equipment of the machine by providing an unnecessarily long register.

High Operating Speed

Control and simulation problems require very high speeds. The necessary calculations must be carried out in real time; the more complex the controlled system is, the faster the computer must be. There is no practical upper limit to the computing speed that could be used if available.

Where the problems are large enough, and these problems are, one high-speed machine is much better than two simpler machines of half the speed. Communication between machines presents many of the same problems that communication between human beings presents.

Great effort was put into WWI to obtain high speed. The target speed was 50,000 single-address operations per second, and all parts of the machine except storage meet this requirement. The actual WWI present operating speed of 20,000 single-address operations per second is on the lower edge of the desired speed range.

Large Internal Storage

A large amount of high-speed internal storage is needed since it is not possible in general to use slow auxiliary storage because of the time factor. In many cases, a magnetic drum can be useful since its access time is short compared to the response times of real systems. Even with a drum there is considerable loss of computing and programming efficiency due to shuffling information back and forth between drum and computer.

Although designed for 2,048 registers of electrostatic storage, WWI was

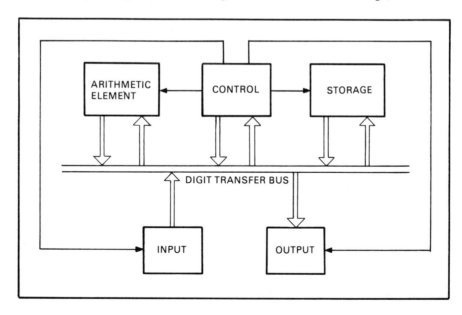

Figure 2. Simplified computer block diagram.

originally placed in operation with only 256 registers available. This number, while small, was adequate for much useful work. In September 1951, a second bank of new model storage tubes storing 1,024 spots per tube was installed. WWI has been operating reliably with these 1,024 registers since December 1951. The tubes in the first bank have been retired from service and will be replaced by new model tubes sometime in the near future. The resulting 2,048 registers will be on the lower end of what the project considers desirable. What the computer business needs, has needed, and probably always will need is a bigger, better, and faster storage device.

Extreme Reliability

In a system where much valuable property and perhaps many human lives are dependent on the proper operation of the computing equipment, failures must be very rare. Furthermore, checking alone, however complete, is inadequate. It is not enough merely to know that the equipment has made an error. It is very unlikely that a man, presumably not too well suited to the work during normal conditions, can handle the situation in an emergency. Multiple machines with majority rule seem to be the best answer. Self-correcting machines are a possibility but appear to be too complicated to compete, especially as they provide no stand-by protection.

The characteristics of the WWI computer may be recapitulated as follows:

Register length	16 binary digits, parallel
Speed	20,000 single-address operations per second
Storage capacity	originally 256 registers presently 1,024 registers target 2,048 registers
Order type	single-address, one order per word
Numbers	fixed point, 9's complement
Basic pulse repetition frequency	1 megacycle 2 megacycles, arithmetic element only
Tube count	5,000, mostly single pentodes
Crystal count	11,000

There are 32 possible operations, of which about 27 are assigned. They are of the usual types: addition, subtraction, multiplication, division, shifting by an arbitrary number of columns, transfer of all or parts of words, subprogram, and conditional subprogram. There are terminal equipment

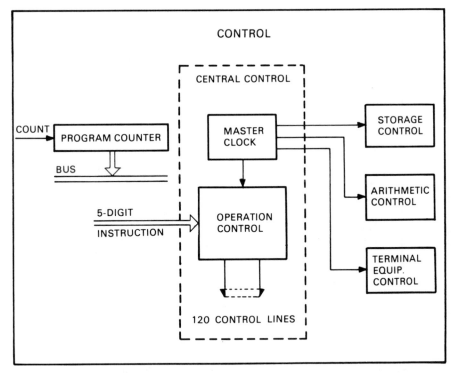

Figure 3. Controls of
the WWI.

control orders and there are some special orders for facilitating double-length and floating-point operations.

One way to increase the effective speed of a machine is to provide built-in facilities for operations that occur frequently in the problems of interest. An example is an automatic coordinate transformation order. The addition of such facilities does not affect the general-purpose nature of the machine. The machine retains its old flexibility but becomes faster and more suited to a certain class of problems.

From March 14, 1951, when we began to keep detailed records, until June 1, 1952, a total of 2,100 hours of computer time was scheduled for applications use. The machine was in successful operation for 85 percent of this scheduled time. Total machine operating time during this period was 5,400 hours; the time not used for applications has been used for machine improvement, adding equipment, and preventive maintenance. WWI is now in operation about 150 hours a week.

Of the 2,100 hours available, 1,100 have been used by the scientific and engineering calculation group, the rest for control studies. The group has run a wide variety of problems, but has spent a large part of its time in training, setting up procedures, and preparing a library of subroutines.

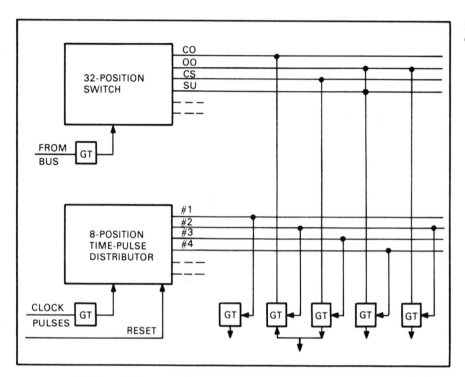

Figure 4. Operation control.

A partial list of the actual problems carried out by the group includes:

1. An industrial production problem for the Harvard Economics School.
2. Magnetic flux density study for our magnetic storage work.
3. Oil reservoir depletion studies.
4. Ultra-high-frequency television channel allocation investigation for DuMont.
5. Optical constants of thin metal films.
6. Computation of autocorrelation coefficients.
7. Tape generation for a digitally-controlled milling machine.

The scientific and engineering applications time on WWI has been organized in a manner patterned after that originated by Dr. Maurice V. Wilkes at Cambridge University. The group of programmers and mathematicians assigned to WWI assists users in setting up their own problems. Small problems requiring only a few seconds or minutes of computer time are encouraged. Applications time is assigned in one-hour pieces two or three times a day. No program debugging is allowed on the machine. Program errors are deduced by the programmer from printed lists of results, storage contents, or order sequences as previously requested from the machine operator. The programmer then corrects his program which is rerun for him within a day or perhaps within a few hours.

Every effort is made to reduce the time-consuming job of printing tabulated results. In many cases a user desires large amounts of tabulated data only because he does not really know what answers he wants and so asks for everything. Such users are encouraged to ask only for pertinent results in the form of numbers or curves plotted by the machine on a cathode-ray tube and automatically photographed. If these results prove inadequate or the user gets a better idea of his needs, he is allowed to rerun his program, again asking only for what appear to be significant results. Figure 1 shows a sample curve plotted by the computing machine showing calibrated axes and decimal intercepts.

WWI System Layout

Figure 2 shows the major parts of any computer such as WWI. The major elements of the computer communicate with each other via a central bus system.

WWI is basically a simple, straightforward, standard machine of the all-parallel type. Unfortunately, the simple concept often becomes complicated in execution, and this is true here. WWI's control has been complicated by the decision to keep it completely flexible: the arithmetic element by the need for high speed, the storage by the use of electrostatic storage tubes, the terminal equipment by the diversity of input and output media needed.

Controls

The WWI controls are divided into several parts, as shown in Figure 3.

The central control of the machine is the master source of control pulses. When necessary, the central control allows one of the other controls to function. In general there is no overlapping of control operation; except for terminal equipment control, only one of the controls is in operation at any one time.

Storage control generates the sequence of pulses and gates that operate the storage tubes. Central control instructs the storage control either to read or write.

Arithmetic control carries out the details of the more complex arithmetic operations such as multiplication and division. The setup of these operations plus the complete controlling of the simpler operations such as addition are carried out by central control.

Terminal equipment control generates the necessary control pulses, delay times, and interlocks for the various terminal equipment units.

The program counter which keeps track of the address of the next order to be carried out is considered as part of control. This is an 11-stage binary counter with provision for reading to the bus.

◁
Figure 5. View of central control.

Figure 6. View of electrostatic storage.

▷

Most of the functions of these subsidiary controls could be combined with the central control. The major reason they are not is that they were designed at different times. The arithmetic element and its control came first, followed by central control. At the time central control was designed, the necessary characteristics of storage control were unknown. In fact, the machine was designed so that any parallel high-speed storage could be used. The form of terminal equipment control was also unknown at this time. Since flexibility was a prime specification, it was felt preferable to build separate flexible controls for the various parts of the computer than to try to combine all the needed flexibility in one central control.

In a new machine we would attempt to combine control functions where possible, hoping to have enough prior knowledge about component needs to eliminate subsidiary controls completely. We still insist on a large degree of control flexibility.

The master clock consists of an oscillator, pulse shaper, and divider that generate 1- and 2-megacycle clock pulses, and a clock pulse control that distributes these clock pulses to the various controls in the machine. It is this unit that determines which of the subsidiary controls actually is controlling the machine. This unit also stops and starts the machine and provides for push-button operation.

The operation control, see Figure 4, was designed for maximum flexibility and minimum number of operation digits, and, consequently, minimum register length. It is of the completely decoding type.

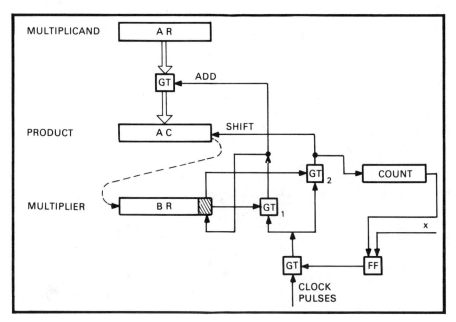

Figure 7. Arithmetic element.

The operation switch is a 32-position crystal matrix switch that receives the 5-bit instruction from the bus and in turn selects one of 32 output lines corresponding to the 32 built-in operations.

There are 120 gate tubes on the output of the operation control. Pulses on the 120 output lines go to the gate drivers, pulse drivers, and control flip-flops all over the machine; 120 is a generous number. The suppressors of these gate tubes are connected to vertical wires that cross the 32 output lines from the operation switch. Crystals are inserted at the desired junctions to turn on those gate tubes that are to be used for any operation.

The time pulse distributor consists of an 8-position switch driven from a 3-binary-digit counter. Clock pulses at the input are distributed in sequence on the eight output lines. The control grids of the output gate tubes are connected to these timing lines. The output of the operation control is thus 120 control lines on each of which can appear a sequence of pulses for any combination of orders at any combination of times. The central control of the machine is shown in Figure 5. The control switch is in the foreground with the operation matrix to the right.

Electrostatic Storage

The electrostatic storage shown in Figure 6 consists of two banks of 16 storage tubes each. There is a pair of 32-position decoders set up by address digits read in from the bus. There is a storage control that generates the sequence of pulses needed to operate the gate generators, and so forth. A radio-frequency pulser generates a high-power 10-megacycle pulse for readout.

Each digit column contains, besides the storage tubes, write-plus and write-minus gate generators and a signal-plate gate generator for each tube. Ten-megacycle grid pulses are used for readout in order to get the required discrimination between the fractional-volt readout pulses and the 100-volt signal plate gates. For each storage tube there is a 10-megacycle amplifier, phase-sensitive detector, and gate tube, feeding into the program register. The program register is used for communicating with the storage tubes. Information read out of the tubes appears in the program register. Information to be written into the tubes must be placed in the program register.

Arithmetic Element

The arithmetic element, see Figure 7, consists of three registers, a counter, and a control.

The first register is an accumulator, AC, which actually consists of a partial-sum or adding register and a carry register. The accumulator holds the product during multiplication.

The second or A-register holds the multiplicand during multiplication. All numbers entering the arithmetic element do so through AR.

◁

Figure 8. View of
arithmetic element.

Figure 9. View of
test control.

▷

The third or B-register holds the multiplier during multiplication. The accumulator and B-register shift right or left. A high-speed carry is provided for addition. Subtraction is by 9's complement and end-around-carry. Multiplication is by successive additions, division by successive subtractions, and shift orders provide for shifting right or left by an arbitrary number of steps, with or without roundoff.

The arithmetic element is straightforward except for a few special orders and the high speed at which it operates. Addition takes 3 microseconds complete with carry; multiplication 16 microseconds average including sign correction.

In Figure 8 are shown several digits of the arithmetic element. The large panels are accumulator digits. Above the accumulator is the B-register, below it the A-register.

Test Control

Test control, shown in Figure 9, is used at present both for operating and for trouble-shooting the computer. The control includes:

1. Power supply control and meters.
2. Neon indicators for all flip-flops in the machine.
3. Switches for setting up special conditions.
4. Manual intervention switches.
5. Oscilloscopes for viewing waveforms. A probe and amplifier system allows viewing any waveform in the computer on one scope at test control.
6. Test equipment to provide synchronizing, stop, or delay pulses at any step of any order of a program, allows viewing waveforms on the fly anywhere in the machine.

An important part of the test facilities is the test storage, a group of 32 toggle-switch registers plus five flip-flop registers that can be inserted in place of any five of the toggle-switch registers. This storage has proved invaluable not only for testing control and arithmetic element before electrostatic storage was available, but also for testing electrostatic storage itself. When not in use for test purposes, test storage participates as part of the terminal equipment system. The toggle-switches hold a standard read-in program; the flip-flop registers are used as in-out registers for special purposes.

NOTES

A Note on Sources

The story of Project Whirlwind was reconstructed from interviews and from letters, memoranda, casebooks, contracts, office and laboratory journals, quarterly reports, and other materials generated by the people involved in the project or representing the organizations and institutions associated with its activities. Many of these documents were collected and held by the Massachusetts Institute of Technology and later by the MITRE Corporation; much of the MITRE collection of Whirlwind papers has been transferred, together with parts of the Whirlwind computer, to the Smithsonian Institution's National Museum of History and Technology in Washington, D.C.

These materials constitute the major sources for the preparation of this study. Selected documents bearing directly upon the historical development of Project Whirlwind were photocopied by the authors for consultation as the history was being researched and written. In addition, the authors' files were supplemented by selected copies of unclassified documents from the files and archives of the Office of Naval Research, the Special Devices Center of ONR, Division VI of the Lincoln Laboratory of MIT, and the MITRE Corporation, a lineal descendant of Project Whirlwind and Lincoln Laboratory.

The authors' working files have been deposited with the History of Science Collections in the University of Oklahoma Library, Norman, Oklahoma, and with the Historical Collections of the Massachusetts Institute of Technology in Cambridge, Massachusetts. Similar and additional materials pertinent to Project Whirlwind may be found in the archives of the MITRE Corporation, Bedford, Massachusetts; the Office of Naval Research, Washington, D.C.; and the Smithsonian Institution. The archives of the MITRE Corporation also contain a large collection of photographs of the Whirlwind computer.

Chapter 1 The Beginning

1. Draft memorandum (anonymous, no date), Whirlwind papers. The contents suggest a Navy source prepared it prior to April 1944.

2. SDD memorandum, J. W. Ludwig to Capt. Luis de Florez, Oct. 11, 1944. Cf. Enclosure D of Bureau of Aeronautics Procurement Directive EN11-27339-45, Nov. 22, 1944: "Data for OP&M," Nov. 20, 1944, by J. B. Van Duzer and R. I. Knapp of SDD.

3. Quoted in Robert L. Taylor, "Captain among the Synthetics," Part I, *The New Yorker*, Nov. 11, 1944, p. 34.

4. Ibid., pp. 34 ff.; Part II, Nov. 18, 1944, pp. 32 ff. See also de Florez's obituary in *New York Times*, Dec. 6, 1962, p. 43.

5. Servomechanisms Laboratory, MIT, "Project Whirlwind, Summary Report No. 1," Apr. 1946, pp. 1–4.

6. Memorandum, Rogers Follansbee, Aircraft Simulation Section, to Director, SDD, subj.: "Analyzer, Flight Characteristics," Feb. 5, 1944.

7. N. McL. Sage to Luis de Florez, Dec. 8, 1943.

8. John R. Markham, Otto C. Koppen, Joseph Bicknell, "Note on a Proposed Method of Ensuring Satisfactory Handling Characteristics of New Airplanes," Apr. 1944, p. 4.

9. Rogers Follansbee, SDD, to J. Bicknell, MIT, subj.: "PBM-3 Operational Flight Trainer Data—Forwarding of," Feb. 5, 1944.

10. Markham, Koppen, Bicknell, "Note on a Proposed Method," pp. 1-6.

11. J. C. Hunsaker to de Florez, Apr. 15, 1944.

12. Memorandum for files [C. P. Andrade], subj.: "Project Whirlwind," June 13, 1946.

13. Navy Department, Bureau of Aeronautics (hereafter, BuAer), SDD, "Specifications for Airplane Stability and Control Analyzer," Aug. 11, 1944.

14. Memorandum, Head of Production Branch, SDD, to Director, SDD, subj.: "Project 2-K—Report on Companies Considered and Facilities Available," Oct. 13, 1944; L. F. Jones, Government Development Section, RCA, to R. I. Knapp, SDD, Oct. 18, 1944; W. S. Hill, General Electric Co., to J. B. Van Duzer, SDD, Oct. 11, 1944.

15. Memorandum, J. B. Van Duzer, SDD, to E. N. Howell, SDD, subj.: "Sources for Project 2-K, Stability Control Analyzer and F7F OFT's," Sept. 18, 1944.

16. Enclosure D of BuAer Procurement Directive EN11-27339-45, Nov. 22, 1944: "Data for OP&M," Nov. 20, 1944, by Van Duzer and Knapp.

17. Memorandum, Luis de Florez to Rear Admiral D. C. Ramsey, BuAer, Nov. 27, 1944.

18. Director, SDD, to Chief, BuAer, subj.: "Airplane Stability and Control Analyzer," Oct. 13, 1944.

19. See Elting E. Morison's essay, "Gunfire at Sea: A Case Study of Innovation," in his *Men, Machines, and Modern Times* (Cambridge, Mass., 1966), pp. 17–44; also his *From Know-How to Nowhere* (New York, 1974).

20. A. J. Marder, *From the Dreadnought to Scapa Flow*, vol. 1, *The Road to War, 1904–1914* (London, 1961), pp. 330-335.

21. Ibid.

22. Mark Sullivan, *Our Times: The United States, 1900–1925* (New York, 1932),

vol. 2, *America Finding Herself*, pp. 557–568.

23. Elting E. Morison, *Admiral Sims and the Modern American Navy* (1942; repr., New York, 1968), passim.

24. Memorandum, Head of Aerodynamics and Hydrodynamics Branch to Chief, BuAer, subj.: "Airplane Stability and Control Analyzer—Comment on," Sept. 5, 1944: Enclosure A to Director, SDD, to Chief, BuAer, subj.: "Airplane Stability and Control Analyzer," Oct. 13, 1944.

25. MIT memorandum, subj.: "Comments on Captain Diehl's Letter with Regard to ASCA," Oct. 2, 1944; J. C. Hunsaker to Luis de Florez, Oct. 4, 1944 (enclosures C and B, respectively, to Director, SDD, to Chief, BuAer, subj.: "Airplane Stability and Control Analyzer," Oct. 13, 1944).

26. Director, SDD, to Chief, BuAer, subj.: "Airplane Stability and Control Analyzer," Oct. 13, 1944. See Enclosure E, memorandum, Ludwig to de Florez, subj.: "Analysis of Project 2-K, Airplane Stability and Control Analyzer," Oct. 11, 1944.

27. Approval initialed on memorandum, Capt. de Florez to Admiral Ramsey, BuAer, Nov. 27, 1944.

28. Memorandum, J. B. Van Duzer, subj.: "Project 2-K, Aircraft Stability Control Analyzer, Conference with MIT representatives," Oct. 18, 1944.

29. Interviews by the authors with Gordon S. Brown, July 6, 1964; Jay W. Forrester (hereafter cited as JWF), July 24, 1964.

30. Ibid.

31. Memorandum, Van Duzer, subj.: "Project 2-K, Aircraft Stability Control Analyzer, Conference with MIT representatives," Oct. 18, 1944.

32. Interview, JWF and Robert R. Everett by the authors, July 31, 1963.

33. JWF, "Hydraulic Servomechanism Developments" (M.S. thesis, Massachusetts Institute of Technology, Cambridge, Mass., June 1945), pp. 1–3.

34. Interviews by the authors with JWF and Everett, July 31, 1963; Kenneth H. Olsen, June 24, 1964; Charles W. Adams and John F. Gilmore, July 3, 1964; Gordon S. Brown, July 6, 1964.

35. N. McL. Sage, MIT, to Chief, BuAer, att'n: Lt. Comdr. E. N. Howell, SDD, subj.: "Proposal for Contract for Development of a Generalized Multi-engined Operational Flight Trainer," May 22, 1945; draft, G. S. Brown to Chief, BuAer, att'n: Lt. J. B. Van Deusen (*sic*), SDD, subj.: "Proposal for Contract for Development of Aircraft Analyzer," Nov. 3, 1944 ("Van Deusen" is Van Duzer).

36. JWF, "MIT Computation Book, No. 36," p. 14; draft, G. S. Brown to Chief, BuAer, Nov. 3, 1944.

37. Enclosure D of BuAer Procurement Directive EN11-27339-45, Nov. 22, 1944: "Data for OP&M," Nov. 20, 1944, by Van Duzer and Knapp; JWF, administrative notes in "MIT Computation Book No. 36," p. 14; memorandum, de Florez to Ramsey, BuAer, Nov. 27, 1944; Navy Department, BuAer, Letter of Intent for Contract NOa(s)-5216, Dec. 14, 1944.

Chapter 2   Computing Problems

1. Interview, Gordon S. Brown by the authors, July 6, 1964.
2. Interview, JWF and Everett by the authors, July 31, 1963.
3. JWF, "Computation Book No. 36," entries of Nov. 2, 1944.

4. Ibid., entry of Nov. 7, 1944.

5. J. R. Markham, O. C. Koppen, J. Bicknell, "Proposed Method of Ensuring Satisfactory Handling Characteristics in Airplanes," April 1944; Navy Department, BuAer, SDD, "Specifications for Airplane Stability and Control Analyzer," Aug. 11, 1944.

6. JWF, "Computation Book No. 36," entry of Nov. 7, 1944.

7. Ibid., entry of Nov. 21, 1944.

8. JWF, "Hydraulic Servomechanism Developments," pp. 4–5. This report was submitted "in partial fulfillment of the requirements for the degree of Master of Science from the Massachusetts Institûte of Technology, Department of Electrical Engineering, June, 1945."

9. Ibid., p. 6.

10. Ibid., pp. 6–7.

11. JWF, "Computation Book No. 36," entry of Feb. 5, 1945.

12. Memorandum, JWF, subj.: "Aircraft Trainee Inspection Trip," Jan. 9, 1945.

13. Servomechanisms Laboratory, "Project Whirlwind, Summary Report No. 1," Apr. 1946, pp. 1–5. See also memorandum prepared but not submitted by JWF, subj.: "Status of Contract NOa(s)-5216," May 8, 1945.

14. JWF, draft memorandum, subj.: "Status of Contract NOa(s)-5216," May 8, 1945.

15. Ibid.

16. Ibid.

17. Ibid.; N. McL. Sage to Chief, BuAer, subj.: "Proposal for ... Development for ... O.F.T.," May 22, 1945.

18. Interview, JWF and Everett by the authors, July 31, 1963.

19. Ibid.

20. JWF, "Computation Book No. 39," entry of May 26, 1945, p. 34.

21. F. L. Alt, *Electronic Digital Computers* (New York, 1958), p. 18.

22. JWF to G. S. Brown, June 22, 1945.

23. JWF, "Computation Book No. 39," entry of June 27, 1945, supplement to p. 54.

24. Interview, Perry O. Crawford by the authors, Oct. 25, 1967.

25. Ibid.

26. Ibid.

27. P. O. Crawford, Jr., "Automatic Control by Arithmetical Operations" (M.S. thesis, Massachusetts Institute of Technology, 1942), pp. 1–2.

28. JWF, "Computation Book No. 39," entry of Sept. 18, 1945, supplement to p. 65.

29. Ibid., entry of Oct. 16, 1945, p. 42.

30. Interview, JWF and Everett by the authors, July 31, 1963.

Chapter 3   The Shift to Digital

1. For a detailed history of the ENIAC project and the efforts of Eckert and Mauchly, see Nancy Stern, *From ENIAC to UNIVAC* (Digital Press, in preparation); J. W. Mauchly, "Mauchly on the Trials of Building ENIAC," *IEEE Spectrum*, Apr. 1975; J. G. Brainerd, "Genesis of the ENIAC," *Technology and Culture*, July 1976.

2. V. Bush, S. H. Caldwell, "A New Type of Differential Analyzer," *Journal of the Franklin Institute* 240 (October 1945): 255–326; S. H. Caldwell, "Educated Machinery," *Technology Review* 48 (November 1945): 31–34.

3. The title of the conference program emitted so formidable an institutional ring as to obscure its historic significance: "Conference on Advanced Computation Techniques, National Research Council, Committee on Mathematical Tables and Other Aids to Computation, Subcommittee Z on Calculating Machines and Mechanical Computation; Cambridge, Massachusetts, October 30–31, 1945."

4. Interview, JWF by the authors, July 31, 1963.

5. Conference Note C6 by Kenneth Tuttle, subj.: "Conference on Techniques of Computation held November 9, 1945," Nov. 14, 1945.

6. Ibid. p. 3.

7. JWF to Office of Chief of Ordnance [U.S. Navy], Nov. 13, 1945.

8. JWF to James W. Walsh, Nov. 16, 1945.

9. Interview, Kenneth H. Olsen by the authors, June 24, 1964.

10. JWF to Henry B. Phillips, Dec. 17, 1945; Engineering Memorandum No. 3, subj.: "Lecture Notes—Part I," Dec. 5, 1945.

11. JWF to John G. Slater, Dec. 17, 1945. Copies of each letter went to Sage and Gordon Brown.

12. Ibid.

13. Conference Note C9 by JWF, subj.: "Outline of Discussion on Digital Computation as Applied to the Aircraft Analyzer," Nov. 28, 1945.

14. Ibid., p. 5.

15. Ibid., p. 8.

16. Ibid., p. 9.

17. Ibid.

18. Sage to Chief, Research and Inventions, Jan. 16, 1946; see also A. P. Bencks, SDD, to Sage, Nov. 27, 1945.

19. Sage to Chief, Research and Inventions, Jan. 16, 1946.

20. JWF to Lt. Comdr. H. C. Knutson, SDD, Jan. 28, 1946.

21. Ibid.

22. Memorandum, JWF to Sage, Feb. 25, 1946; memorandum, Sage to JWF, Mar. 16, 1946.

23. Navy Department, Office of Research and Inventions, Contract Number N5ori-60, June 30, 1945, "Task Order I—Constituting a Part of Contract N5ori-60 with the Massachusetts Institute of Technology and superseding BuAer Letter of Intent for Contract NOa(s)-7082." (The documents do not explain the apparent $60 discrepancy between the two totals.)

24. Navy Department, Office of Research and Inventions, SDD, "Specifications for Project RF-12 Known as *WHIRLWIND*," revised Mar. 20, 1946.

Chapter 4   Preliminary Design Efforts

1. JWF to N. McL. Sage, Jan. 7, 1946.

2. Conference Note C-10 by JWF, Feb. 11, 1946.

3. Administrative Memorandum A-1, JWF to Engineers of Project 6345, Feb. 27, 1946, subj.: "Present Status of Contractual Relations with Navy as Regards DIC 6345."

4. Interview, JWF by the authors, July 31, 1963.

5. Engineering Note E-8, subj.: "Cockpit Program," Mar. 1, 1946. Also Administrative Memoranda A-3, subj.: "Electronic Staff," Mar. 5, 1946; A-7, subj.: "Progress Reports," Mar. 15, 1946; A-9, subj.: "Reports, Schedules and Meetings," Mar. 18, 1946.

6. Report 64, "ASCA Equations," originally dated Oct. 31, 1945, revised Apr. 4, 1946, for Project 6345.

7. Engineering Note E-14, subj.: "Mathematics Group," Apr. 12, 1946.

8. Administrative Memorandum A-3, subj.: "Electronic Staff," Mar. 5, 1946. Conference Note C-12, subj.: "General Meeting of Staff Members of Project 6345," June 10, 1946.

9. Engineering Note E-13, subj.: "Block Diagrams Group," Apr. 3, 1946, p. 1.

10. Ibid.

11. Ibid., p. 2.

12. Ibid., pp. 3–4.

13. Ibid., pp. 4–5.

14. Conference Note C-19, subj.: "Part I—Report of Lab. Work—S. Dodd"; "Part II, Report of Proposed Storage Tube Program—J. W. Forrester," Oct. 23, 1946.

15. Note C-22, subj.: "Discussion of a Parallel Computer," Nov. 6, 1946.

16. Note C-24, subj.: "A High-Speed Parallel Digit Multiplier," Nov. 20, 1946.

17. Note C-12, subj.: "General Meeting of Staff Members of Project 6345," June 10, 1946, p. 2.

18. Ibid.

19. Ibid.

20. Note C-25, subj.: "Pre-Prototype Computer," Dec. 2, 1946.

21. Ibid.

22. Ibid.; memoranda M-43, subj.: "Pre-Prototype Status, Report," Dec. 10, 1946, and M-52, subj.: "Notes and Block Diagrams for the Pre-Prototype Computer," Dec. 27, 1946.

23. Memorandum M-47, subj.: "Pre-Prototype Computer Meeting," Dec. 17, 1946.

24. These were the first in the "L" series of reports issued by the project. Report L-1 appeared as Memorandum M-108 but was shortly changed to: Report L-1, J. W. Forrester and R. R. Everett to Director, Special Devices Center, subj.: "Digital Computation for Anti-submarine Problem," Oct. 1, 1947. Report L-2 appeared as: Limited Distribution Memorandum L-2, J. W. Forrester and R. R. Everett to Director, Special Devices Center, subj.: "Information System of Interconnected Digital Computers," Oct. 15, 1947. Although entitled "Memorandum," the items in this series rapidly became known as "L-reports." The "Special Devices Center" replaced the "Special Devices Division" in the reorganization accompanying the creation of the Office of Naval Reasearch.

25. Interview, JWF and Everett by the authors, Oct. 26, 1967.

26. Report L-1, p. 1.

27. Report L-2, p. 2.

28. Ibid., p. 12.

29. "Project Whirlwind Summary Report No. 9," June 1948, pp. 12–13.

30. JWF to Sage, subj.: "Amendment No. 4 to Project Whirlwind Contract N5ori-60," Feb. 2, 1948; JWF to Director, SDD, att'n Charles Doersam, Mar. 2, 1948.

31. Memorandum, Perry Crawford to Director, SDC, subj.: "Whirlwind Program," Dec. 18, 1947.

32. Proposed Work Description for Whirlwind Procurement, Aug. 16, 1948, corrected by Perry Crawford, Aug. 16, 1948.

33. Interview, C. Robert Wieser by the authors, June 16, 1965.

34. Memorandum for the files, Perry Crawford, subj.: "Conference on Project Whirlwind Held at Navy Department, 22 September 1948," Nov. 2, 1948.

35. For information on the cockpit's acquisition, see Comdr. Noel Gayler, to Commanding General, Wright Field, Sept. 18, 1947, and n. 37 below.

36. Memorandum, Code 424 (Fred D. Rigby) to Code 100, subj.: "Report from C. V. L. Smith to Head of Mathematics Branch," subj.: "Recommendations concerning the Realization ..." Nov. 18, 1948.

37. Memorandum, C. H. Doersam, Jr., Computer Section, to Director, SDC, subj.: "B-24 Fuselage for Project Whirlwind; Disposition of," Oct. 25, 1948; memorandum, Survey and Surplus Property Review Board to Head, Building and Ground Units, subj.: "Surplus Property, Instructions for Disposal of," Dec. 3, 1948.

Chapter 5   Pressure from ONR

1. JWF to Director, SDC, subj.: "Semi-annual Review of Contract N5ori-60" p. 2, Jan. 28, 1947.

2. Ibid., p. 1.

3. Ibid., p. 2.

4. Ibid., p. 1.

5. Ibid., p. 4.

6. Letter of Intent for Contract NOa(s)-5216, Dec. 14, 1944; Task Order No. 1, Contract N5ori-60, June 30, 1945; Amendment No. 4, Jan. 21, 1948, and Amendment No. 6, Sept. 29, 1948, Task Order No. 1, Contract N5ori-60; Directive, Chief of Naval Research, to Director, SDC, Feb. 8, 1949.

7. Interviews by the authors with: JWF and Everett, July 31, 1963; G. S. Brown, July 6, 1964.

8. JWF, "Computation Book No. 45," entries of Nov. 27, 1946–Dec. 10, 1948, pp. 89–91, 134–135. See also the following items by Perry Crawford: confidential memorandum, subj.: "Project Whirlwind," Nov. 4, 1947; memorandum to Director, SDC, subj.: "Whirlwind Program," Dec. 18, 1947; memorandum to Director, SDC, subj.: "Report on Visit to MIT on 9 January 1948," Jan. 12, 1948.

9. Idem, "Report on Visit to MIT on 9 Jan. 1948," January 12, 1948; anonymous memorandum from ONR files, subj.: "Report on Conference with Dr. Mina Rees and Dr. John Curtiss at Sands Point, 15 September 1947"; JWF to Capt. D. P. Tucker, ONR, July 23, 1948; interview, Norman Taylor by Howard Murphy and K. C. Redmond, Aug. 8, 1963.

10. Anonymous memorandum on "Conference with Dr. Mina Rees and Dr. John Curtiss . . . 15 September 1947."

11. JWF to Lt. Comdr. H. C. Knutson, SDD, Jan. 28, 1946; J. W. Forrester, Hugh R. Boyd, R. R. Everett, Harris Fahnestock, R. A. Nelson, Report L-3: "Fore-

cast for Military Systems Using Electronic Digital Computers," Servomechanisms Laboratory, MIT, Sept. 17, 1948; R. R. Everett, "The Whirlwind I Computer," revised text of a paper presented at the joint AIEE-Institute of Radio Engineers Conference, Philadelphia, Pa., Dec. 10-12, 1951 (see above, Appendix B).

12. Memorandum, Perry Crawford to Director, SDC, subj.: "Discussion of Project Whirlwind at ONR Conference on 28 October 1947," Oct. 29, 1947.

13. Memorandum, JWF to N. McL. Sage, subj.: "Warren Weaver, Visit to Laboratory, February 15, 1947," Feb. 19, 1947; JWF, "Computation Book No. 45," p. 27; Warren Weaver to Chief of Naval Research, att'n Mina Rees, Feb. 10, 1947; Weaver to Chief of Naval Research, att'n Mina Rees, June 26, 1947.

14. Anonymous memorandum for the files, Aug. 26, 1947.

15. Anonymous memorandum on "Conference with Dr. Mina Rees and Dr. John Curtiss . . . September 15, 1947."

16. Ibid. Task Order No. 1, Contract N5ori-60, June 30, 1945; Amendment No. 6, Task Order No. 1, Contract N5ori-60, Sept. 29, 1948.

17. Memorandum, Perry Crawford to Director, SDC, subj.: "Discussion of Project Whirlwind at ONR Conference on 28 October 1947," Oct. 29, 1947.

18. Ibid.

19. "Project Whirlwind, Summary Report No. 2."

20. JWF to Director, SDC, att'n Capt. G. M. O'Rear, Nov. 21, 1947.

21. JWF to H. L. Hazen, Mar. 10, 1947.

22. JWF to Director, SDC, att'n Capt. G. M. O'Rear, Apr. 23, 1948.

23. Weaver to Chief of Naval Research, att'n Mina Rees, Feb. 10, 1947.

24. JWF to Director, SDC, att'n Capt. O'Rear, Nov. 21, 1947.

25. Memorandum No. 94, W. S. Loud to JWF, R. R. Everett, P. Franklin, subj.: "Suggestions for Further Work," Aug. 6, 1947; Memorandum M-124, Philip Franklin to JWF and R. R. Everett, subj: "Location of Target from Combined Observations," Oct. 21, 1947.

26. Memorandum M-160, P. Franklin to JWF, subj.: "Mathematical Work of Project Whirlwind," Nov. 12, 1947.

27. Servomechanisms Laboratory, MIT, "Project Whirlwind, Summary Report No. 3," Dec. 2, 1947; JWF to Commanding Officer, Boston Office, ONR, subj.: "Participation of Mathematicians and Scientists in Project Whirlwind Activities," Jan. 30, 1948; JWF "Computation Book No. 45," pp. 86–87.

28. Memorandum M-41, subj.: "Floor Space Required . . ." Nov. 29, 1946; JWF to N. Sage, Nov. 29, 1946.

29. Jackson and Moreland to Sage (copies to Profs. Forrester and Stever), Mar. 11, 1947.

30. JWF to Director, SDC, att'n H. C. Knutson, Apr. 14, 1947.

31. JWF to Director, SDC, att'n Perry Crawford, Apr. 18, 1947.

32. See JWF, "Computation Book No. 44" (Oct. 10, 1946–Mar. 14, 1948); "Summary Report No. 1," Apr. 1946.

33. Conference Note C-14, Project Whirlwind, Oct. 9, 1946.

34. JWF, "Computation Book No. 45," entry of Mar. 17, 1947, p. 29; entry of Aug. 29, 1947, p. 52; entry of Oct. 10, 1947, p. 79.

35. See Francis J. Murray, *The Theory of Mathematical Machines* (New York, 1947).

36. Memorandum, JWF to R. R. Everett, subj.: "Professor Murray's Visit,"

Nov. 3, 1947; memorandum, H. H. Goode, SDC, to Director, SDC, subj.: "Trip to Boston, Mass., 7–9 November 1947; Report of," Nov. 12, 1947.

37. F. J. Murray, "Report on Mathematical Aspects of Whirlwind," submitted to Director, SDC, Nov. 21, 1947.

38. John von Neumann to Mina S. Rees, Dec. 10, 1947.

Chapter 6   Breaking New Trails

1. Servomechanisms Laboratory, MIT, "Project Whirlwind (Device 24-x-3), Summary Report No. 3," Dec. 1947, p. 2. Hereafter cited as "Summary Report No." Beginning in November 1947, these reports were submitted on a monthly basis to "the Special Devices Center, Office of Naval Research, under Contract N5ori-60."

2. Ibid., p. 3.

3. Ibid., p. 5.

4. Ibid.

5. Interview, JWF by the authors, July 24, 1964.

6. "Summary Report No. 3," Dec. 1947, p. 8.

7. Ibid., No. 6, Mar. 1948, p. 19

8. Ibid., No. 15, Dec. 1948, p. 19.

9. Ibid., No. 3, Dec. 1947, p. 7.

10. Ibid., No. 5, Feb. 1948, p. 3.

11. Ibid., No. 9, June 1948, p. 8.

12. Ibid., No. 10, July 1948, p. 2.

13. Interview, JWF by the authors, July 31, 1963.

Chapter 7   Problems of Federal Assistance

1. Memorandum, Perry Crawford to Director, SDC, subj.: "Trip to Boston, Mass., 8 January 1947 to 10 January 1947; report of," Jan. 28, 1947; anonymous SDC memorandum for the file, subj.: "SDC Computer Section Comments on Reference (a)," Aug. 26, 1947; W. R. Mangis to Director, SDC, and to Commanding Officer, Boston Branch Office, ONR, subj.: "Contract N5ori-60 (M.I.T.)—Assignment of Contract Administration Responsibilities," Oct. 2, 1947.

2. Memorandum, Perry Crawford to Director, SDC, subj.: "Report on Visit to MIT on 9 January 1948," Jan. 12, 1948; Amendment No. 6, Task Order No. 1, Contract N5ori-60, Sept. 29, 1948; T. A. Solberg to Director, SDC, subj.: "Contract N5ori-60 Task Order I Massachusetts Institute of Technology; change in cognizance of," Feb. 8, 1949.

3. Memorandum, N424 (Mina Rees) to N101, subj.: "Responsibility for Computer Research and Development," Jan. 28, 1949.

4. *Annual Report of the Secretary of the Navy for the Fiscal Year 1947* (Washington, 1948), p. 82.

5. N. McL. Sage to JWF, June 10, 1948.

6. JWF, "Computation Book No. 45," entries of Nov. 27, 1946 and Dec. 10, 1948, pp. 134, 151.

7. Sage to JWF, June 10, 1948.

8. Ibid.

9. Amendment No. 6, Task Order No. 1, Contract N5ori-60, Sept. 29, 1948; Sol-

berg to Director, SDC, subj.: "Contract N5ori-60 Task Order I Massachusetts Institute of Technology; change in cognizance of," Feb. 8, 1949; Amendment No. 7, Task Order No. 1, Contract N5ori-60, Mar. 31, 1949.

10. See Kent C. Redmond, "World War II, a Watershed in the Role of the National Government in the Advancement of Science and Technology," Charles Angoff, ed., *The Humanities in the Age of Science* (Rutherford, N. J., 1968), pp. 166–180. For an excellent history of the federal government and science, see A. Hunter Dupree, *Science in the Federal Government: A History of Policies and Activities to 1940* (Cambridge, Mass., 1957).

11. *Annual Report of the Secretary of the Navy—Fiscal Year 1940* (Washington, 1941), pp. 25–27; see also the *Report* for FY1939, pp. 24–25.

12. Dupree, *Science in the Federal Government*, p. 333.

13. U. S. Congress, Senate, Committee on Military Affairs, *The Government's Wartime Research and Development, 1940–44*, Report from the Subcommittee on War Mobilization, Part 2: "Findings and Recommendations," 79th Cong., 1st sess., Senate Subcommittee Report No. 5, pp. 5, 56–67, 70–71. U. S. Congress, House of Representatives, Hearings before a Subcommittee of the Committee on Government Operations [on Research and Development], 85th Cong., 2nd sess., July 14, 15, 17, and 18, 1958, Part 2—Military Research Representatives.

14. *Annual Report of the Secretary of the Navy for the Fiscal Year 1942* (Washington, 1942), p. 11; "The Bird Dogs: The Evolution of the Office of Naval Research," *Physics Today*, 14 (August 1961): 31–32.

15. U. S. Congress, House of Representatives, Committee on Naval Affairs, *Hearing on H. R. 5911 (ex-4317), to Establish an Office of Naval Research in the Department of the Navy*, 79th Cong., 2nd sess., March 26, 1946, pp. 2821–2822. *Annual Report, Fiscal Year 1945: The Secretary of the Navy to the President of the United States* (Washington, 1946), pp. 30–31; see also the Secretary's *Annual Report* for 1946, pp. 66–73.

16. Hearing . . . to Establish an Office of Naval Research, pp. 2834–2837.

17. Ibid., pp. 2840–2857.

18. *Physics Today*, 14 (August 1961): 33–35

19. *Hearing . . . to Establish an Office of Naval Research*, p. 2847; John E. Pfeiffer, "The Office of Naval Research," *Scientific American* 180 (February 1949): 11–15; Carrol W. Pursell, Jr., "Science and Government Agencies," in David D. Van Tassel and Michael G. Hall, eds., *Science and Society in the United States* (Homewood, Ill., 1946), pp. 245–246.

20. U. S. Congress, House of Representatives, Committee on Interstate and Foreign Commerce, *Hearings on H.R. 942, H.R. 1815, H.R. 1830, H.R. 1834, and H.R. 2027, Bills relating to the National Science Foundation*, 80th Cong., 1st sess., March 6 and 7, 1947, pp. 208, 231–254.

21. Task Order No. 1 to Contract N5ori-60, June 30, 1945, and amendments No. 4, Jan. 21, 1948; No. 6, Sept. 29, 1948; No. 9, July 1, 1949. Interview, JWF and Everett by the authors, July 24, 1964.

22. Task Order No. 1, Contract N5ori-60, June 30, 1945, and amendments No. 3, June 26, 1947; No. 4, Jan. 21, 1948.

23. JWF, "Computation Book No. 45," p. 35.

24. Letter (illegible signature) to MIT, subj.: "Contract N5ori-60, Task Order 1, Proposed Cost-plus-fixed-fee Subcontract to Sylvania Electric Products, Inc., in the aggregate amount of $319,576.75," Sept. 22, 1947; Prime Contract No. N5ori-60, Subcontract No. 1, DIC Project No. 6345, Revision No. 1, Sept. 24, 1947.

25. Enclosure A, "Proposed form of letter for budget request to Office of Naval Research," JWF to F. L. Foster, DIC, MIT, Aug. 14, 1947; F. L. Foster to Commanding Officer, Boston Branch Office, ONR, subj.: "Contract N5ori-60, Budget for Fiscal Year 1947–48," Aug. 15, 1947; memorandum for files, J. B. Thaler, Procurement Officer, SDC, subj.: "Status of Contract N5ori-60 with Massachusetts Institute of Technology and N6ori-133 with McKiernan Terry Corp.; Summarization of facts and events leading thereto," Oct. 23, 1947.

26. Memorandum, J. B. Thaler, SDC, to H. W. Fitzpatrick, Chief Accountant, ONR, subj.: "Contract N5ori-60, Task Order 1, Massachusetts Institute of Technology; Financing thereof," Nov. 3, 1947.

27. JWF to Sage, subj.: "Amendment No. 4 to Project Whirlwind Contract N5ori-60," Feb. 2, 1948.

28. Ralph D. Booth to James R. Killian, Jr., Aug. 26, 1948.

29. Memorandum, Perry Crawford to Technical Director, SDC, subj.: "Project Whirlwind, Fiscal requirements of," July 22, 1948.

30. Memorandum, C. H. Doersam, Jr., to Perry Crawford, subj.: "Project Whirlwind 24-x-3, Budget estimate of," Oct. 24, 1947; memorandum, Crawford to Technical Director, SDC, July 22, 1948; J. R. Ruhsenberger, SDC, to Chief of Naval Research, att'n Code N101, subj.: "Project Whirlwind, Contract N5ori-60, Financing of," Aug. 18, 1948.

31. Ruhsenberger to Chief of Naval Research, Aug. 18, 1948.

32. Amendment No. 6, Task Order No.1, Contract N5ori-60, Sept. 29, 1948.

33. Solberg to Director, SDC, Feb. 8, 1949.

34. U. S. Congress, House of Representatives, Subcommittee of the Committee on Appropriations, *Hearings on the Department of the Navy Appropriations Bill for 1949*, 80th Cong., 2nd sess., p. 968; Amendment No. 6, Task Order No. 1, Contract N5ori-60, Sept. 29, 1948; Ruhsenberger to Chief of Naval Research, att'n Code N101, subj.: "Project Whirlwind, Contract N5ori-60, Financing of," Aug. 18, 1948.

35. U.S. Congress, Senate, Committee on Armed Services, Hearings on S. 1560, "To facilitate the performance of research and development work by and on behalf of the Department of the Army, the Navy, and the Air Force, and for other purposes," 80th Cong., 2nd sess., March 12, 1948, p. 28.

36. Ruhsenberger to Chief of Naval Research, att'n Code N101, subj.: "Project Whirlwind, Contract N5ori-60, Financing of," Aug. 18, 1948; Procurement Directive Nr-720-003/7-22-48, Contract N5ori-60, Task Order No. 1, Aug. 11, 1948, attachment C to Clearance Memorandum prepared by J. B. Thaler, SDC.

37. Solberg to Compton, Sept. 2, 1948.

38. Sage, "Memorandum of Conference between Dr. Compton and Messrs. Killian, Forrester, Foster and Sage on Project Whirlwind," Sept. 8, 1948; Compton to Sage, Sept. 8, 1948.

39. Ibid., Booth to Killian, Aug. 26, 1948; Henry Loomis to T. A. Solberg, Sept. 10, 1948.

Chapter 8   Collision Course

1. JWF, H. R. Boyd, R. R. Everett, H. Fahnestock, and R. A. Nelson, "Forecast for Military Systems using Electronic Digital Computers, Report L-3," Servomechanisms Laboratory, Sept. 17, 1948, p. 8. The first version prepared by the same authors was entitled, "A Plan for Digital Information Handling Equipment in the Military Establishment, Report L-3," Servomechanisms Laboratory, Sept. 14, 1948. The "L" reports were sometimes entitled memoranda; hence the references in notes 13–16 below.

2. Report L-3, Sept. 17, 1948, p. 4.

3. Ibid.

4. Forrester, Boyd, Everett, Fahnestock, and Nelson, "Alternative Project Whirlwind Proposals, Report L-4," Servomechanisms Laboratory, Sept. 21, 1948, p. 2 and passim.

5. Interview, JWF by the authors, Oct. 26, 1967.

6. Memorandum from J. B. Thaler to Director, Contract Division, SDC, subj.: "Trip to Office of Naval Research . . . 20 September 1948 concerning Contract N5ori-60; Report on," Sept. 24, 1948.

7. Ibid.; JWF, "Computation Book No. 45," pp. 134–135.

8. Interview, Perry Crawford by the authors, Oct. 25, 1967.

9. Memorandum, Thaler to Director, Contract Division, SDC, Sept. 24, 1948; JWF, "Computation Book No. 45," pp. 134–135.

10. Ibid.; Solberg to Compton, Sept. 29, 1948.

11. Ibid.

12. Compton to Solberg, Oct. 7, 1948.

13. JWF, Memorandum L-5: "Project Whirlwind, Principles Governing Servomechanisms Laboratory Research and Development," Oct. 11, 1948 (copies to: Dr. K. T. Compton, Dr. J. R. Killian, Mr. Henry Loomis, Mr. N. McL. Sage, Dr. G. S. Brown, Mr. Ralph Booth). This "L" report covered three single-spaced typewritten pages.

14. JWF and Robert R. Everett, Memorandum L-6: "Comparison between the Computer Programs at the Institute for Advanced Study and the MIT Servomechanisms Laboratory," Oct. 11, 1948 (copies to: President's Office (2), Mr. N. McL. Sage, Prof. G. S. Brown, Mr. Ralph Booth). This "L" report covered six single-spaced typewritten pages.

15. Memorandum L-5, p. 1.

16. Memorandum L-6, pp. 2, 5.

17. Memorandum, Hugh R. Boyd and Robert A. Nelson to JWF, subj.: "Detailed Estimates of Costs Project Whirlwind, Applicable to Period from November 1948 through June 1950," Nov. 4, 1948; Memorandum L-8, JWF to N. McL. Sage, subj.: "Cost Trends, Contract N5ori-60," Nov. 19, 1948; memorandum, JWF to Sage, subj.: "Budget Adjustments," Dec. 1948.

18. JWF, "Computation Book No. 45," entries of Nov. 2 and Dec. 6, 1948, pp. 141, 146.

19. Ibid., No. 49, entry of Dec. 9, 1948.

20. Amendment No. 7, Task Order No. 1, Contract N5ori-60, Mar. 31, 1949.

21. Sage to ONR, Dec. 10, 1948; Rees to Sage, Feb. 23, 1949; memorandum,

Harris Fahnestock to JWF, subj.: "Comments on Letter Dated February 23, 1949 from Dr. Rees to Mr. Sage," Mar. 15, 1949; JWF, "Computation Book No. 49," entries of Jan. 12 and 13, 1949, pp. 15–17. See also Memorandum L-10 (draft), JWF to Sage, subj.: "Analysis of Whirlwind Program," Jan. 13, 1949.

22. JWF to C. V. L. Smith, May 20, 1949; Sage to Head, Computer Branch, Mathematical Science Division, ONR, June 14, 1949; C. V. L. Smith to Sage, July 18, 1949; Amendment No. 9, Task Order No. 1, Contract N5ori-60, July 1, 1949; M. S. Stevens to Head, Computer Branch, subj.: "Supplementary Information on Request for Funds for Contract N5ori-60 (NR048 097)," July 27, 1949; file memorandum, JWF, subj.: "Air Traffic Control Project," Mar. 10, 1949; JWF, "Computation Book No. 45," entry of July 28, 1948, p. 121; ibid., No. 49, entry of Mar. 10, 1949, p. 36.

Chapter 9   R&D Policies and Practices

1. JWF, Memorandum L-10: "Analysis of Whirlwind Program" (draft), Jan. 13, 1949, p. 1.

2. "Summary Report No. 15," Dec. 1948, p. 2.

3. Ibid.

4. "Summary Report No. 16" (Jan. 1949), No. 17 (Feb.), No. 18 (Mar.).

5. Ibid., No. 18, pp. 14–15.

6. Interviews by the authors.

7. JWF, Memorandum L-5: "Project Whirlwind, Principles Governing Servomechanisms Laboratory Research and Development," Oct. 11, 1948, p. 2.

8. Ibid.

9. JWF and Robert R. Everett, Memorandum L-6: "Comparison between the Computer Programs at the Institute for Advanced Study and the MIT Servomechanisms Laboratory," Oct. 11, 1948, p. 2.

10. Memorandum L-5, p. 1.

11. Ibid., p. 2.

12. Ibid., p. 1.

13. Memorandum L-6, pp. 1, 2.

14. Ibid., p. 2

15. Ibid.

16. Ibid.

17. Ibid.

Chapter 10   Crisis and Resolution

1. JWF to J. B. Pearson, Deputy Director, ONR, Dec. 2, 1949; memorandum, H. R. Boyd to JWF, subj.: "Budget Basis," Dec. 15, 1949.

2. R. J. Bergemann, to Head, Computer Branch, ONR, subj.: "Project Whirlwind Progress: Comments on," Dec. 22, 1949.

3. Memorandum, C. H. Doersam, Jr., SDC, subj.: "Contract N7 ONR-38902, Project Hurricane, recommendation of termination of," Nov. 1, 1950; report, C. H. Doersam, Jr., to Code 920, subj.: "Trip Report to Raytheon Manufacturing Com-

pany on 8 November 1950," Nov. 20, 1950; internal note, Samuel Nooger, Head, Engineering Branch, SDC [ca. Nov. 21, 1950].

4. Memorandum, C. V. L. Smith to Code 434, subj.: "Letter of J. W. Forrester, dated 2 December 1949, on the future financing of digital computer work at M.I.T.," Jan. 16, 1950.

5. R. J. Bergemann, "Record of Visits, January 1950–June 1950," Jan. 12, 1950; C. V. L. Smith, "Summary of Conference on Trip," Jan. 12 and 13, 1950.

6. E. R. Piore, ONR, to J. A. Stratton, Feb. 3, 1950; C. V. L. Smith to JWF, Mar. 2, 1950: JWF to Stratton, Mar. 3, 1950.

7. Interview, JWF by the authors, Oct. 26, 1967.

8. Mina Rees to Kent C. Redmond, July 15, 1964.

9. C. V. L. Smith to George R. Stibitz, Dec. 13, 1948; Mina Rees to Harold Hazen, Dec. 28, 1948; Hazen to Rees, Jan. 10, 1949; Hazen to Rees, Jan. 12, 1949; JWF to Rees, Jan. 17, 1949; Rees to Joseph E. Desch, Jan. 31, 1949; "Memorandum of Conversation with Dr. Alan Waterman," Mar. 7, 1949.

10. C. V. L. Smith to JWF, Aug. 19, 1949.

11. JWF to Smith, Aug. 26, 1949.

12. Research and Development Board, Committee on Basic Physical Sciences, "Report of the Ad Hoc Panel on Electronic Digital Computers," PS 13/5, Dec. 1, 1949. (Hereafter referred to as the preliminary report.)

13. JWF, Memorandum L-17: "Comments on the Report of the Ad Hoc Panel on Electronic Digital Computers of the RDB Committee on Basic Physical Sciences," Servomechanisms Laboratory, Jan. 13, 1950.

14. JWF, Memorandum L-11: "Information on Whirlwind I as Requested by Lt. Cmdr. Rubel, Research and Development Board . . . 7 February 1949," Servomechanisms Laboratory, MIT, Feb. 15, 1949; JWF, "Notes for RDB Committee Meeting," Aug. 29, 1949. In addition, memoranda L-3 and L-12 and Air Traffic Summary Report No. 1 were made available to the panel.

15. JWF, Memorandum L-16: "Discussion of the Comments on Project Whirlwind made by the Ad Hoc Panel on Electronic Digital Computers of the Basic Physical Science Committee of the Research and Development Board," Servomechanisms Laboratory, Jan. 13, 1950.

16. Memorandum, Code 434 to Code 102, signed by A. E. Smith, Acting Head, Computer Branch, ONR, subj.: "Confidential Report of the Ad Hoc Panel on Electronic Digital Computers, RDB, Comments on," Dec. 20, 1949.

17. Diary note, A. T. Waterman, subj.: "Whirlwind Conference Held at Massachusetts Institute of Technology," Mar. 6, 1950; C. M. [Carl Muckenhaupt], "Record of Visits January–June, 1950," Mar. 6, 1950.

18. Diary note, Waterman, Mar. 6, 1950; memorandum, C. V. L. Smith, "Summary of Conference on Trip," Mar. 6–7, 1950.

19. Ibid.

20. Memorandum, N. McL. Sage, Apr. 7, 1950.

21. Sage to Chief of Naval Research, May 5, 1950; Memorandum D-23, JWF to Head, Computer Branch, Mathematical Science Division, ONR, subj.: "Request for Funds for Contract N5ori-60 for the Period July 1, 1950 through June 30, 1951," May 3, 1950.

22. C. V. L. Smith to Sage, June 26, 1950.

23. JWF to Sage, July 6, 1950; Sage to JWF, July 11, 1950.

24. Memorandum for File 6345, Paul V. Cusick, MIT, Oct. 6, 1950; Amendment No. 12, Task Order No. 1, Contract N5ori-60, Nov. 14, 1950.

25. Sage to Chief of Naval Research, Feb. 23, 1951; interview, JWF and Everett by the authors, Oct. 26, 1967.

26. JWF to Chief of Naval Research, Sept. 25, 1951; Memorandum A-124, JWF to laboratory personnel, subj.: "Change in Laboratory Name," Sept. 20, 1951; Memorandum A-25, H. R. Boyd to "6345 Personnel," subj.: "Moving to Barta Building," Sept. 8, 1947.

27. Amendments No. 13 and No. 14, Task Order No. 1, Contract N5ori-60, June 28, 1951.

28. Ibid., No. 16, Mar. 26, 1952; No. 19, Apr. 18, 1951.

29. Interview, JWF by the authors, Oct. 26, 1967.

30. Research and Development Board, "Report on Electronic Digital Computers by the Consultants to the Chairman of the Research and Development Board," PS 13/8, June 15, 1950.

31. JWF, Memorandum L-24: "Statement of Status of Project Whirlwind Prepared for the Research and Development Board," Servomechanisms Laboratory, May 10, 1950.

32. "Report on Electronic Digital Computers by the Consultants to the Chairman of the Research and Development Board," June 15, 1950, p. vi. (Hereafter referred to as the final report.)

33. Ibid., pp. vi–vii.

34. Ibid., p. viii.

35. Cf. preliminary report (Dec. 1, 1949), p. 9, and the final report (June 15, 1950), p. 9.

36. Cf. preliminary report, p. 44, and final report, p. 45.

37. Cf. preliminary report, pp. 8, 23, and final report, pp. 9, 22.

38. Cf. preliminary report, p. 9, and final report, p. 9.

39. Cf. preliminary report, pp. 11, 39.

40. Cf. preliminary report, p. 34, and final report, p. 33.

41. Cf. preliminary report, p. 15, and final report, p. 13.

42. Preliminary report, p. 53.

43. Final report, p. 54.

44. Ibid.

45. Ibid.

46. Preliminary report, p. 39.

47. Final report, p. 40.

48. Ibid., appendix 4.

Chapter 11   ADSEC and Whirlwind

1. Gen. Hoyt S. Vandenberg to Dr. Vannevar Bush, Dec. 9, 1947.

2. Memorandum M-1810, A. P. Kromer, subj.: "Minutes of Joint MIT-IBM Conference, Held at Hartford, Connecticut, January 20, 1953," Jan. 26, 1953.

3. Vandenberg to Bush, Dec. 9, 1947.

4. W. L. Barrow, Chairman, Panel on Radar, Committee on Electronics, RDB, to

Normal L. Winter, Executive Director, Committee on Electronics, RDB, Jan. 5, 1948.

5. *History of the Air Force Cambridge Research Center*, 1 July–31 December 1953, vol. 19, part 1, pp. 247–252.

6. Ibid., 249–250, citing La Verne E. Woods, "The Lincoln System," *ADC Communications and Electronics Digest* 4 (Jan. 1954): 4–11.

7. C. L. Grant, *The Development of Continental Air Defense to 1 September 1954*, *USAF Historical Studies: No. 126*, pp. 14–18.

8. *Operational Plan, Semiautomatic Ground Environment System for Air Defense*, HEDADC, Mar. 7, 1955, p. v.

9. Memorandum for DCS/C, DCS/P, DCS/O, and DCS/M, HEDUSAF from General Muir S. Fairchild, VCS, USAF, subj.: "Air Defense Technical Committee of the Scientific Advisory Board," Dec. 15, 1949, cited in *History of Air Force Cambridge Research Center*, vol. 15, part 1, appendix 11.

10. Valley to Dr. Theodore Von Karman, Nov. 8, 1949.

11. Ibid.; General Muir S. Fairchild to Commanding General, Air Material Command, subj.: "Air Defense System Engineering Committee, Scientific Advisory Board to the Chief of Staff, U.S. Air Force," Jan. 27, 1950.

12. ADSEC Report, "Air Defense System," Oct. 24, 1950.

13. General Hoyt S. Vandenberg to Dr. James R. Killian, Jan. 19, 1951.

14. R. R. Everett, C. A. Zraket, and H. D. Benington, "SAGE—A Data Processing System for Air Defense," reprint from *Proceedings of the Eastern Joint Computer Conference* (Washington, D. C., 1957), p. 148.

15. JWF, "Computation Book No. 49," entry of Jan. 20, 1950, p. 77.

16. Interview, George E. Valley by the authors.

17. JWF, "Computation Book No. 49," entry for Jan. 27, 1950, p. 83.

18. Ibid.

19. Dr. Stever was at that time an associate professor of aeronautical engineering. Dr. Draper was director of the MIT Instrumentation Library and in 1951 became head of the Department of Aeronautics.

20. JWF, "Computation Book No. 49," entry of Jan. 30, 1950, p. 84.

21. Ibid., entry of Feb. 21, 1950, p. 88.

22. Ibid., entry of Feb. 15, 1950, p. 86.

23. C. R. Wieser in Lincoln Laboratory, "Quarterly Progress Report, Division 6–Digital Computer," June 1, 1952, pp. 6–9.

24. Wieser, "Digital Computers in Control System," Report R-181, Servomechanisms Laboratory, Apr. 27, 1950.

25. Wieser in Lincoln Laboratory, "Quarterly Progress Report, Division 6—Digital Computer," June 1, 1952, pp. 6–9.

Chapter 12 Phasing into Operation

1. "Summary Report No. 20, Third Quarter, 1949," p. 9.

2. Testimony of JWF, Mar. 8, 1960, in records of Patent Interference No. 88,269, "In the United States Patent Office before the Examiner of Interferences, Jay W.

Forrester v. Jan A. Rajchman," pp. 27–28.

3. Ibid., p. 31.

4. JWF, "Coincident-Current Magnetic Computer Memory Developments at MIT," p. 2. This paper was given at the Argonne National Laboratory Computer Symposium, Aug. 4, 1953. Cf. JWF, Memorandum M-70: "Data Storage in Three Dimensions," Apr. 29, 1947.

5. "Project Whirlwind Summary Report No. 17," Feb. 1949, p. 7.

6. Ibid., p. 8.

7. Interview, JWF by the authors, July 24, 1964.

8. Interview, Everett by the authors, July 31, 1963.

9. W. N. Papian to T. M. Smith, Feb. 12, 1968.

10. Memorandum, Everett to JWF, Jan. 9, 1950; Memorandum L-18, H. R. Boyd to JWF, subj.: "Estimated Cost of Standard Storage Tubes (January 1950)," Feb. 15, 1950.

11. "Summary Report No. 20, Third Quarter, 1949," pp. 17, 27.

12. Memorandum L-18, Feb. 15, 1950, p. 1.

13. JWF to J. A. Stratton, Mar. 3, 1950, p. 1.

14. Ibid.

15. Ibid., pp. 3–4.

16. JWF to Stratton, Sept. 28, 1950, p. 1.

17. Ibid., p. 2, which bears the date "Sept. 23, 1950."

18. W. N. Papian, Report R-192, "A Coincident-Current Magnetic Memory Unit," Sept. 8, 1950, abstract.

19. JWF, Report R-187, "Digital Information Storage in Three Dimensions Using Magnetic Cores," May 16, 1950.

20. Testimony of W. N. Papian, Patent Interference No. 88,269. The proposal pointed out that this problem was "at present in the center of interest for highspeed digital computers like Whirlwind. Here simple yes-no devices are required that can switch in fractions of a microsecond and lend themselves to a three-dimensional storage of information."

21. "Summary Report No. 23, Second Quarter, 1950," p. 15.

22. "Summary Report No. 24, Third Quarter, 1950," p. 6.

23. Ibid., p. 24.

24. JWF to Stratton, Jan. 18, 1951.

25. JWF, "Computation Book No. 49," entry of Feb. 1, 1950, p. 84.

26. C. R. Wieser in Lincoln Laboratory, "Quarterly Progress Report, Division 6—Digital Computer," June 1, 1952, pp. 6–9.

27. JWF, "Computation Book No. 49," entry of Apr. 12, 1950, p. 102.

28. Directive, John H. Marchetti, Director, Radio Physics Research, to Col. Mitchell, R. E. Rader, Dr. Hollingsworth, Dr. Spencer, Dr. Samson, Dr. Foster, and Mr. Davis, June 29, 1950.

29. Memorandum, Robert E. Rader, Chief, Air Defense Group, Base Directorate, Radio Physics Research, subj.: "Transfer of Personnel to Air Defense Group," July 5, 1950; memorandum, Rader to George E. Valley, Oct. 31, 1950.

30. "Summary Report No. 6," April 25, 1950–July 25, 1950, submitted to Watson

Laboratories, Air Material Command, under Contract AF 28 (099)-45, p. 2.

31. "Conclusions—Scientific Advisory Committee Meeting, January 19, 1951," Contract AF 119 (122)-458, Jan. 20, 1951; Memorandum A-117, H. Fahnestock, subj.: "New Funds under Contract AF 19 (122)-458, DIC 6889," May 7, 1951.

32. Wieser in Lincoln Laboratory, "Quarterly Progress Report, Division 6—Digital Computer," June 1, 1952, pp. 6–9.

33. JWF, "Computation Book No. 49," entries of Feb. 1, 1951, pp. 135, 136; "Summary Report No. 9, January 25, 1951–April 25, 1951," submitted to Air Force Cambridge Research Laboratory under Contract AF 28 (099)-45, p. 1.

34. Ibid., p. 23; Wieser in Lincoln Laboratory, "Quarterly Progress Report, Division 6—Digital Computer," June 6, 1952, pp. 6–10; Memorandum M-1515, D. R. Israel, subj.: "Interception Experiments with Bedford MEW," June 11, 1952.

35. Memorandum M-2092, Wieser to JWF, subj.: "Experimental Interceptions with Bedford MEW Radar," Apr. 23, 1951.

36. Hoyt S. Vandenberg, Chief of Staff, USAF, to George E. Valley, Jr., Chairman, ADSEC, May 28, 1951.

37. "Summary Report No. 23, Second Quarter, 1950," p. 5.

38. "Summary Report No. 20, Third Quarter, 1949," p. 28.

39. Ibid.

40. "Summary Report No. 22, First Quarter, 1950," p. 21.

41. "Summary Report No. 25, Fourth Quarter, 1950 and First Quarter, 1951," p. 5.

42. Ibid., p. 6.

43. Ibid., p. 5.

44. Ibid.

Chapter 13 The End of the Beginning

1. Memorandum A-124, JWF, subj.: "Change in Laboratory Name," Sept. 20, 1951; JWF, "Computation Book No. 49," entry of Oct. 1, 1951, p. 139.

2. Interview, JWF and Everett by the authors, July 31, 1963.

3. JWF, Memorandum L-32: "Project Lincoln, Division VI Program, July 1952–June 1953," Jan. 7, 1952.

4. Memorandum A-131, H. Fahnestock, subj.: "Accounting Procedures, DIC 6886," Mar. 26, 1952; JWF in Lincoln Laboratory, "Quarterly Progress Report, Division 6—Digital Computer," June 1, 1952, pp. 6–7. Memorandum M-1356, subj.: "Laboratory Personnel," Jan. 1, 1952.

5. Memorandum L-173, JWF, subj.: "Organization and Tasks of Division 6," Nov. 16, 1954.

6. Interview, John C. Proctor by the authors, July 13, 1964.

7. Memorandum A-147, subj.: "Division 6 Move to Lexington," May 26, 1953.

8. Interviews, Fahnestock and Proctor by the authors, July 15 and 13, 1964.

9. Memorandum L-32, JWF, Jan. 7, 1952; Memorandum L-45, JWF and Everett, subj.: "Condensed Summary of FY 54," June 10, 1952.

10. MIT, "Problems of Air Defense, Final Report, Project Charles," Aug. 1, 1951: 96–122; C. R. Wieser in Lincoln Laboratory, "Quarterly Progress Report, Division

6—Digital Computer," June 1, 1953, pp. 6–11; "Brief Summary of Activity Planned by Project Lincoln during FY/53," PLA-126, Jan. 9, 1951.

11. Schedule to Contract No. AF 19 (122)-458.

12. HEADC, "Operational Plan, Semiautomatic Ground Environment System for Air Defense," Mar. 7, 1955, p. vi.

13. Memorandum L-86, C. R. Wieser, subj.: "Cape Cod System and Demonstration," Mar. 13, 1953.

14. "Brief Summary of Activity Planned by Project Lincoln during FY/53," PLA-126, Jan. 9, 1951; Memorandum L-45, JWF and Everett, June 10, 1952.

15. Memorandum L-32, JWF, Jan. 7, 1952.

16. Memorandum M-1810, A. P. Kromer, subj.: "Minutes of Joint MIT-IBM Conference, Held at Hartford, Connecticut, January 20, 1953," Jan. 26, 1953, p. 3.

17. Memorandum L-64, C. R. Wieser, subj.: "ADEE Steering Committee Meeting at Colorado Springs, October 7, 8, 1952," Oct. 10, 1952; Memorandum L-66, Arthur Kromer, subj.: "Discussion of Contract Status with IBM," Oct. 17, 1952; JWF, "Computation Book No. 53," entry of Nov. 3, 1952, p. 9,; Memorandum L-71, D. R. Brown, subj.: "Group Leaders' Meeting, November 24, 1952," Nov. 24, 1952.

18. Major General D. L. Putt, Vice Commander, HEDARDC, to COMRADC, subj.: "Revision of Command Policy pertaining to ADIS," May 6, 1953; Lt. General Earle E. Partridge, Commander, ARDC, to Dr. Harlan Hatcher, President, University of Michigan, May 6, 1953.

19. Memorandum L-64, Wieser, Oct. 10, 1952; Memorandum L-65, JWF, Oct. 13, 1952; Memorandum L-71, Brown, Nov. 24, 1952.

20. Memorandum L-86, Wieser, Mar. 13, 1953.

21. Lincoln Laboratory, "Quarterly Progress Report, Division AF-24 6—Digital Computer," Dec. 15, 1953, p. iii.

22. Memorandum L-129, D. R. Brown, subj.: "Group Leaders' Meeting, December 7, 1953," Dec. 7, 1953.

23. "Project Whirlwind Summary Report No. 28, Fourth Quarter, 1951," p. 11.

24. Ibid., p. 11.

25. Memorandum L-36, Everett, subj.: "Second Bank of 1024-Digit Storage Tubes for WWI," Apr. 3, 1952.

26. "Summary Report No. 35, Third Quarter, 1953," pp. 5, 32–33.

27. Ibid., p. 33.

28. Memorandum M-1810, Kromer, subj.: "Minutes of Joint MIT-IBM Conference . . . January 20, 1953," Jan. 26, 1953.

29. Memorandum M-1321, B. E. Morris, subj.: "Fourth Meeting on Air Defense Computer," Nov. 8, 1951, p. 4.

30. Memorandum L-45, JWF and Everett, June 10, 1952.

31. Memorandum L-30, JWF and Everett, subj.: "Digital Computers for Air Defense System," Oct. 5, 1951.

32. Memorandum M-1327, D. R. Brown and B. E. Morris, subj.: "Summary of First Four Meetings on Air-Defense Computer," Nov. 9, 1951.

33. Memorandum L-32, JWF, Jan. 7, 1952.

34. Memorandum, Everett and Fahnestock to JWF, subj.: "Senior Staff Meeting," Mar. 5, 1952.

35. Memorandum L-34, H. Fahnestock, subj.: "Group Leaders' Meeting, March 26, 1952," Mar. 27, 1952.

36. Memorandum L-46, D. R. Brown, subj.: "Group Leaders' Meeting, June 9, 1952," June 11, 1952.

37. Memorandum L-37, D. R. Brown, subj.: "Group Leaders' Meeting, April 7, 1952," Apr. 9, 1952.

38. Memorandum L-46, June 11, 1952.

39. Memorandum L-66, Arthur Kromer, Oct. 17, 1952; JWF, "Computation Book No. 53," entries of Oct. 17, 1952, pp. 1, 2, 4.

40. JWF, "Computation Book No. 53," entry of Oct. 27, 1952, p. 7.

41. Ibid., entries for Oct. 17, 1952, pp. 1, 2, 4.

42. Ibid., entries of Oct. 22, 27, 1952, pp. 6–7; Memorandum M-1739, A. P. Kromer, subj.: "Summary of IBM-MIT Collaboration, October 27, 1952, to November 30, 1952 inclusive," Dec. 3, 1952; Digital Computer Laboratory, MIT, Purchase Requisition, DIC-L 33210, Dec. 4, 1952.

Chapter 14   A Retrospective

1. JWF to C. W. Farr, Dec. 18, 1967.

2. Ibid.

3. Ibid. See also K. C. Redmond and T. M. Smith, "Lessons from 'Project Whirlwind,'" *IEEE Spectrum* 14 (Oct. 1977): 50–59.

4. Interview, Everett by authors, Oct. 26, 1967.

5. *Scientific Manpower—1957,* National Science Foundation Document No. NSF-58-21 (Washington, 1957), p. 25.

INDEX

Adams, Charles, 190
Ad Hoc Panel, *see* Defense, U. S.
    Department of
ADSEC, *see* Air Defense Systems
    Engineering Committee
Aeronautics, Bureau of (U.S. Navy),
    see Navy, U.S.; Special Devices
    Division
Aiken, Howard, 30, 69, 84
    and Mark I, 29, 31, 34
    (*see also* Harvard Mark I)
air defense computer, *see* AN/FSQ-7
Air Defense System Engineering Committee
    (ADSEC), 172–176, 190, 198
    created (1949), 172, 179
    studies of air defense, 191, 192–194,
        201–202, 203–204
    See also "Valley Committee"
Air Force, U.S., 60, 103
    and national defense (1950s), 169–173
    requests laboratory at MIT, 172 (*see also*
        Lincoln Laboratory)
    Scientific Advisory Board (SAB), 171–173
    and Whirlwind I and II, 128, 130, 156–158,
        166–168, 176, 186, 190–191, 212, 213,
        215
    Willow Run Research Center, 203
Air Force Cambridge Research Laboratories
    (later Center), 172, 175, 190, 191, 192,
    203, 212
Air Materiel Command, 172
Airplane/Aircraft Stability and Control
    Analyzer (ASCA), 80, 192,
    beginning of project (1944), 2, 4–6, 8,
        12–13, 17, 19–20, 45, 66, 218

"breadboard model" cost, 13, 17
and "convergence" of traditions, 29
Forrester's work with, 14–17, 19–20, 22–23,
    25, 45, 52, 83, 217
    and digital concept, 26, 27–28, 32, 33,
        39–41, 49, 60, 67
freedom of operational choice for, 8, 219
operating speed requirements, 84–85, 181
simulator cockpit and problems, 5, 15, 16,
    20, 32, 48–49
    cockpit junked, 46, 59, 60, 147, 223
work abandoned, 47, 179
See also contract(s); Whirlwind project
Air Research and Development Command
    (U.S. Air Force), 103
Allegheny Ludlum Company, 183, 184
American Telephone and Telegraph
    Company, 6
analog device(s), 16, 34
    design and development of, 15, 23, 25, 27,
        32, 40, 45, 60
    vs. digital device(s), 28, 33, 39–41, 42, 45,
        47, 197
AN/FSQ-7 (air defense computer,
    "Whirlwind II"), 215
    contract problems of, 212–213
    design and design problems of, 210–211
    Systems Office for, 199–200
antiaircraft defense, 171
    computer technology and, 27
    for merchant ships, World War II, 9
    See also early warning systems; radar
antisubmarine warfare, *see* submarines
Archibald, R. C., 26, 32, 33, 217
Armament Branch (ONR), *see* Office of

271